SEXUAL PATHOLOGY

Opinions from Medical Journals

"An excellent topographical survey of diverse manifestations of sexual behavior, giving a recapitulative and illuminating digest of work done in this field mainly from the standpoints of description, correction, and criminological medicine."

—*Journal of Nervous and Mental Disease*

"Magnus Hirschfeld will be remembered as one of the great pioneers in the study of sex. . . . The value of a treatise on the pathology of sex depends obviously upon its reflection of the experience of the author. In this instance the author's experience has been unusually extensive."

—*American Journal of Psychiatry*

"Covers a wide range in the field of sexual abnormality. . . . Highly recommended to the profession."

—*Connecticut State Medical Journal*

MAGNUS HIRSCHFELD, M.D.

Magnus Hirschfeld was born in Germany in 1868, the son of a prominent physician. After extensive preparation at five universities, and several years of general practice, he became the first physician to specialize in psychosexual diseases. Later he helped establish the Medical Society for Sexual Science.

In 1918, with many years of specialized practice behind him, Dr. Hirschfeld founded the famous Institute of Sexual Science, in Berlin. This was soon taken over by the government as the Magnus Hirschfeld Foundation. In succeeding years the Institute was visited for research and study by thousands of physicians and scientists from all over the world. In connection with the same Institute, Dr. Hirschfeld proceeded to set up the first German Marriage Consultation Bureau, which became the pattern for similar institutions in many other countries.

In addition to his other activities, Dr. Hirschfeld was a medico-criminal expert of note, specializing in cases that involved aberrations of the sexual instinct.

Between the years of 1921 and 1932, he called five meetings of the International Congress for Sexual Reform on a Scientific Basis. The meetings were organized by the World League for Sexual Reform, an organization founded by Hirschfeld together with August Forel and Havelock Ellis.

A bibliography of Dr. Hirschfeld's writings includes more than two hundred titles, among the most important being: *Natural Laws of Love,* based on more than 10,000 questionnaires filled out by men and women who came to him for advice; *Sexual Knowledge,* based on thirty years of research, published in five volumes; *Sexual Pathology,* a study of disorders of the sexual instinct; and *Men and Women—The World Journey of a Sexologist.*

Commenting on Dr. Hirschfeld's recent death, *The New York Times* refers to him as, "the author of many works which are considered standard books on sex analysis and sex psychology . . . authority on sex problems and pioneer advocate of sexual 'reform.' "

Norman Haire, himself noted for his achievements in the field of sexual knowledge, tendered this tribute, ". . . the noble work of ameliorating the needless sexual misery of a large proportion of humanity lay ever nearest the heart of Magnus Hirschfeld. . . . What stands out, is his scientific achievement, his establishment of Sexology as a recognized branch of medical science and medical practice, his contribution to the knowledge of that science, not only within the bounds of the normal, but even more in the domain of sexual pathology . . . splendid scientific and humanitarian work."

SEXUAL PATHOLOGY

A STUDY OF DERANGEMENTS OF THE SEXUAL INSTINCT

by

MAGNUS HIRSCHFELD, M.D.

AUTHOR OF: *Natural Laws of Love; Sexual Anomalies; Men and Women—The World Journey of a Sexologist; Sexual Knowledge;* etc.

FORMER: President, World League for Sexual Reform; Director, Institute of Sexual Science

AUTHORIZED TRANSLATION BY JEROME GIBBS

Originally Published in 3 Volumes

The courts of our country have gone on record as sanctioning rational sex education.

They did so in the Stopes case (United States District Court), as well as in the Dennett case (United States Circuit Court of Appeals).

In the latter case Federal Judge Augustus N. Hand stated:

". . . The old theory that information about sex matters should be left to chance has greatly changed. . . . It may reasonably be thought that accurate information, rather than mystery and curiosity, is better in the long run and is less likely to occasion lascivious thoughts, than ignorance and anxiety."

NEW YORK • EMERSON BOOKS, INC. • 1947

REVISED EDITION, 1940
Second Printing, 1944
Third Printing, 1945
Fourth Printing, 1947

CONTENTS

v

Worship of the phallus and the vulva. Anus sniffers. Genital fetishists. Fetishism of the extremities. Shaking and kissing the hand. Movement fetishism. Dance voyeurs. Erotic and anti-erotic significance of eyeglasses, canes, and umbrellas. Perfume fetishism. A woman collar-button fetishist. Fetishism for red cockades. Divorce because of a *flannel* fetishism. Differential diagnoses of handkerchief theft and handkerchief fetishism. Divorce action because of corset fetishism. A woman's hypererotic condition as the result of leather and spiral puttees. The large group of shoe worshippers. The metastrophic significance of shoes. Fetish scars. Retroussé and disrobing fetishists. Bed fetishism. Fetishism for *sleeping* women. *Sexual color madness.* Costume and uniform fetishism. Stimulating dress. Fetishism for animal skins, such as furs and leather. The fetishistic basis of zoophilia. *Idiotic* desecrators of animals. Love of dogs and cats. Erotic fixation on a canary bird and a parrot. Onanism with animals. Lambitus and coitus performed by animals on humans. *Zoosadism.* Crocodiles and snakes as sexual objects. Transmission of diseases through caressing animals. Religious sodomy. Why is the punishment of lewdness with animals unnecessary? A man who had an affair with an old *oak tree.* Erotic fixation upon objects from the mineral world. Case of crystal fetishism, etc.

The *quantitative* variations of the sexual urge. The sexual-pathological plus and minus groups. The *strength* of eroticism conditioned by the *inner secretions.* Where does sexual *excess* begin? The sexual temperament. Sexual athletes. Relation of the *direction* of the urge to the *strength* of the urge. Dissimilarity of the libido with bisexuals when directed to the same or to the opposite sex. Ability to control the urge. Prepubic and postclimacteric sexual desire. Relation of libido and potence. Capacity for sexual impressionability and possibility of sexual expression. The "corpses' sweetheart." Sexual rhythm. Ebb and flood of the sexual hormone waves. Sexual temptations. Influence of foods, luxuries, and drugs upon the strength of the urge. Love-frenzies, satyriasis, nymphomania, and man-craziness. Faust's "in enjoyment I thirst again for desire." Polygamous and monogamous forms of hypereroticism. Polyeroticism. Humans with genitals and genitals with humans. Sexual polypragmasy. Influence of hypereroticism upon the physical and psychic health. Case of a married polyerotic person. Oral genital-intercourse. Prostitutes because of passion. Hypererotic conduct. Sexual supernecessity with women. Lust-

CONTENTS

of corpses. Salome types. Forms of bodily hypereroticism. Priapism. Erections without participation of the sexual urge. Amorous desires of aging persons and erections with a full bladder. Gonorrheal priapism. Aphrodisiacs. Anal effects of an erection. Peripheral stimulation of the pleasure bodies. Erections and ejaculations with hanged and beheaded persons. Priapism through exhaustion. Leucemic priapism. Toxic priapism. Priapism through long enduring stimulation of the erection center. Illness of involuntary losses of semen. Spermatorrhea at urination of defecation. Conception of sexual overstimulation.

The mechanism of sexual potency. The fourfold genital innervation. A general consideration of fertility. Testimony in cases of adoption. Divisions of impotence. Impotentia coeundi and generandi. Cerebral eroticization. Contestation of marriage because of aspermatism and andrinism. Organic and functional impotence. Absolute and relative impotence; matrimonial impotence. Our fourfold division into impotentia cerebralis, spinalis, genitalis, and germinalis. Lack of sexual appetites. Anti-erotic effects of tiring and toxic stuffs. Fleeing into solitude from sexual temptations. Depotentizing effects of alcohol. Influence of cocaine, coffee, lead, nicotine upon the potency. Impotence as the result of acute or chronic illnesses. Frame of mind and sexuality. Antieroticism of the woman. Impotence as the result of anomalies of the urge. Impotence on an antifetishistic basis. Reports concerning a reëstablishment of a marriage in a case of temporary impotence. Autosuggestive impotence. Impotence because of inhibitions. Defective sexual sensations in the man and in the woman. Why does the woman more often not have a feeling of pleasure than the man? Anorgasm and frigidity. Difference in the pleasure curve of the man and of the woman. Cold women. Relative and absolute frigidity. The individualistic character of the sexual reflex. Harmony of the nervous system. Baffled pleasure in sexual intercourse. Ejaculatio precox. Spinal impotence. Sexual centers in the spinal cord and the sympathicus. The motory conduction in the nervi erigentes. The independence of the erection and ejaculation proceedings from the will. The complicated blood and muscular apparatus of the member. Defect phenomena at being shot through the loins and the gradual rehabilitation. Tabic impotence. Case of impotence with multiple sclerosis. Testimony of an impotent man in approving a divorce action. Psychogenous limitation of nervous impotence. Genital impotence. Lack of the penis. Ability of hermaphrodites for coition and generation. Abnormal smallness and largeness of the penis. Doubling of the penis (diphallus). Difficulties of cohabitation through hypospadia and epispadia. Significance of phimosis. Real and apparent shortening of the foreskin band. Obstacle to coitus through paraphimosis. Shots through the penis. Fractures and luxation of the penis. The skinned and torn penis. Tying off of the penis. Foreign bodies in the urethra. Freezing and burning of the member. Herpes progenitalis. Cavernitis. Chorda penis. Plastic induration of the penis. Ossification processes in the member. The Fournier illness. Edematous, varicose, and elephant-iastic thickening of the member. Impotence through condylome, ulceration, and swellings of the penis. Corneous formations of the penis. Slipping in of the penis. Ability of cohabitation of feminine hermaphrodites. Membranous closing of the vulva. Cicatricose growing together of the vagina. Depotentizing effect of hanging breasts. Pruritus vulvae. Vaginal stenosis. Abnormally thick and resistant hymen. Second closing membrane. Lack of the vagina. False vagina. Double vagina. Cohabitation in the mouth of the fallen womb. Inability of cohabitation because of pain-ful inflammations in the annexes. Germinal impotence. Causal relationship between psycho-sexual-pathological and general con-stitution. Ability of cohabitation and generation of eunuchs. In-flammation of the testicles as the main cause of azoospermy. Gonorrheal sterility. Necessity of seminal examination with dis-puted paternity. Artificial fertilization through testicular punc-ture. Lack of semen in conditions of exhaustion. Quantitative and qualitative destruction of germs through alcohol. Temporary sterilization through Roentgen rays. Asthenic and deformed sperma. Semen-destroying substances. Procedure of obtaining in-disputable sperma. Red, green, and yellow colored semen. Coitus without ejaculation. Aspermy after constant acts of coition. Pains with orgasm. Germinal impotence of the woman—lack of eggs. Impassableness of the conducting channels. Sexual diseases as the most common cause of female sterility. Shriveling of the womb. The fetal, infantile, and pubescent uterus. Later develop-ment of the uterus. Inability of reception. Stenoses of the mouth of the womb. Impotentia concipiendi, gestandi, and parturiendi.

PREFACE

In 1844 there appeared in Leipzig, in *Latin,* the first "Psychopathia Sexualis." Its author was the Ruthenian physician Heinrick Kaan. About forty years later (1886) Krafft-Ebing, the famous psychiatrist at the university at Graz, published his epochmaking textbook under the same title. Since then, many more years have gone by, years in which the knowledge concerning sexual science has been enriched far more than in the interval which lay between Kaan and Krafft-Ebing.

In the meanwhile Krafft-Ebing's "Psychopathia Sexualis" has gone through many editions. The original scope of this excellent work was considerably increased, but it could not avoid the fate of being outdated, to which even the best book on the subject is destined, *when natural science, in general, advances so rapidly.*

The literature which has appeared since Krafft-Ebing's great work in the field of sexual science, is very comprehensive. In part, the authors have chosen *limited* fields, in that they have treated only of *individual disorders* of sexual psychopathology; in part, they have chosen a wider field in that they have included the *whole* of sexual life. Only very few have treated the *sexual-pathological phenomena* for themselves alone. If I increase the number of the latter it is because my professional activity in a practice of *twenty years* has afforded me a quite unique mass of material.

PREFACE

This book did not originate at a desk in the editorial room, but in the consulting room. Living experiences were the sources from which we drew. Moreover, I was able to base my statements upon *examples* which *I had* myself observed and investigated, and seldom needed to draw upon outside casuistic arguments.

In the preface to the first edition of the "Psychopathia Sexualis," Krafft-Ebing says: "The medical profession should devote itself to an industrious study of all human forms of life."

He also states that whoever makes psychopathology of the sexual life the object of a scientific discourse, is face to face with a dark side of human life. However, it tends to make amends for the moral philosophers and aesthetics to be able to trace back to *morbid stipulations* what is offensive to their ethical and aesthetic minds. Since this thought was expressed, three decades have gone by without its being possible to bring *the pathological in sexual life to general appreciation.*

Yet in this book one will search in vain for *complaints* and *accusations.* I have been very careful to avoid everything which might be regarded as a lack of cool objectivity. The facts speak for themselves.

I dedicate this book to the spirit of Krafft-Ebing. If my "Sexual Pathology" may fulfill the same purpose for our time that his "Psychopathia Sexualis" did for his, then will be attained the goal at which I have aimed.

MAGNUS HIRSCHFELD, M.D.

SEXUAL PATHOLOGY

SEXUAL SYMBOLISM

THE POWER of attraction which one person exercises upon another never proceeds from the whole person. It is much more often only single spiritual and physical qualities, sometimes in a lesser, sometimes in a greater number, which attract and hold; in fact it not rarely happens that it is only one single quality in a person by which the love of another person is attracted. Blemishes and defects in a person are thus scarcely regarded objectively as such, but rather, because of the preference, are subjectively wholly overlooked.

This partial attraction, attraction of partiality, is called "individual fetish magic" by Krafft-Ebing, and is regarded as the "germ of all sexual love." As there is a physiological fetishism, so also there is a pathological fetishism which stands opposed to it and which in its crudest form is characterized by the fact that some object, quite apart from its wearer, as for example a lock of hair or a shoe, may cause a sexual stimulus of the strongest type. Between these two extremes, the normal partial attraction on which depends the great law of sexual selection, and the morbid partial attraction which has to do only with an isolated char-

15

acteristic, there lies the wide domain of passionate affection in which, though the senses may be focused on some one thing in connection with the person to whom it belongs or of whom it is a part, this thing or part is not to be overestimated as it far less often occurs that the person is loved on account of this specific characteristic, than that this characteristic is desired as belonging to the person on whom it is found.

Binet, on the basis of these observations, differentiated between a minor and a major fetishism; with the minor, the erotically attractive part stands well in the foreground both in regard to sexual sentiments and activity, but does not eliminate the wearer to whom more generally the infatuation is transferred. With the major fetishism, such a transfer is the exception to the rule; there is instead an absolute substitution in which the attract-part even though it be an inanimate object, steps completely into the place of the person loved. The name comes from Binet, who wrote of the subject in his work "Du Fétichisme dans L'Amour" in the *Revue Philosophique,* and introduced this conception of sexual pathology to science. This word is usually connected with the Portuguese "feitiço" which means a charm, a kind of magical token somewhat as an amulet, talisman, or the relique in religious veneration, or also, as an idol, whereby one must remember that primitive man conceived of these lifeless objects and symbols as being inwardly animated natures. As early as the year 1769 there had appeared in Paris a book with the title "Du Culte des Dieux-fétishi" which dealt with the worship of many strange things to which a fetishistic characteristic character was attributed. The term fetishism has prevailed because the other no less definite expressions such as "sexual partiality" or "sexual idolatry" have not

16

been used. The name suggested by Eulenberg, ''sexual symbolism,'' has been little used also, although it has the advantage of revealing the inner nature of the phenomenon, for, as we shall see, fetishism has to do with action through concentrated symbols in association with an imaginary idea. The Portuguese root word, moreover, is derived from the Latin ''factitius,'' from ''facere,'' to make, and so conveys the idea of an artificially produced conception. One philologist has proposed that instead of symbolism, the word metabolism be used, from the Greek word ''metaballo,'' which means to exchange or replace, a well-coined, well-turned, clear word, since, indeed, the whole proceeding is one of substitution. The expression which I coined in ''The Natural Laws of Love,'' partial affection, with its antonym partial aversion, is objected to on the ground that the expression is incapable of transformation, and especially allows of the forming of no derivative words. For this conception of partial aversion, literature has adopted the expressions ''antifetishism'' and ''fetish hate.''

Fetishism is related to antifetishism as something positive to something negative, as affection to disaffection, as like to dislike, as love to hate. Although fetish hate occasionally assumes quite violent forms, can even result in criminal violence, yet basically it is usually only a disguised fetishism, in which the feeling of displeasure arises from the absence of the desired sensuous perception. To give an example, the antifetishistic aversion of many women to the man's full beard usually springs from a fetishistic partiality for a smooth face; the positive sign, the male characteristic of the beard, develops a negative; the negative, lack of a beard, takes on a positive form in proportion to the lack of femininity and ability to react in a feminine manner, of

17

the loving person. *Antifetishistic idiosyncrasy plays an important rôle as the cause of spiritual impotency.* I here want to quote two observations which I published in a collection in the *Neurologisches Zentralblatt* under the title, "Ueber Horror Sexualis Partialis":

One of the cases belongs to a medical colleague. He is thirty-five years old, married, thoroughly heterosexual, strongly libidinous. His aversion is concerning the female breasts. It is so strong that such expressions as "bosom," "breast," "Mammae," and all others of this sort, discomfort him terrifically. It costs him a great effort to pronounce the word "breast," and he seeks every means of avoiding it. This aversion for even the word is as widespread as it is characteristic of antifetishists; in such cases of fetishistic concentration, it corresponds to word-magic. His wife, my colleague states, often sings the beautiful composition of Heine's poem, "Whene'er I look into your eyes." He feels an anguished trembling before the line "And when I lean upon your breasts;" he is ashamed before his wife, who knows nothing of his aversion, and does not breathe freely until the ominous passage is over. The image of drops of milk flowing from a mammary gland, not only the sight of it, but even the very thought of it, causes him to vomit. The sight of a woman *en décolleté,* a nursing mother, a large-bosomed woman, and paintings such as the Titian "Venus" make him nauseous. Window displays of the corset shops seem to him *the height of indecency.* In his profession as a physician, this aversion has caused him repeated difficulties. Thus with women he would undertake percussion and auscultation only from the rear. One woman consulted him about a carcinomatous tubercule in the breast; he was unable to look at it, and sent

18

her without examination to a specialist. In order that the necessity of seeing this hated part of the body might not arise so often, he became a children's doctor. He was unable to give any explanation for his strange and painful antipathy. That it could have arisen from some special incident, a ''choc fortuit,'' he considered out of the question; he had investigated into that quite thoroughly, but could discover nothing to which his antipathy could be attributed.

An analogous case of a fetish hate is that of the following woman:

A woman of the better class, about forty years old, told her husband that she would divorce him if he carried through his intention of growing a full beard. The patient is absolutely heterosexual, feels strongly drawn to men who come up to her tastes, has been very much in love with one man for many years, but still, as long as she can remember, has had an unmistakable hatred for full beards. ''Even as quite a young girl,'' she writes, ''I was disturbed when I read newspaper advertisements recommending some beard-raising preparation, in which the beard was spoken of as 'the greatest ornament' or 'the greatest pride of a man.' I cannot express how horrible a beard, whether long or clipped, light or dark, is to me. I admit,'' she continues with characteristic irony, ''that it saves considerable washing of collars and shirts, and even quite horrible neckties can be worn under cover of a beard; that, however, can have no bearing on the question as one of good taste. I could never, never love a man with a full beard. Though some few have this growth of beard, are not most of the men of genius clean-shaven? Caesar, Napoleon, Goethe, Luther, Schiller, and many other intellectual heroes had no

19

beards. Is it not absolutely forbidden the priests of the Catholic Church in order that they may be able to bring to expression a certain spiritual surplus? I think, and this is not meant frivolously, that even the head of Christ on the cross would be more gripping and stirring if the lips, sad and distorted by pain, were not covered with the full beard. To me the full beard is a sign of brutality and violence; I love only the fine proud human nature, and on that account the full beard is to me loathsome in the very last degree.''

One notices the urge toward an intellectually objective view of purely subjective feeling, and further, that in both cases, with thoroughly heterosexual persons, the fetish hate is directed against such secondary sexual characteristics as the beard of the man and the breasts of the woman, as are considered especially typical and attractive indications of sex. This allows general conclusions as to the psychosexual peculiarities of the personalities obsessed by an antifetishism, and even conclusions along the line that they are not absolute types of their sex.

The number of fetishes is unlimited. From head to foot there is no tiny spot on the body, and from head-covering to foot-wrapping there is no little fold of attire from which a fetishistic attraction cannot arise. Since it is so often concerned with such extraordinarily small peculiarities, as a certain sort of a smile or a peculiar type of carriage, it happens that that which attracts as well as that which repulses is not rarely buried in the depths of the subconscious, or is realized only as a purely aesthetic matter of taste. The first doubt as to whether or not there is an erotic undercurrent mixed with this feeling for the beauty of some object, usually emerges

20

at the time of puberty, when a feeling of shame is mixed with the feeling of pleasure. Then the young man or young girl instinctively begins to feel ashamed of the pleasure which is felt at the sight of a beautiful foot or shoe, they blush at the mention of it, and suppress expressions about it, because they would be painful to them.

In this connection there is a diagnostically very important difference of significance in whether the person craves the thing on his own body or on some other person. The real fetishist is interested in the part, or the thing, either on his own body or on some other person. Usually he himself wears the opposite of what attracts him in another; if he loves women with short hair, then he has the desire to let his own grow long; if he has a craving for patent leather, laced, or buttoned shoes on women, then he himself will usually wear clumsy elastic-sided slip-ons, buckled shoes, or boots. It may happen that a fetishist puts on a piece of clothing for which he has a fetish, but usually only in passing, seldom for a long time. If on the other hand the passion is for velvets and silks, pearls and diamonds, or even to having women's clothing on his own body, then the craving falls into the range of narcissism, transvestitismus, or zisvestitismus. Admittedly, fetishes have been often put on, in order to ensnare the fetishists; prostitutes especially have used these lures in great numbers since olden times.

There are cases, to be sure, in which it is hard to differentiate the diagnosis of automonosexualism and fetishism; in the effort to bring the desired object into the closest possible contact with his own body, it is put on for a longer or shorter time, but *not* as with transvestitism or zisvestitism as a projection of a certain personality, but as an apparently exciting sexual object in itself. I will give an example of a case in which the desire to see the fetish on other people passed over immediately to a desire to possess and wear the object himself. The letters which are quoted are very valuable because they afford us an insight into the single-purposed train of thought of many fetishists who are interested only in questions which are in more or less relation to their fetish. In the case of such people the fetish is the nucleus around which their whole life is built in concentric circles. K., who comes from an uneducated class, writes:

"I would like to ask you whether it would be unnatural for me if I should acquire for myself some women's boots, with quite a high leg, as are now in fashion, in order that when things are critical with me I could put them on for a quarter or half hour. If I always have these shoes before me only in my mind, in my imagination, I believe that this will do me more harm than if I had them actually; if I could say to myself that I had the most elegant ones possible at home, then perhaps I would not be disturbed by those on the feet of the women, at which I always have to keep staring when I am on the street, though to be sure, only the most elegant highly polished ones with quite high heels. The lust has been aroused in me beyond all measure by the high women's shoes which are now in fashion, so that I must put a pair on in order to be freed. Otherwise I get terrible headaches; when I have on a pair of women's shoes, then I feel as happy as a king."

Another letter reads: "I have suffered since my youth from a morbid prepossession for women's lace shoes and for women's boots with very high heels. I have always been held back from carrying through my passion by the feeling of the unnaturalness of the desire, but now it has been made even stronger through the fashion developments in women's shoes, with the inserts, the buckles, the buttoned shoes, and the spangled shoes with all imaginable attractive details. I contracted this passion through seeing them. There was a variety troupe at the annual Fair, and before the beginning of the performance, beautiful young girls kept coming out on a ramp before the house, in ball costumes. The girls wore laced ballroom slippers. One of the girls had to climb up on a stool, where there was an iron upright next to her. I was twelve years old at the time I saw all this. The leader made the girl get on the upright, and suddenly the girl had her hips on it and she was stretched out from it like a balance. Her hair fell loosely down, and her beautiful shoes caused such a commotion in my head that I didn't know where I was. When I got home, I immediately put on a pair of my sister's shoes like those I had seen.

"Years went by without my knowing what this was, until one day I read in the newspaper about a girl who cut buttons. From the editorial remark on this, I learned that I also was a fetishist. I have no more peace. I would like very much to buy a pair of women's shoes with very high legs and high heels to wear myself. But always at the last moment I have hesitated about sending in the money, because they must be made to order, and it comes to a matter of about thirty-five marks, at which price one concern will supply them. If I only knew of some place where I could get a second hand pair, that was almost new, at a lower price. I find that it does me more harm when I have the shoes before me only in imagination than when I am actually able to wear them for a quarter or a half hour, after which *I have peace again for about three months.* I want quite high-heeled women's boots with high legs, and some spangled shoes, as for fancy dress.''

The craving of the fetishist is never for a thing in all its phases, but it is violently desired only if it be of some particular character. In most cases the organs of sense turn instinctively to the part desired (one who is experienced in these things can draw important conclusions from just the direction of a person's glance). The senses remain fixed lustfully on this part, though, only if it possesses certain peculiar properties. There is never a person who loves beautiful eyes who is attracted by every eye, but only to those which cause the reaction to which he is subjectively attuned; eyes of a certain sort, shape, color, and even set, as those with long lashes. Just as the organ of sight craves only impressions of a certain type, so also the ear is seeking certain notes and tonalities, and the organs of smell and feeling are not satisfied with any and every, but only with certain particular perfumes and touch sensations. So that from sexual partiality there arises a specialization of sexual partiality which causes extraordinarily great differentiations. The erotic conception of beauty has a wholly personal coloring, it being questionable anyway whether there is such a thing as objective beauty, much as the aesthetes have tried to lay down laws of harmony for forms, colors, and tones. If, however, such rules may have an objective reality in aesthetics, in the erotic there are no such things as absolute laws of beauty, so that the generalizing expression, ''Love is blind,'' shows a complete ignorance of the elementary laws of sexual psychology.

24

Almost without exception the special form of the characteristic sought for is such as in its peculiar composition belongs to either one sex or the other, and even in this sex to only a small part, or even to quite isolated individuals. It is clear that these people can be quite dissimilar among themselves if only the attracting requirement, whether it be a facial expression or a peculiarity of bearing, be there. Since these people, insofar as the other features are concerned, may be blond or dark, large or small, strong or weak, in short, totally different, the lovers themselves often believe that they feel attracted toward quite different types of people, as in truth the people are except for the fact that they all possess a "certain something," and this, which they have in common and which is typical, is the attraction.

The details of sexual partiality are uncommonly minute and manifold, as is easy to see when one collects together the passions of a great number of persons who have been questioned in relation to fetishes for just one particular part of the body. Thus, to give an example, the widespread attraction of the hair is relative to not only its color and the thickness of the hair on the head and body, on its odor, its softness or harshness, but also on the manner of the coiffure. One man likes it hanging free, another likes it braided close to the head, and a third likes the hair parted.

Here is an example of a hair fetishist. The patient, who had been under my observation for over ten years, is a high ranking civil servant, fifty years old. From his reports is the following:

When the patient was seven years old, one evening the children were already in bed when a servant girl came in and embraced them all because she was leaving.

25

This moment is still clear in the mind of the patient, how he clenched his hands in her hair. *With the entrance of puberty the sight or touching of a beautiful part aroused sexual excitement.* From then on, however, relief of this feeling was confined to the hair on men's heads, the hair of women did not draw his attention at all any more, and even with men only the smooth brownish-black hair through which a part must be drawn. Also it depended on where the part began in the front; if it were too far to one side, it was not so pleasing although this was not of such great importance. Patient had a preference for young, bashful boys, who must yield to his wishes quite naturally, though he found especial relief for his condition of sexual excitement, among hairdressers. His procedure was as follows: He stood behind the person concerned, moistened the hair with oil and a pomade which he always carried in his pocket as he did also a comb, and then he drew a part. *In drawing the part in the hair he would come to an ejaculation,* but even the stroking and smoothing of the hair with his hands would give him relief in a moment, especially if he should come lightly into contact with the back of the other person with his own body while tracing the part. He did not uncover his sexual organs, although he said that this would give him even greater pleasure, but he omitted this from a feeling of shame. He himself had a part far back on his head, and dressed his hair very often. But he got more pleasure when he could dress some one else's hair. Just the sight of a part would cause him to run after the person and accost him. When as a young officer he would approach a girl to flirt with her, he would make a very handsome part in his hair; at the decisive moment he would turn his part towards her as a symbol of his highest sexual feel-

26

ings. The cutting of a lock of hair as a remembrance is incomprehensible to the patient, although he can conceive "that he would take a lock of hair from a very dear friend who was dying and whom he would never see again, to have as a keepsake." His main association of ideas runs by way of the sight of a beautiful part back to remembrances of some wonderful hours when he allowed some young people to part his hair "as an expression of his highest gratitude and feeling within the world in which he moved, which was as a closed ring, whose central point was a brownish-black part lying smoothly and neatly combed, the center of light of the great system, in which only little light reveals the life in the great stretches of darkness." The patient, who has become quite a character through his conduct, frequents various drinking places, especially a few in which he is known as "the barber." These drinking places do not bespeak his aristocratic upbringing and family, but are the popular milieu in which he feels happiest.

From what has been said, it will be clear that the differentiation between a minor and a major fetishism, between a healthy and a morbid fetishism, is not at all easy to draw. It is certainly a very popular fetish to carry a lock of hair of the girl a man loves, in a locket, and one can scarcely find anything morbid in this. If, as in a case I have run across several times, a man calls several hundred bunches of hair his own, keeping them all tied separately with bright silken ribbons having the names of the former possessors from whose pubes these hairs came, then one starts thinking a bit and cannot help seeing a sign of pathological fetishism in such a craze for collecting.

That fetishism has little in common with an objective

27

sense of beauty, allowing that there is such a thing even,
is shown by the countless examples in which fetishists
become passionately interested in deformed, crippled,
and mutilated parts of the body, an inclination which in
the field of clothes fetishism corresponds to a prepossession for ragged clothes and broken-out shoes. I had
one case in my practice, a companion to the love of the
philosopher Cartesius for squinting women, one patient
who had a great affection for the staring eyes of women
suffering from morbus Basedowii. Many men are also
quite ''keen for'' lame and hunchbacked women, and
occasionally women for limping and deformed men, especially for such as have lost a limb in the war. The following case of crutch fetishism was observed by Dr. A.
Kronfeld and myself:

Dr. S., writer, of Dutch extraction, thirty years old,
was sent for consultation by his wife. He insisted that
in marital intercourse she walk on crutches and then
take the crutches into bed with her; he at the same time
would be on crutches also. Patient declared that his first
sexual excitement had been bound up with the fact that
at the age of five he had seen a boy who walked on
crutches. Since that time *the sight of crutches had
aroused a fascinated sexual desire in him.* Because of
this fact, for many years women as such had entered
his mind as sexual beings. Since puberty he had delighted
in the idea of crutches, had also bought some at different
times, but always after a short time had burned or
thrown them away from shame or disgust. This feeling
did not last very long however, and he always bought
new ones. He experienced special pleasure when he went
out on them secretly in the evening. It was not the
thought of having the sympathy of the passers-by, but

28

he was excited by the crutches themselves with their soft padding for the armpits. He had lived a chaste life until marriage. His present wife was his first love. She is sixteen years older than he and aside from her intellectual charm, attracted him through the fact that she always wore such rich furs, which also worked an erotic charm on him. In the beginning she had treated him with a complete understanding. He had been especially happy in his married life when his wife gripped him under the armpits to support him, because he was very weakly, or when he would support her in the same way while climbing stairs. Of late however the wife has felt that her husband's crutches are a slight upon her own erotic value, an objection which is often raised by wives in respect to the fetishes of their husbands.

The stooped, long and lanky but weakly man revealed nothing unusual in his nervous system. Psychically he was a weak, sensitive, easily offended character, of fine poetic feelings and great impressionability. Treatment by suggestion accomplished considerable temporary result.

We will let the curious crutch fetishists speak for themselves; one, who is by no means the only one I have observed, writes:

"I was born on the fifteenth of May, 1890. My father, at the time of my birth, was about forty-six, and my mother thirty-three, both, to my knowledge, thoroughly normal. When I was five and a half years old my father took us to live in R. There I used to see from our window every day a young boy of about twelve who played on the street and who, because of his crippled right leg, used a crutch. *I could not take my eyes off him,* but experienced in watching the boy what was to me at that age an inexplicable attraction. I also remember the time while we were in R. that walking with my mother I often used to see a certain well-dressed man who used crutches, but as I can still remember, apparently showing off just as much as I later did myself.

"After my father's death my mother moved to Berlin. Then, when I was eleven, I walked for the first time on crutches. I cannot say exactly when it was; it may have been a bit later, when I was fifteen. This latter I consider more probable. At any rate I remember active abnormal sensations from this time on . . . at fourteen and a half I had a very serious case of meningitis and cerebrospinal meningitis. . . . From that time on, at great intervals, I used to make myself crutches out of broomsticks and such things, and walk on them secretly in my own room. Later, when I was a student, first in Kiel and then at three different times, I bought crutches and by this time, usually late at night, I would go out on them in the streets secretly for long stretches of time. There was an exception during the period before I became acquainted with my present wife. I had so far overcome my feeling of shame in public . . . it was during the winter of 1917 . . . that during the time I was taking my bar examinations in L., with the exception of a few steps in the courtroom, I walked about during the daytime on crutches for about a fortnight.

"Until I was twenty-six I had never been with a woman. Also I never discovered any signs of homosexuality. I always had a terrible fear of intercourse. I was prevented from finding a companion on the streets partly through the bashfulness which had been bred into me, partly through fear of discovery, and partly through my

30

very scanty pocket money. So I masturbated, usually once, rarely twice, every night. *As a stimulus I would imagine beautiful women wrapped in furs and walking on crutches.*

"During the time of my engagement, though I lived in the same house as my fiancée, I did not have intercourse with her, but with a terrible effort I stopped masturbating. The desire for that is gone! Or at least my will is stronger than every urge. On the other hand I cannot prevent an erection at the sight of normally built and well-dressed people, especially women, walking on crutches. At the sight of beggars or people who have limbs amputated, I have no sensation at all. In the same way I have an erection whenever I feel furs. But this happens only when I wrap my wife in her furs, or cover her with a fur robe for her afternoon nap, or turn up the fur collar of my coat.

"Since the time of my marriage . . . I was married in June of this year . . . both these abnormal sensations have been limited to my wife, whom I love exceedingly and whom I won with great difficulty. Furs and crutches! My wife is thirteen and a half years older than I! But we have tested each other out, twice we separated in anger, we were driven together for the third time, and are happy! Only one thing, and therefore my confession. What has made me cry aloud and has made me want to walk on crutches again is not only the fascination of the sexual sensation. It is a feeling of bodily fatigue which I have, for example, when I have to stand for a long time in the street car, when I have to walk a long way on foot, and so on. It is a wish in my brain which is stronger than I and torments me into an irritable nervous state. Then there is one thing more. My wife once told me that she herself, on account of some rheumatic trouble, had

31

to walk on crutches for some months in Aachen. And now, because she is naturally anemic and weakly, I cannot help thinking of that time, and I wish fervently that she would just once do what I want and come to me wrapped in her furs and walking on crutches, and go walking with me!

"One more thing, to close. I am not as potent sexually as I should be if quite normal, and, as far as my wife and I can judge, my testicles are actually somewhat dwarfed. I cannot have intercourse more than once, at the very most twice, in the space of an hour. It often happens that I need a very long time before the first discharge. This is especially the case when I have been working very hard at some intellectual task. Then, in order to assist me, my wife takes hold of me under the arms, or tells me about the time when she was on crutches. This always helps. But despite her love, my wife cannot fully understand my thoughts and wishes. She is unhappy when I have an erection as a result of conversation about furs or crutches. She, who despite the difference in our ages is sexually the stronger of us, feels that through these thoughts I am robbing her of part of my love. And that is *not true*.

"But my wife is almost forty-four years old. Luckily, as otherwise the difference of age would be very troublesome, I am not strong sexually, and in ten years or even less I will be leading a sexually wholly abstemious life. And I believe that later on when the sexual excitement weakens, my wife will also better understand such aids as the crutches. But that is not yet the case. We are both still young, and the years should be a riot of happiness, with no shadows, with mutual understanding and complete fulfillment of what the soul craves . . . this alone is my desire.

32

"My wife has just bought herself a long, soft, seal fur-piece, at my request. But my longing for crutches! I cannot persuade her to go on crutches, and she does not of herself wish to renew the time at Aachen. These two last sentences contain my sad lot."

Here again one notices the change of focus from an autistic to a fetishistic viewpoint. What is even more remarkable in this case is the feeling of weakness arising from the desire and pleasure of crutches. This one sees very often. Thus people with a fetish for cold believe that they suffer from heat, and actually do suffer. People with a fetish for pressure take refuge in neuralgic pains which disappear after pressing or squeezing. It is not easy to decide whether the organic trouble is at the root of the fetishistic inclination, or whether the fetish is the primary cause of the painful sensation which can be appeased and relieved only by the fetish. It was already known before the World War through cases described by Lydston and Krafft-Ebing, that a fetishistic attraction could emanate from men with amputated arms and legs. Bloch in his "Sexualleben" mentions a man who had a fetish for hermaphrodites. This man, a riding-master, was obsessed with the idea of finding a hermaphrodite with whom he could have sexual intercourse. I also know of cases in which men feel attracted toward women who have some defect of speech, as a lisp; and also one woman who was especially attracted to men who stuttered. Even absolute illnesses such as chlorosis, jaundice and consumption are fetishistic objects, and, which is most remarkable of all, even venereal diseases are not excluded. One aristocratic lady who came to me was sexually aroused by warts, callouses, and particularly by corns. Fetishes for wooden legs have been ob-

33

served, and lovers of women with a strong growth of beard. Quite some time ago I ran across what was to me the most remarkable case of all, a man who had a passionate inclination to pregnant women. He would search through the streets for women who looked hopeful, and would often follow them for long distances. The further along the pregnancy was, the more his sexual urge was aroused.

It seems that in all cases of attraction to deformities and defects, of which many more examples could be cited, sympathy should not be underestimated as a motive for the affection.

One patient writes characteristically: "Four years ago I became acquainted with my husband R., a Swiss by birth, and terribly hideous, as was also his sister, both of whom had been orphaned for years. I met him at a party. At once I liked him because he was ugly. I always like ugly people because they are usually shunned by others, if they have some infirmity, and I have always found true golden hearts in them. So-called beautiful men, on the contrary, are out and out repulsive to me."

There are men and women who are erotically captivated beyond all by the *helplessness* of others. They derive pleasure as much out of serving as commanding these people. The majority of marriages which seem inexplicable because of social, physical, and other differences, can usually be explained on the grounds of a fetishistic attraction.

But how is this latter to be explained? In 1887, in the *Revue Philosophique* (Paris, No. 8) Binet set forth the thesis that here a "choc fortuit" produced the effect of a psychic trauma, and almost all authors in this field

34

since then have adopted similar viewpoints, with but relatively minor modifications. So Ziehen speaks of "determining" experiences, and the Freudian school also lay a great weight, and to our mind too great a weight, on "accidental factors" and "infantile impressions." Freud himself has repeatedly appealed against the erroneous reproach that through his emphasis on infantile impressions, he has denied the importance of the hereditary constitutional considerations. He writes:

"Such a reproach springs from a narrow need for causality of the people, which wishes to be satisfied by a single thing produced in opposition to the already familiar forms of reality. Psychoanalysis has said a lot about the accidental factors in etiology, and but little about the constitutional factors, it is true, but only because it has something new to contribute to the first, while little is known now which was not known before about the second. We refuse to say that there is any contradiction in principle in the two etiological motives; we assume rather an orderly coöperation of both for the creating of the observed effects. Both together determine the fate of the person, rarely, almost never, is one of these forces alone. Only in individual and isolated cases can the share of activity of each be allotted. The range of variation in the amounts of the two factors will, to be sure, also have its extreme cases. We will estimate the share of activity of the constitution and of experience, according to our understanding, and will reserve the right according to changes in our understanding."

However, whoever examines the writings of the psychoanalysts without bias will not be able to escape the im-

35

pression that the whims of exogenous fate are assigned an irrelatively larger rôle than the inner "demons" of the sexual constitution.

Krafft-Ebing also, who rejected Binet's theory in regard to homosexualism, masochism, and sadism, makes an exception here, because insofar as regards fetishism he accepts the doctrine of "accident agissant sur un sujet prédisposé." By "accident" is meant any sort of a chance happening, while "predisposition," as Binet expressly stated, can be understood only as meaning *a general nervous hyperesthesia.* To me the hypothesis of occasional connection, whose representatives *do not refute the constitutional and endogenous* in favor of the "predisposition," seems wholly inadequate in its present form. It actually has to do with the supposition that a new and enduring sexual attraction and excitement is limited primarily by the attracting object, and not through the peculiar constitution of the sexual organ of reception . . . a theory which has not yet, and still cannot be proven. For though it is too obvious to require proof that the first contact of the muffled sense of sex with that which is its fate releases sensations of desire, yet when we compare the ubiquity of sexual attractions with the rarity of individual sexual reactions, when we notice the *enormous electiveness* which rules human sexual urges, and when we realize that the very same object which will set one person into the highest ecstasies will leave millions of others *unaware and without any reaction,* then it is manifest by all the rules of logic that it can be only *the constitution of the sexual psyche,* of the central nerve organ, of the *specific constitution* which decides. What we consider attractive *depends on particular features of our internal make-up,* not upon the attraction as such.

36

In love there is no accident, *everything is according to law*. We are accustomed to term as a *chance* event one in which two sets of causes cross each other. In the cases before us there are the accidental external causes and the constitutional internal causes. However, even when in a concrete case a sequence is indicated in which an animate or inanimate object calls forth the first libido, it is still not proven that the inclination was attained, "determined," by this experience, for it must have begun at some time, and have been first expressed in this connection at some time. The theory is still in the air; as Krafft-Ebing says in agreement with Binet himself, "The cause through which the association arose is, as a rule, forgotten. Only the result of the association remains known." Certainly as regards a partial attraction, it cannot be claimed without further proof to support the supposition that a prepossession for eyebrows which grow together, Manchester trousers, cigarettes, or the smell of Russian leather is hereditary, but it is just as unfounded to believe that after some object which is in almost daily use has played a rôle in a chance, almost never-realized experience in a person's youth, this object through that experience should acquire a lifelong and so decided sexual significance. Here obviously many complicated circumstances must come into the consideration, which stand in a *very intimate* if not always immediately clear connection with the direction of the constitutional urge. *As with every sexual reaction, so also with fetishism, the question is in the end one of a reaction limited by the endocrines.*

That infantile impressions cannot be influential here to any decisive degree is shown also by the fact that fetishists often incline to objects which in their youth were absolutely not present. Experiences of World War I have been very instructive on this point. Soon after its appearance, the "field gray" uniform became an exceedingly strong fetish for many women, and this in many cases caused an antifetishistic feeling towards the gayly-colored uniform of peace times. In the second year of the war an old lady came to me, who, as she expressed it, had become "quite bothered" by the leather gaiters of the officers; a homosexual lawyer, forty-five years old, was aroused from 1914 on to the highest pitch of sexual excitement by the Iron Cross. People without these decorations left him quite cold. Even the simple black-and-white striped ribbon of the order caused an erection. Supposing that the chance sight of the leather or iron object could have had the same effect upon every and any neuropath, in these cases and the many similar ones which could be cited, one is forced to say with Moebius that "every explanation can only be superficial."

In the following I wish to repeat the explanation which I gave in my "Wesen der Liebe" (p. 152) for fetishism in its many kinds and degrees. First of all, the character of a particular personality which determines the direction of his life is primarily inborn. The often quoted sentence of Horace about the eternal recurrence of human nature which is not to be cast out even with a pitchfork, is one of the truest maxims of biology. To be sure, habits and circumstances of life, education and all sorts of accidents and experiences are of the greatest importance for the external course of a life, but the stamp of the individual remains. *Corresponding to the nature of the personality is also that of the sexual urge and love in its own peculiar and individual essentiality, inborn in every person, a dowry of nature, for good or for evil.* The person and his love are an *inseparable* unity. But not only is the general direction of the

38

urge, no matter toward which sex, based on the nature of the individual, but also the special prepossession for the groups of people of this sex who are characterized in the particular manner. It is not a matter of chance whether a man will love a girl who is thoroughly submissive to him, and whom he will support, or an older woman, his intellectual superior, upon whom he will depend; or a woman marry a gushing youthful type of boy, or a man who is set in his ways, *but this depends upon the particular inner nature of the lover.*

If however, it is some particular characteristic which excites especially, as the eye, the foot or head-covering, then this *part in its particularity* will be regarded as something chiefly characteristic of the direction of the feelings, as a measure true of the type can be regarded as a *concentrated symbol.* The partial attraction, then, is not based on any chance occurrence but upon the particularity of the psychosexual nature. These complicated associations and anastomosized nerve connections are etiologically more difficult to grasp than the direction of an urge towards a sex, a type, or an individual.

I agree thoroughly with my friend Professor Lippshuetz in Dorpat, that the problem with fetishism is much the same as with the conditioned reflexes described by the physiologist Pawlow in his work on the psychic secretions of the salivary glands. Just as the digestive glands begin their secretion before the mouth and stomach have taken in the apparently appetizing food, indeed at the mention or sight of it, even at the mention of something else which is often in a very distant connection, in the same way there is a secretion of the sexual glands at the sight or the oral, written, or pictorial representation of an object which is calculated to satisfy the much more peculiarly individual feeling of sexual hunger.

39

My colleagues occasionally set me the question: Is fetishism also somehow connected with the inner secretions? This is then to be answered in the affirmative insofar as the psychosexual character and receptivity of the one person, and the conceptions which he has in this connection, depend upon the particular mixture of the male and female characteristics; this however is especially dependent upon the relations and influences of the andrase and the gynase upon the nerve center. Thus it is also with the capacity for reaction to a fetish, and so in the last analysis fetishism and antifetishism are caused by the endocrines and inner secretions. There is, to be sure, an association of ideas, but this does not arise fortuitously, as Binet and Krafft-Ebing believe, but through such conceptions as must, without this being realized, connect the subject with the object as the aim of his desire. It is a fascinating task to follow up this highly personal train of thought. We will explain in a few cases how the connections were formed between the fetishist and his fetish.

A few years ago I was visited by the spiritual leader of a sect who confessed with great reluctance that he had an unhappy inclination to *high heels,* on women's shoes. He felt this passion to be a great humiliation, but he could not refrain occasionally from asking prostitutes, for a price, to allow him to *kiss* their heels. About the same time a former officer wrote me: "My passion: Women of the Amazon type, dark eyes, full black hair, full figure, short, high feet, and relatively large girth in the joints of the limbs. A voice which as far as possible has that huskiness which often comes to people who are in the open a lot, especially in the south, and which speaks of health, love of life, and a certain high spirit.

Much leather, creaking if possible, in the clothing, especially the belt and shoes. A woman's foot in a leather shoe or boot, of the French high-heeled type which was the fashion in the seventies, has a great effect upon me, or a woman with such footgear getting wet or wading in water. The attraction, naturally, will be increased or diminished to nothing, through the accompanying spiritual and intellectual factor. So I am a shoe and boot fetishist only in the sense that this gear must be on the foot of the woman who is already sympathetic to me, in which case it will symbolize to me above all *the idea of womanly energy and decision.* Have had intercourse only with women, and on the whole very seldom, probably never without the concurrence of the circumstances mentioned above, but also not without the important spiritual motive. After release from a formal marriage which was contracted without any consideration for my own wishes and so ended unhappily, I took another wife. My companion knows my taste, satisfies it partly through her own natural characteristics, and also consents partly from love insofar as her nature allows. And after my first wife's apparent aversion to my 'abnormality' (apparently for lack of love) and now in its place the willingness (dictated by true love) to do these same things, my nature, blighted from youth by its delicacy, has emerged, and . . . at the age of fifty-two, I am about to become a father.''

A teacher writes: "I suffer from a fetish for the sound of shoes, and am forced to follow women whose shoes creak when they are walking. The rhythmic sound of fine shoes excites me sexually to a great degree, and I delight in this sound until there is an ejaculation. This reminds one of the case reported by Moraglia, in which a

41

man would have an ejaculation through having a prostitute, naked but for her shoes, sit opposite him and make creaking movements with her shoes.''

How to explain the strong passion of the men belonging to the type described above, for a special sort of women's shoes? The basic motive is heterosexual. The Amazon woman is the opposite of their own nature, which the officer describes himself as ''mild and timid.'' The connection arose in their minds between the high-heeled leather boots on the woman's foot and a really brisk, determined stride. This gradually became the concentrated and concentric symbol of the type, and indeed finally became so strongly so that these boots were in a visual or acoustical capacity the *conditio sine qua non* for their sexual stimulation.

Another patient laid less emphasis upon the shoes than upon the woman's walk. ''I can recognize in a person's walk,'' he writes, ''how the person values himself. And for that reason, if a woman walks proudly, it flatters my ambition to please a person who thinks so highly of herself. It excites me excessively when I see a woman who does not take little tripping steps, but walks with her feet right on the ground and lifts her feet gravely and springily like a horse. I like best of all to walk arm in arm through the streets with a woman who consciously has this pride in herself. I always think when such a briskly walking woman prefers me and allows me to walk with her, that all other people must envy me because so powerful a personality, who knows well the admiration she deserves, should have chosen me from among so many.''

42

Very characteristic of this version of partiality are the following lines of an arm fetishist, who writes:

"For me, who loves beautiful people in full possession of their creative powers, the arm is a fetish. To me it is the essence of a personality that is sympathetic to me; in it is expressed the fullness of strength, which intoxicates me, of a proud, stately, commanding individual. It is the symbol of energy, of powerful activity, which I love in a person dear to me."

As the last instructive example I add the "theory" of a nail fetishist, giving the various objective reasons for his intense passion. He argues thus:

"Regarded purely objectively, a beautiful hand, especially a woman's, is something splendid. Imagine even the rosy shining nails of a slim rosy finger, ending in a snow-white long, smooth, round-filed or even sharp-filed point, through even this alone the hand can gain beauty and charm. Many, to be sure, may say that to them these 'talon like points are displeasure, offend their aesthetic sensibilities; that, however, is probably just a matter of taste, since I must also say that a hand with short fingers and square-cornered nails can be made considerably more lovely through the filing of the ends in the shape of a thorn, as Vatsyayana has already said. Max Dessoir, and to my mind justly, deals with the aesthetic motivation of fetishistic love in his treatise 'On the Psychology of Vita Sexualis.' He says, '*In pathological degeneracy the aesthetic motive leads to fetishistic love.*' Although the pleasure does not remain at the same pitch, but is more widely specialized, it tapers

43

off to such a degree that beautiful hair, for example, or
. . . to return to my own prepossession . . . a beautiful
hand with beautiful nails is in itself enough to arouse
considerable passion. For practical reasons, because of
the laborious work with the hands, we men have been
accustomed to cut our nails short. That we call 'culture.'
The beasts have claws. We men must distinguish ourselves from the animal kingdom by having our nails
clipped short. That is the general idea. But we men,
insofar as we do not belong to those classes who have to
do heavy work with their hands, should profit by the
example of the Japanese who, aside from their general
care of the body, have also a definite regard for the care
of the hands and the nails. Up to now, to be sure, the
prevailing impression of a manicure was coupled with
thoughts of the demimonde hungry for a man, or the
useless members of the 'four hundred.' The ones who are
least manicured belong to the 'golden mean.' For the
last few years fortunately, there has been considerable
progress compared with former years. In ancient times
great weight was laid on the care of the hands and nails
by the Egyptians, the Greeks, and the Romans, and, as
can be seen from their drawings and paintings, by the
people of the Oriental culture, the Japanese, Chinese,
and Siamese—as still today—and more recently the
Turks, Persians, etc., and of the Europeans, particularly
the French, Italians, English, and Hungarian women,
and not least, let there be thanks, our German women!
They all work away at the care of their hands, often
with the most delicate of cosmetics.

"The habit of pointing the nails which has just recently arisen is to my mind no mere fad, but it has a
deep psychological basis. The woman who carefully
tends her nails and has them long and pointed wishes

44

thus to express to the man who becomes desirous of her
. . . that is the only aim of a woman, it lies deep in her
nature. . . . 'These enticing perfumed hands, these
long snow-white nails, I will allow you to kiss them, beloved, if you are a fetishist! With these white, sharp-
pointed nails I will scratch you; if you prefer a gentler
sort then I will titillate and brush against you quite
lightly with these beautiful shimmering cool nails which
I will round off just a bit so that there may be no wound,
if you are a masochist. And thus will not only your
sexual urge be satisfied, but also mine will blaze up into
a frenzy; for I am a sadist!' ''

From these last remarks it follows that next to the
sense of sight, it is the sense of touch which hopes for
pleasure from the long nails which this *apparently
metastrophic fetishist regards as the corporeal symbols
of a woman who would treat him according to her whim.*
The arguments of this nail fetishist, in turn, afford us
a good insight into the way these people try to generalize
aesthetically on their particular inclination, and, further,
how the fetish becomes for them, usually without their
realizing it, the point of departure for their circle of interests and studies, slipping gradually further and
further away from the original central point. The following letter of a Russian gerontophile is also a good confirmation of the symbolic interpretation of fetishism.

"I love silken neckcloths, because to me they *symbolize
the soul,* which can only be *compared to a silken fineness,*
and the nature of the *beloved.* I feel the same way about
a beard. It must be very well kept, soft, and reach down
to the chest, because only through that is the full su-

45

periority of the male to be recognized. And gray in color, because only this color beard gives a man dignity.

"A scrubby beard and a woolen neckcloth, if they were not actually repulsive, would at least leave me quite indifferent. If the beard of one whom I loved should become scraggly through neglect, then I would quickly make it soft, and smooth as silk, again, as though I feared that the superiority of his worth might suffer forfeiture through this degradation. And if he should wear a woolen neckcloth, I would quickly replace it with another of silk, because to me his gentle soul could be reflected only through this latter. Lacking both of these symbols which so delight me, I am incapable of arousing any sexual feeling."

Finally one last example in which the fetish comes to expression as the exciting symbol for the endocrine sexual constitution:

Mr. B. Z., student of political economy, twenty-one years old, shows a peculiar form of fetishism, namely a strong sexual reaction toward rubber air cushions. Mr. Z., whose feminine nature had been noticed by his family for a long time without their having any idea of the true reason for it, observed in himself quite suddenly, about the end of his fourteenth year, a strange urge to handle rubber air cushions, to blow them up tight, and hold them against his body. He was totally unable to figure out the reason for these mysterious manipulations, since he had no knowledge whatsoever about sexual things. The urge, purely instinctive, to be surrounded by air cushions, to be in permanent bodily contact with them, kept growing stronger and stronger and after a short time led to a

46

deep depression because no relief appeared. One evening, about four weeks after, the first ejaculation occurred. That evening, as always, he had blown the air cushion up tight, while in bed, and then had spontaneously laid it upon his body so that the region of the abdomen and genitals was stimulated by it. The stimulus arising from the fetish was mainly of a tactile nature; there followed later, secondarily, through association, an erotic excitement from the mere odor of rubber, as it was typical of the smell of the air cushions. The air cushion could exercise certain effects only in a visual manner, while its acoustical effects were none.

The imaginative conception which entered with the first spontaneous act of onanism, which was repeated daily with but few interruptions during the next six years, had always the same basic motif: a large, strong, fat man, who was put into some situation or other with masochistic tendencies. The ideas which brought the most pleasure, of plump thighs and a fat body, were evoked by pressing and touching the smooth, full-blown air cushion. It is remarkable how in later years the symbolizing of the desire for a live partner led more and more to a substitute. Finally an adequate sexual object not being available, Mr. Z. put on a very large man's suit which he filled out with the help of an air cushion, and a deliverance and sexual relief resulted from the spectacle in a mirror, in which he saw not himself but the object of his sexual cravings. Air cushions were always used as stuffing, because other things, such as down pillows, had no sexual effect. The first sexual impulse, as related, occurred at fourteen. A memory complex could be traced which springs from the age of eight and had a certain relation with the air cushion fetishism. At this age Z. saw an air cushion for the first time, and in one of the following days, in a humorous act at the circus, saw a man who was blown up like a rubber ball. The two experiences interested him greatly at the time, but were forgotten until taken up again by the psyche as a sexual motive upon the entrance of puberty.

This infantile impression, however, is not to be considered a sort of "choc fortuit" which was in any way directional for the sexual constitution; rather it is the sexual psyche, already limited in the germ by the endocrines, and whose feminine component here greets us in the form of a homosexual masochism, which at *so early a time accepts the sensory impression as adequate.*

If, after the general consideration of the nature and causes of fetishism, we turn to the *individual forms of partial attraction,* then we soon recognize that the extraordinary wealth of the phenomena in this field make possible division to fit the most differing points of view. Because every part of another's body can cause, and every part of one's own body can receive a fetishistic stimulus, we are in a position to differentiate as well according to the *source of stimulus,* the object, and the *reception of the stimulus* in the subject. The points of reception of the fetishistic sexual excitement divide themselves according to the different organs of sense, so that, as the question is of visual, aural, olfactory, gustatory, or tactile stimuli, one can differentiate between *optical, acoustical, olfactory, gustatorial, and tactual fetishism.*

One class of these sexual stimuli works on the organs of the bodily surface which are capable of reaction through the medium of the air, the other through direct contact. There are, therefore, distant fetishistic stimuli, which reach the retina, the eardrum, or the olfactory surfaces of the mucous membrane, and proximate stimuli

48

which touch the skin and the tongue membrane. These two groups of distant and proximate attractions show still other physiological differences. The distant attraction is almost always the one to which the sense turns first. It precedes the proximate and so is primary, while the essentially stronger, proximate attraction usually enters only as secondary. In the normal course of procedure, it works as desire only if *a prepossession* has been established through the distant sexual attraction.

The causal connection usually is that, causally and temporally, the conception, aware through the distant cognition, is the primum movens. On this primary stimulus everything else follows as a chain of reflexes, or better, as steps of reflexes, now repressed, now not repressed. We will try to illustrate the proceeding. A sense impression, arousing desire, forces its way to the nerve center; the feeling which then arises causes a reaction on the motor nerve tract; this reaction returns from the periphery to the nerve center as a new and stronger stimulus. The internal raising of the desire is transformed on the motory nerve cords into a new action, whose operation again presses inwardly as a heightened feeling of desire. And thus it goes, from without on the sensory track inwards, from within on the motory track outwards, and then always further centripetal-sensory, centrifugal-motory, now known, now unknown, now interrupted, now not interrupted, in steps, until through the summation of the stimuli there is an increasing erotization of the brain cells and so gradually the peak of desire is reached unless a stop has been called on one of the lower steps by the interference of some external or internal influence.

The organ of sense of longest range, in a living creature, is the one which guides him in his sexual life. The

49

sequence for humans is: sight, hearing, and smell. This applies equally to physiological and pathological attraction. The eye is especially the medium of human love. Possibly because through its use in the erotic realm, the involuntary seeking and pursuing of sexual stimuli, it has become for us the chief receptive station for beauty. With other creatures, other senses take this leading position, and always, with every animal, his most delicate organ is also erotically the most sensitive perceptive organ. With many the sense of hearing stands in the first place. Thus we know that many male birds woo their mates exclusively with their voices, often during the night. Although the gay plumage of the male bird has the same effect upon the females in the birdworld that a gay uniform has upon many a human female heart, yet the female will be lured from a much greater distance by the songs of the male who, according to her judgment, sings the sweetest. In the animal world, attraction through scent plays a large rôle, and also elsewhere where the sense of smell is highly developed. Very many animals have glandular organs whose secretion is solely for the purpose of attracting the male. The male will follow the scent of this perfume, which is pleasing to him, for unbelievable distances; insects will come for miles to the place where the sweet smelling female is. Many animals become absolutely intoxicated through smelling so that finally, in the ecstasy of smelling, there is scarcely time for the sexual act. If smell and sound impressions are the most important with those animals whose strongest sense is that of smell and hearing . . . and the majority of mammals belong to these . . . with the human their efficacy falls far behind that of the eye. We can see this from the fact that in erotic literature, in the descriptions of a beloved object, the description of

50

the outwardly *visible* charms takes up the greatest amount of space. The question of how the beloved smells, tastes, feels and what noises emanate from it, is very rarely dealt with and then only in a subordinate manner, in the higher realms of poetry.

Unconsciously the visual organ of the human is continually on the search for its fetish; involuntarily, whether out-of-doors or in a closed room, it focuses on such sexual impressions as are in tune with its desire, and which are of great value to its pleasure. At the same time the eye tries to avoid antifetishes. I once had a patient, a traveler, who usually missed his train because he could not bring himself to sit in the same compartment with a person who was repulsive to him . . . his antifetishism was corpulence even to the slightest degree. In no small agitation, he would seek, in car after car, for the thinnest looking people. *In the indecision caused by the pursuit of his fetish,* it was not seldom that the train left before he could find a carriage whose occupants pleased him. But one of the precautionary measures which we always meet when the question, in nature, is of love, is that not just one of the senses functions for distant sexual impressions, but several. Nature does not deprive the deaf and the blind of love. So we see that when the eye is dimmed, another organ of sense fills the empty place.

I give the statements of an officer who was shot in the forehead and deprived of his senses of sight and smell. Before his injury it was almost exclusively the optical and olfactory senses through which the sexual stimuli found their way into his consciousness. When these two important centers of sense were lost to him through the severe wound, he began to notice that more and more,

51

as he himself expressed it to me, "the stream of sympathy which formerly came by way of the eye, passed over to the ear." "The hearing was, even before this," he wrote, "very finely developed, but it often neglected the duty of warning which was transmitted to it through the loss of the eye. Since my affections have been conducted through the hearing, I believe that I go more surely than before." The melodious sounds of the voice, pronunciation and sentence structure are now the things that attract him. Through his present affections has also come a feeling of differentiation of the qualities of the skin, especially the shape of the hand, a narrow, soft hand with small, thin fingers leaves him cold, while powerful hands with heavy fingers arouse his excitement. *In this way the type to which he feels attracted remains exactly the same, and he himself is very surprised that his senses of hearing and touch should be able to choose the same type of beloved people as did formerly his senses of sight and smell.* Victor Cherbuliez once said, "For people born blind, a woman's beauty is in her voice." And also Havelock Ellis spoke of how important a means of stimulus the voice is to the blind, when he quoted from an American doctor, James Cooke, who had written a book on the voice as the "index of the soul."

It also happens, not rarely, with people in full command of all their senses, that another organ of sense takes precedence of attraction over the eye. In a love letter which was placed at my disposal are the following lines which I would like to append at this point: "If I attempt to visualize the first hour I found you, I know that your attraction was felt at the same time by both the ear and eye. But I intentionally mention the ear first, because, before I saw you . . . you were holding a

52

conversation, and many people were sitting between us
. . . your wonderful melodious, softly shaded, and facile
voice went through me, almost physically . . . it seemed
to me that never, outside the realms of my dreams, had I
ever heard such tones. Then for the first time I saw you,
and my eyes sought your mouth from which had come
such sounds of music!'' After seeing the raptures with
which many ladies rivet their attention upon certain
singers on the stage, and their rejoicing over them after
the singing, no one can doubt that there is a considerable
erotic element in this. Wedekind's ''Concert Singers'' is
thoroughly true to life. But there are also antifetishistic
idiosyncrasies connected to a considerable degree with
the sense of hearing. Not seldom this antipathy is directed against dialect. A man at some function falls in
love with a woman who, in his eyes, is the epitome of
all feminine beauty. Almost intoxicated with her appearance, he finally manages to be introduced to her. But at
the first sentence of her conversation, when he hears the
strong Saxon dialect, not only does his affection vanish,
but so strong a revulsion sets in that he leaves immediately. This man had always been powerfully attracted
by certain German dialects, such as that of Berlin or
Hanover, while others, especially the Saxon and East
Prussian, had aroused a strong feeling of displeasure in
him.

Defects in speech are responsible just as often for
fetishes as antifetishes. One of my patients, a very
effeminate, metastrophic person, was erotically affected
to the highest degree by a deep woman's voice. Also
others of the noises emitted by people, the sound of their
step, their gasps of breath, even such dissonant sounds
as snoring, sometimes give rise to sensations of desire in
lovers. I heard one of the most peculiar examples of

acoustical sexual stimulus from a sixty-year-old man who told me that for a long time he could remember nothing that so strongly aroused him sexually as "rumbling body-noises." An old lady on my records was set into a state of sexual excitement by the tread of heavy soldiers' boots on the hard pavement. In the quiet of her room she would listen for this sound, and became more and more tense as the steps approached her dwelling. When a troop of soldiers marched by in rhythmic step, she frequently began to masturbate.

Also in the realm of acoustical fetishism is the sexual effect of word sounds. Women have at different times testified in divorce proceedings that their husbands forced them to pronounce strongly obscene words during the act of intercourse, or else they did it themselves, because only thus could they arouse their sexual excitement. One patient, a magistrate by profession, said that his sexual desire is never so much aroused as when he is addressed as "Du" (corresponding to the familiar "you" in English) by some girl of the common people. Apparently here again there is a metastrophic complex. The fascination emanating from certain titles of nobility, even when they are suspect, is very widespread. Women fall into this title fetishism more often than men. A very effeminate man, twenty-four years old, declared as follows: "The title 'Count' or 'Baron' rouses me completely from my sexual indifference. My dreams are usually as follows: I am staying in Berlin; in a wine parlor I become acquainted with a thirty-two-year-old Count who is quite to my taste. I go to his home with him. It is a wonderfully fitted-out place. It becomes night. He takes me into his bedroom. He proposes that I should stay with him always. I explain that this cannot be because I have a position which I cannot afford to lose,

54

While he is speaking to me, servants come in who address him, with very devoted mien, as 'Count.' He will not let me go. I must stay as his guest. I feel very happy about it, and wake up at his last word in a pollution, and then realize that it is only a dream.''

As regards the sense of smell, I could cite a number of cases in which this sense dominated over the others. Thus a lady once showed me a piece of Russian leather which she carried tied to a ribbon under her blouse. In strong superlatives she explained to me the significance which the smell of the leather held for her. The erotic affection for her husband, who had been a surprisingly ugly man and died early, had been totally ruled by smells, especially ''the man's smell of the mixed odors of tobacco and Russian leather.'' Even now she still smells at her dead husband's clothing which still gives off this ''sweet aroma'' to some extent. It would require a great deal of control for her to resist a man who should lure her with this attraction. In another case a woman had her husband, who was at the front, send her his shirts, in order that through smelling them she might excite herself to an orgasm.

If the law is correct that the erotic capabilities of attraction through an organ of sense are in direct proportion to its sensitivity and specialization, then with the human being the sense of smell would rank third. It takes a middle position between the distant attractions, eye and ear, and the proximate attractions, skin and mucous membrane, since it is not a mere aerial disturbance that meets the nerve ends, but corpuscular elements, indescribably fine particles of exceedingly small weight, which disturb the nasal mucous membrane. It is known that with many peoples, as those of Central Asia, there is instead of a lip or tongue kiss, a smell or nose kiss, while for the means of distant attraction, eye and ear, there is nothing analogous to the kiss. In general, with the human being, the sense of smell plays more of a limiting and warning rôle; it serves more in sexual aversion than attraction. Many people say that any and every perceptible odor emitted by a person whom they love, is unpleasant to them. There are here also, to be sure, many individual divergences, since it is always true in love life that every rule is nothing more than a general cross section, because of the enormous personal coloring. In love life the main bodily odors to be considered are the exhalations of the hair follicles, sweat, tallow, and the glands of the mucous membrane. These, according to the intensity and quality of the scent, which differs widely in individual cases, usually secrete much more activity in a state of sexual excitement than when at rest. We notice that for many people the exhalations more often result antipathetically than sympathetically, but, on the other hand, it must be mentioned that very strong erotic excitement is able to prevail over the unpleasantness of the odors. It is evident that even unsympathetic impressions, in the case of strong love, can awaken feelings of desire, which, to be sure, usually have a masochistic basis. Thus I know of a case in which a girl was violently in love with an athlete, who suffered from a foul-smelling ozena. In the beginning this obnoxious odor was exceedingly painful to her, but her passion was so strong that not only did she become accustomed to it, but even missed and sought for it. In another case the pungent reek of a cavalryman's sweating feet caused a strong revulsion in a lady of high standing, and later a feeling of the strongest desire. Here one can almost speak of an antifetish-fetishism.

56

Many authors who busy themselves with osphresiology conclude, from the large rôle which bodily exhalations play in the animal world, that the same must hold true with humans. This is a faulty conclusion, because, as we know, the human sense of smell is, of and in itself, much less strongly developed than this sense in animals. This is anatomically proven as the smell center, the scent-lobes, in the animal brain are much larger than in the human brain, and the glands which form the attracting scents—they are found in part, in humans, in the glandulae vestibulares majores—are functionally completely atrophied.

From the observations of Schiff, Fliess, and others, it may be concluded that there are certain sexual points in the erectile tissues of the nose which are in correlation with the proceedings of the sexual sphere. From this arises the probability that there are erogenous zones in the nasal mucous membrane such as we have long known to exist in the sensory sphere of the skin. May this not also be true in the other organs of sense? It is possible, even, from analogy, probable, but at present we are lacking the ways and means of supporting this conjecture by direct observation. The presence of erogenous zones in the organs of sense raises the question of whether or not the special quality of feeling which differentiates the feeling of love from the other feelings, may not be bound up to certain sexual terminal bodies, constructed according to the principle of specialization, which are present in the organs of sense. If the leading physiologists of today have declared, with von Frey, their belief in the existence of a certain sense of pain which is characterized by the point of pain, then, after all we have learned about the specific quality of sense impressions, it does not, after all, seem wholly improb-

57

able that there may also be for the *sexual feeling special receiving stations, sexual points* within the different organs of sense, of a peculiar sensitivity and receptivity.

According to this interpretation, the sense of taste, the fourth of the human senses, is relatively least of all a sexual point. With men and women the feelings of desire arising from this are more an individual matter than a general matter true of the whole species, while with many animals, next to smelling, licking plays the important sexual rôle; next to the nose, the tongue. The tongue is by no means excluded in the love life of the human; the tongue kiss, cunnilinctus, and penilinctus, which are by no means the only acts belonging to this group, go to prove this fact. But, as the mucous membrane of the tongue has many more tactile than taste buds, it is still to be determined whether the sense of touch is not much more involved in this form of excitement than the sense of taste. That it is not altogether excluded is proven by the fetishistic prepossession, incomprehensible to the normal person, for licking, sucking up, and swallowing human secretions be they almost without taste or smell such as saliva, and blood, or quite sharply odored and flavored as the urine, sweat, vaginal mucous, *preputial sebums, and feces*. The desire to bring the tactile buds of the mouth into contact with the mucous membrane of the genitals not seldom has an *elementary compulsory character which excludes every other form of activity as inadequate*.

The real proximal sexual sense of the human does not lie particularly in the zones of the mouth and genitals, but in the skin generally. Can we speak here also, as with the other organs of sense, of partial attraction and of pathological fetishism? With humans, in principle, the possibilities of a tactile excitement have as a hypothesis

58

a distant prepossession. The contact is not in itself enough; it must proceed from a body or part which possesses an erotic power of attraction. Only when this distant attraction precedes can there arise that sensation which Werther describes: "Oh, how the fire coursed through my veins when my finger unexpectedly touched yours, when our feet met under the table! I drew back as though from fire, but some mysterious power drew me forward again." It may well be that many bodily contacts which are today general customs among relatives and friends, were, when they first arose in ancient times, sexual skin contacts. This applies even to the custom of shaking hands which is today so common. In speech, which is more conservative even than custom, the man still asks today for a woman's "hand" in marriage, and she gives him her "hand for life." As with these contacts of the hands, so it also is with linking the arms, even with the kiss. Embracing and kissing on the cheeks, hand, and even on the mouth, as is done in greeting and taking leave of relatives and friends in many countries quite generally, has sunk to a demonstration of affection with no sexual significence attached to it.

What a difference, though, between the short, fleeting pressure of the hands of two friends greeting each other, and the long fervent pressure of two people who love each other, which causes a stream of pleasant vibrations from the point of contact, through the line of neurons, to the nerve center. How different the barren kiss of etiquette from that contact of the lips in which the consummation of the nerve stimulus leads to a hyperemization irradiating far into the body. In one of my previous books a man compared the love kiss which he received from any other person but his wife, to "soup without salt." It is because of this great difference between erotic and non-erotic attraction that contact, by persons whose characteristics leave the organs of sense and the imagination indifferent or repulsed, will also seem indifferent or repulsive to the sense of touch. The sort of feeling resulting from the contact, often hard to define, but always definitely felt, is thus differentiated by whether the reaction is of an erotic or non-erotic nature, whether or not the sexual chemism is set into action. If the former be the case, then even a very light contact of the foot, the fingertip, the knee, or elbow can arouse a real feeling of desire; if the people be unsympathetic, then the feeling will be unpleasant; if indifferent then the feeling will be one of indifference, that is, being of no consequence, will not come into the active consciousness. If Chamfort once defined love as "l'échange de deux fantaisies et le contact de deux épidermes," or Dante in the "Purgatorio" said that seeing and feeling were the two channels through which love attracted, then it must be said that here the question does not deal with coördinated, but with subordinated proceedings, because feeling does not only follow seeing outwardly in point of time, but also inwardly stands in a subsequent causal relationship to it.

As regards partial attraction in the cutaneous region, it must first of all be mentioned that certain parts of the skin are apparently more sensitive sexually than others. These are the erogenous zones—the term "zones érogenes" originally occurs in the French. There are, in the main, eight parts of the bodily surface, four of which are covered with hair, and four covered with mucous membrane, which are felt as especially sensitive subjectively, and often at the same time, as particularly stimulating to the object. The four hair covered parts are the hairy skin of the head, the region of the beard,

60

armpits, and genitals, which are really areas of sexual charm not only for the sense of sight but also for the sense of smell. Quite similar are the four positions of the bodily surface which are characterized by a tender and thinner overskin which stands midway between the ordinary epidermis and the mucous membrane covering the inner canals (regio labialis, mamillaris, genitalis, and analis). The breast nipples are in the leading position among the places which reduce sexual resistance. It must have been an experienced connoisseur of love who wrote in the "Chansons de Roland," "The man loves with his heart, the woman with the tips of her breasts."

Outside the eight points named, there are still other points of sexual excitement where the overskin is stretched especially taut and lies directly over the bones and muscles with but little fatty tissue under the skin. In humans the special points of sensitivity are the palm of the hand, the soles of the feet, the fingertips, the tips of the toes, the knees, elbows, and the region of the loins.

Further erogenous zones, with many people, are the inner side of the thigh, the nape of the neck, the shell and lobe of the ear. Here again there are individual peculiarities which *presumably are characterized anatomically by a dense accumulation of sexual terminal nerve bodies in certain places*. To add two unusual cases which belong properly to this group, I cite the case of one man who said that he derived a feeling of sexual desire through tweaking the outer corners of his eyes, another through the insertion of a finger into his ear. Both aroused these parts artificially for purposes of masturbation.

It is not without reason that the sense of touch has been termed "the least intellectual of the senses, aes-

61

thetically the least significant.'' There is no doubt that among the higher forms of life tactile impressions are not formed with such great individual differences, nor do they leave such specialized impressions in the imagination and the memory as the stimuli received through the eye, ear, or sense of smell.

The skin always has a quite different feeling also according to the sex, age, and individual nature of the person, and experience shows that great weight is often laid upon the character of the skin, whether, for example, it be flabby or hard, smooth or rough, as a factor of erotic or non-erotic significance. *The fetishist can be exceedingly attracted by a particular skin contact, and the antifetishist be repulsed.* Thus stroking hair, both that growing on a human body, as a woman's playing with a man's beard, and that taken from animals, fur-pieces, usually causes a fetishistic stimulation of desire. Another natural cause of attraction and repulsion is the temperature of the skin; thus I know one patient who goes off in a high passion at contact with cold hands, while warm hands, on the contrary, leave him quite indifferent. In another case a man was obsessed by the urge to occupy a seat which had been left immediately before by a woman. He was able to do this quite easily and without being noticed even in the most crowded cars of the street cars and the trains. The warmth still clinging to the seat from the woman's buttocks often caused an erection. To sit in a seat left warm by a man, caused him great distaste, and in the end was absolutely impossible for him. In hotels, on the railways, and in other such places he would often use the women's toilets, which not rarely brought on reprimands. The following passage tells of a case of cold fetishism which has been under my observation for years:

62

"My interest in scanty clothing is always still very strong, and it is not surprising, since my wife has the same interest, that we frequently speak of it, so that my emphasis on the idea of hardening oneself has undoubtedly been transmitted to some extent to my wife. At least she does not think that she came to the idea wholly by herself. But there is a complete harmony of our opinions in this matter. The only difference is that with me the *thought and sight of such clothing or of pictures of it, causes a sexual stimulation,* which is naturally not the case with my wife. And she has absolutely no idea that it is so with me, knows absolutely nothing of these rather perverse feelings. In this respect she is as pure and innocent as a child. If I should occasionally make a drawing representing a girl on the ice with bare arms and shoulders and naked legs, she regarded it as a joke, for since she is in favor of children having bare legs and low-cut clothes in the winter, she naturally does not take seriously the exaggerations to which my heated imagination inclines. These moments of sexual excitement, which cause such phantasies and simultaneous masturbation, are more prevalent at times when intercourse with my wife is not possible because of one reason or another.

"The phantasies are exclusively concerned with one thing . . . half matured girls in the scantiest of clothing in winter. Moreover, when I was in Partenkirchen in the winter of 1915, I once followed my urge in the presence of my wife, and under trees heavily laden with snow, *took a bath at several degrees below zero in the half-frozen Partnach,* which was exceedingly gratifying to me, while my wife considered it a stupid little boy's stunt 'of which she had not thought me capable.'

"After one year of service at the front, I was assigned to local garrison duty. Our military office, in which I worked, looked out on the schoolyard of a secondary children's school. I was interested to find out how many of the young boys wore short socks in the wintertime. For the same purpose, I stood at noontime at the entrance to the girls' school to find out how many of them were dressed according to my ideas.''

I should like to remark here that very many constraining conceptions, especially many forms of fear or desire of contact—folie de toucher—which usually appear to have come from out of the air and formerly defied every attempt at explanation, in the last analysis have their roots in the sex life. Thus many people have come to me who suffered from a constraining fear of the customary shaking hands in greeting and taking leave of a person. While they were talking to any one, the thought haunted them that they would probably have to endure the painful handshake. If it did occur, then when they got home, they would wash and scrub their hands for hours. It assumed the appearance of an exaggerated fear of infection; in reality, however, it showed an extended fetish hate for the hands of both sexes. I was asked advice some time ago by the parents of a girl who had been charged with assault because she had given a severe blow on the chest, resulting in a hemorrhage of the lungs, to a pulmonic invalid who was standing beside her with his wife. The girl, who had a position at a bank, testified as follows: Since the overcrowding of the means of transportation, she had been in a continual state of turmoil. If a man stood close beside her, so that she felt his body against hers in any way, she literally felt "touched in the most unpleasant manner." She had to exercise the greatest control not to become

64

physically violent towards the man. The displeasure, the qualms, were so great that she finally had to decide to walk the long distance to work, since the crowds had become so thick on the streetcars due to the wartime conditions. If a woman stood near her, she did not have these feelings of distaste; on the contrary, it was usually a feeling of pleasure, but contact with a man was unbearable. She granted that the invalid who had crowded up against her in leaving the car had done so unintentionally, but she *had given him the blow just as unintentionally;* it had happened absolutely of itself, out of self-defense. The girl, who wore her hair short and had a strongly neuropathic and virile make-up, was acquitted.

What is probably the most painful of all is when this sexual fear of contact extends to the sexual organs of the other sex. One man, in himself thoroughly heterosexual, had to take steps for a divorce because any contact of his body, and especially his penis, with the female genital organs was impossible. He compared the feminine organs with "a toad which he could not bring himself to touch." With women also, and not only with homosexual ones, an analogous fetish hate is found, directed against the male penis.

Thus some time ago a woman came to see me, quite frightened and despairing, and reported the following: She herself was thirty-two years old, mother of a ten-year-old illegitimate child; she had suffered since its birth from an inflammation of the uterine ligaments. A year before, she had fallen in love with a twenty-one-year-old man to whose persuasions to marriage she had finally yielded. Since the bridal night he had forced her to take hold of his member with her hand, as only thus could he attain an erection. This, however, was impos-

65

sible for her; she did not deny him intercourse, but the *contact of her hand with his penis filled her with horror* and an indescribable feeling of loathing. She lived in constant fear of this desire of her husband's, and on account of it had repeatedly left him for short periods, as was the case at this time also. She wanted to know whether *his desire of the contact or her fear of the contact* was morbid. Continuance of the marriage was impossible for her in these circumstances, even in the face of the danger that her husband might realize his threat and kill her if she did not stay with him.

For the most part, a person's taste in general, his whole outlook on the world and life, his conduct in life, is dependent upon his fetishistic focus. A man who has a prepossession for Oriental types and Oriental clothes, will travel to the Orient and enjoy its customs and usages; a woman who values in people a certain robust good humor, will be interested in the fashions and time which especially expressed this, as the Biedermeier period. A man who writes that he is especially interested in the "great ladies of the time of Moses," will be strongly anti-Semitic, while some one who says that everything round, fat, and dark in a woman is hateful to him, will come to this same conclusion rather in an associative way. *Beneficial sensations from attracting colors and forms of parts of the body and pieces of clothing are transferred to everything which has even remotedly to do with it.* Thus the whole world is full of symbols. Of many examples in my experience I single out one of my favorites: An aristocratic, single Dutch lady had a passionate prepossession for seamen at work. From their firm movements, their wideset legs, their tattooed chests, the picturesque dirty sailors' costumes,

66

the sounds of drawing in the hawsers, the tossing and catching of bales while loading or unloading cargo, the smell of tar and seaweed, there streamed a magnetism which she could not do without. In order to indulge her fetishism, she lived exclusively in harbor towns, and in the hotels located down along the wharves. She had her bed placed so that from early morning she could look out over the scene, which was erotically exciting to her. In the evenings she would often put on simple clothes and go into the quite common dance halls of the sailors, where she was taken for some shopgirl. She danced tirelessly with the sailors, to whom she would snuggle up quite close. She played her rôle very cleverly, and was never found out.

Erotic partial attraction plays a large rôle also in the choice of a profession, as people usually know themselves. E. T. A. Hoffmann, in his novel "Das Fraeulein von Scuderi," gives a crude but very instructive example, in which he describes a case of jewel fetishism, which is quite common with both sexes. This man, Cardillac by name, became a dealer in precious stones because of his prepossession. He was famous for his work, but those who wanted him to do their work had to wait a long time and stand for a good bit of incivility at delivery, because Cardillac could not bring himself to part with the jewels. It even went so far that, driven by this urge, he waylaid and murdered customers who had taken back their jewelry at night, in order that he might regain possession of it.

Cardillac considered this passion inherited and related the following:

"Wise men often speak of the strange impressions which affect pregnant women, of the wonderful influence which such vivid, but unwilled impressions from without have upon the child. I have been told a curious story about my mother. About eight months before I was born, in company with some other women she was a spectator at a splendid court banquet which was given in the Trianon. There her glance fell upon a cavalier in Spanish garb with a brilliant jeweled chain around his neck, which held her spellbound. She could not bring herself to stop gazing. *Her whole being was consumed with a desire for the sparkling stones which seemed supernatural treasure to her.*

"Many years ago, when my mother was still unmarried, this same cavalier had made attempts against her virtue, but had been repulsed with aversion. My mother recognized him again, but now it seemed to her that in the radiance of the shining diamonds he was a being of a higher sort, the epitome of all beauty. The cavalier noticed the longing, fiery glance of my mother. He believed that now he was to be more fortunate than he had been before. He was able to approach her, even more, to lure her away from her companions to a lonely spot. There he flung his arms about her passionately. My mother reached for the beautiful chain, but in that same instant he collapsed and drew my mother with him to the floor. Whether it was that he had a sudden stroke, or through some other cause, it suffices that he was dead.

"My mother's attempts to untwine herself from the death clasp of the corpse's still arms were in vain. With its hollow eyes, whose power of sight had been extinguished, directed on her, the dead man rolled with her on the floor. Her piercing cry for help finally was heard by those passing at a distance, and they hurried to her and rescued her from the arms of her gruesome lover. The shock caused my mother a severe illness. People

68

gave her and me up for lost, but she regained her health and the delivery was more fortunate than one could ever have hoped. But the horror of that frightful moment had affected me. My bad star had arisen, and had shot off sparks *which kindled in me the strangest and most fatal passions.*

"Even in my earliest childhood shining diamonds and gold jewelry attracted me above all other things. It was considered as a natural childish inclination. But it revealed itself as quite another thing, for as a boy *I stole gold and jewels whenever I was able to get hold of them.* Like the most experienced connoisseur I differentiated by instinct between real jewelry and imitation. Only this attracted me; imitation gold, as well as coined gold, I left unregarded. My father's most terrible punishments were of no avail before this inborn desire. *Just to be able to handle gold and diamonds, I turned to the goldsmith's profession.* I worked passionately, and was soon the foremost master at the trade.

"Now began a period in which the innate craving, suppressed for so long, arose powerfully and grew with might, destroying everything else. As soon as I had finished a piece of jewelry and delivered it, *I fell into a state of unrest, into a state of despair,* which stole away my sleep, health, and cheerfulness. Day and night the person for whom I had done the work appeared before my eyes, adorned with my jewelry, and a voice whispered into my ear, 'It is yours, it is certainly yours, what right have the dead to diamonds!' Finally I set myself to the art of stealing. I had entrance into the house of the great; no lock could resist my skill, and soon the jewelry on which I had worked was again in my hand. But even that did not disperse my unrest. That sinister voice made itself heard again and mocked me

and cried: 'Ho, ho, a dead man is wearing your jewelry!'
I do not know myself how it came about, that I had such
an inexpressible hate for those persons for whom I had
made jewelry. *Yes, in my innermost soul there raged a
desire to murder them, before which I myself quaked
with terror.*"

If we consider the focus of fetishism upon the attracting object, then we must recognize one feature of differentiation which has struck all investigators of this
phenomenon, and which is so marked that it permits a
division into two almost equal groups of fetishism: the
exciting stimulus proceeds either immediately from some
part of the body, or else from some piece of clothing
covering some part of the body. In this sense Krafft-
Ebing had already differentiated between fetishism for
some part of the body, and fetishism for clothing or some
other inanimate object. In my "Natural Laws of Love"
I myself drew a distinction according to whether the
attraction was an immediate part of the person, or a
separable thing, of inherent or adherent attraction. Between the extremes of these two groups of sexual attractions, stands the coherent attraction, by which we understand purposeful changes or adornments on the body,
such as rings of gold, silver, or other metals which are
put through the ears or nose or on the fingers; tattooing
or painting with cosmetics, powder, ink or charcoal,
which is by no means confined to the lower races of
people; even the addition of scars on the skin as the
artificial face scars of the aborigines of South Australia,
or the similar duel scars of which the German student
is so proud, can have a fetishistic significance.

Whether a part of the body will be more often craved
in its natural or in its changed—clothed—condition,

70

is a matter which depends upon which is the condition in which people *will more often catch sight of it*. Thus it is not to be doubted that the hand is often, and the glove relatively less often, a fetishistic sexual object, while on the other hand the shoe relatively often, and the bare foot seldom, exercises this exciting influence. Krafft-Ebing saw that the reason for this was that the hand is usually seen bare, and the foot usually covered. Also we observe that the new appearance and wide spread of some object, such as is caused by fashion or some disturbance in the age, such as a war, brings with it the appearance of many fetishists who are uncommonly keen for this new thing, as the markings or parts of a field uniform. Thus one lady consulted me recently for whom the wound stripes exercised a high degree of sexual stimulus.

That the fetish is not always present from the time of youth, as is commonly believed to be the case, is a fact which experience teaches since a thing may become a fetish at an advanced or even old age just as easily as at the time of puberty. Thus people traveling in other countries on their vacations often become acquainted with objects of common use which they had never known of before, and to which they react fetishistically. For example I know of one effeminate man who had long passed fifty, who after his first trip to London acquired an incurable fetishism for the short swagger-sticks which most of the English officers carry. All these cases throw a helpful light upon the origin of fetishism which *depends upon the subconscious associative elaboration of a sense perception according to the individual sexual constitution*. There can be no talk of "accident," but only of *a reciprocal action, in accordance with law, between the subject and the particular object*.

71

There are two things through which this physiological proceeding acquires a basically pathological character, first, through the almost *exclusive concentration* of the imagination upon the *one* part, and secondly through this important circumstance, that the sexual relief is usually not sought or found through intercourse with the *possessor of the fetish,* but it is more often desired and accomplished through *manipulations of the fetish itself* which is stroked, squeezed, touched with the lips and tongue, brought into the closest possible contact with the body and finally with the genitals, until there is an orgasm, usually *without mutual contact of the organs of copulation.* With excitable persons there is often an ejaculation from even mere caressing of the fetish with the hand. *Through this extragenital activity the major fetishism presents one of the most serious disturbances to relief.* Characteristically Krafft-Ebing speaks only of the fetishism of the male for the charm of the female, but it is even as widespread among females for the charms of the male.

If we examine the enormous number of individual fetishisms according to certain points of view, then we come to a differentiation which is not only as obvious as the division into parts of the body and articles of clothing, but is also just as practical and feasible as this: a division according to *regions of the body.* There are three main groups to be distinguished: fetishism of the *head, the torso, and the extremities.*

Head Fetishism

The hair is one of the parts of the head which most frequently exhales fetishistic influences. Here there is

72

first of all a *visual* fetishism, but also the senses of taste and smell play a small part, and to a great degree, the sense of hearing, through which one can become pleasantly aware of the delicate sound of the lightly rustling hair. Of the particular qualities of the hair, the color, length, and dress acquire special fetishistic significance, but also at times an antifetishistic significance; furthermore the smooth or curly, soft or scrubby characteristics of the hair cause now an unmeasured attraction, and now a strong aversion.

The man who clips locks of hair can also be regarded as a type of fetishist, who is so infatuated with one essential part of the female body, of quite peculiar characteristics, that he would not even stop at violence to come into possession of it. I had the opportunity to become personally acquainted with one of the best known hair-despoilers of our time, St. As nearly all fetishists, he was, despite good intellectual capabilities, a hereditarily handicapped psychopath. When he was arrested at one time in Hamburg, thirty-one locks of hair were found at his lodging, all tied in gay ribbons and marked with the day and hour when they were clipped. The following passages, which describe the case, are taken from the records of the Hamburg police department, from which the public prosecutor Wulffen drew extracts for his book "Sexual Criminals."

About his sex life, St. testified the following, which should afford a full insight into the pathological condition of the psyche of the hair-despoiler. He did not seem to know what really drove him to clipping hair. *It was the hair alone that he loved, not particularly the person to whom it belonged.* So it is quite comprehensible that he cut his sister's hair. From the beginning he dreamed

73

of hairs and tresses of hair. He still often dreams of this. He did not know when he first had a sexual feeling in connection with it; it seemed to him that he did *not* have a sexual feeling when cutting the hair. *It may probably have been more of an urge to which he gave way,* without knowing what caused it. He was enlightened as to sexual matters *at his first trial.* He had never had sexual intercourse with a woman; he felt estranged from and repulsed by any one whom he knew to have had intercourse with women. It was especially distasteful to him when anything of this sort was spoken of in an obscene way. On this account he *joined the moral society Ethos.* The impulse here was as natural as it is common, to compensate for pathological sexual impulses through antisexual fanaticism. After his acquittal, he made a firm resolution never again to yield to his unnatural desire. In this he succeeded for a year, but in June, 1917, he was backsliding again. He was afraid that he could no longer resist this unhappy desire; he was willing to accept any sort of help, from whatever quarter it might come. Here in the asylum he felt safe, but was never completely at peace. He kept asking when quiet would rest in his agonized soul. In the summer semester of 1907 he was alone and independent in Br. There things grew worse again. He had foreseen that in the excitement of a festival he would be able to clip a few tresses of hair quite easily, and this thought had troubled and obsessed him for weeks beforehand. He had had no scissors in his possession since he was in Berlin, not even a pair of nail scissors. At two different times, two weeks before the festival, he walked up and down before a store and debated with himself as to whether or not he should buy a pair of scissors, but in the end conquered his desire. A few days later, however, he bought the scissors,

74

and that was his downfall, as now the excitement kept growing stronger and stronger. He often wanted to throw away the scissors, but he did not do this, in order "to show that in spite of the scissors" he was strong enough to resist his urge. On the day of the festival *he wandered alone through the streets, noticing only hairs and tresses of hair,* carefully avoiding several acquaintances whom he chanced to meet. *Despite great excitement,* he was able to control himself on this day. But the next day he succumbed. In the evening there was a great celebration at the castle, and there he snipped several tresses. The first he did not succeed in cutting through entirely, because it was too thick and heavy, and the same happened with the second. Then he chanced upon a large girl with wonderful, long, loose-falling hair; the hair was in marvelous waves down to her knees. He was terribly excited. He grasped into the thick of it, and just then the girl drew the whole of her glorious hair forward over her shoulder. This was a hard blow to him, yet he did not move from the spot, thinking that she would let her hair fall back again. When he saw that this would not happen, he tore himself away, and searched around further, but all the girls had their hair over the front of their shoulders. Finally he tore one girl's hair back over her shoulder and snipped off a lock. Towards the end of the festival he was in a terrible state of excitement, due, in large part, to anger at not having been able to secure the beautiful hair he had most wanted. *While making these explanations to the experts, St. was visibly excited and carried away.* Then on the next day, after his memory had reawakened he complained that he was thinking incessantly of long locks of hair. When he lay down, he saw locks of hair dangling from the bed, could not go to sleep, had erections, thought to himself:

75

"Can there really be so long and thick a lock of hair?" He measured out on his body how long it could probably be. He imagined that the wearer of it was sleeping before him, stepped up to the bed, took hold of the lock of hair, that he felt its splendid fullness, pressed it to his lips and nose, breathed in its fragrance, and finally took his scissors and cut it off. Then he groaned and sighed; the battle not to give way to the physical urge would not let him sleep; he lay now on his side, now on his back; all to no good. Then in the darkness came locks of hair from all sides, endlessly, the real ones which he knew, as well as the ones he had only contemplated; the excitement grew, and a great unrest seized him. He forced himself to be still and to lie there quietly. In vain. The old phantasies came again, the old pictures: the castle and the girl with the long tresses passed by, whole cities were pillaged, Berlin, Hamburg, Brunswick, London, Stockholm, and always more and more beautiful tresses were carried off, from the schoolyard and from the streets. *The hairs were carefully combed and plaited, every lock was tied above and below with a ribbon and was marked with the name and age of the wearer, as well as the place of birth and the hair-color of the parents,* and besides that whether the hair had ever been cut. This is in accord with the manner in which hair-despoilers typically preserve their sexual symbols. Often St. had the feeling that his whole pillow was made of locks of hair, and was strewing perfumed hairs over him. He buried his face in it, and he played with, and fanned locks of hair about his breast, his arms and his face. Then, after he had had an ejaculation through onanism, he felt quite weak, and not until some time later, with the ebbing of the excitement, was he able to go to sleep, usually not for about an hour. *If he buried his face in the*

76

hair which attracted him, an ejaculation often resulted immediately.

The relief emphasized here, from the fetish itself, quite apart from the person, is what, in this case, distinguishes the pathological or major fetishism from the physiological. St. was acquitted in Berlin, as in Hamburg, because aside from the high degree of disorder in his sexual urge, there were also other considerable disorders apparent which prevented his free decision, in the sense of the law. Several years after his last trial before a German court, a Spanish paper was sent to me from Montevideo, from which it seemed that the unhappy fellow had again yielded to his passion in Buenos Aires and had been placed in an insane asylum there.

This article, in the *Diario del Plata* of September 28, 1912, contained so many remarkable details, with the complete texts of the opinions of the Argentine doctors, that I would like to give a translation of the original here.

"The Chief of Police of Buenos Aires decided this afternoon that the German engineer R. S. should be committed to the asylum, in agreement with the decision returned by the psychiatrist who had him under observation. As will be remembered, while on a streetcar on the Santa Fé street near the Plaza Italia, S. snipped a lock of hair from the head of the daughter of one of the ambassadors accredited to the Argentine Republic. He fled immediately, but was soon captured at the request of the brother of the young lady. The characteristics of the peculiar illness can be best drawn from the report already mentioned, which we will give."

77

The report reads as follows:

"Of the many people who have been brought under observation at the asylum, there have been few who afforded so much interest as R. S. The remarkable feature of his illness is not its rarity, or the rarity of its coming to light, but the circumstance that it seldom happens that a patient, in one of the cases placed under medical observation, knows his own degeneracy as this man does, admits it without restraint, and at the same time makes no trouble whatsoever in submitting to the long and rigorous observation and treatment which this case demands.

"In an interesting piece of writing which the asylum is preserving, S. reports that even before he had reached the age of ten his attention was drawn to locks of women's hair, and even to the hair of his own sister. This document reveals how great his moral sufferings were from this, the feeling of shame he endured, and the efforts which were made by both him and his family to suppress this desire.

"R. S. is a German, twenty-nine years old, and has an engineer's degree from one of the universities of his native land. He is an intelligent man, orderly in his habits, understanding and sympathetic in his appearance. He realizes his condition, the natural foundations and significance of his aberrations, and is completely in accord with all measures which the physicians have tried in his treatment.

"S. was committed to the asylum for the offense of having snipped a lock of hair from Miss G. M. In the following we quote a few extracts from his autobiography, which will give a clearer picture than could our attempts at interpretation, of his first impulse, the irre-

78

sponsibility of his inclination, his conflict with the police, the development and characteristics of his illness, its unavoidable consequences, and the attempt at cure.

"S. says: 'It is extraordinarily hard for me to write this, and I suffer exceedingly under the shame of my aberration, and the reproaches it draws down upon me. I was between fifteen and seventeen years of age when I first cut a lock of woman's hair, and then it was the hair of my sister. My mother and sister both learned that I had done this, but attached no great significance to the matter. Even as a child, I used to follow for long distances in the streets after girls who had long pigtails, fearing all the while lest they should ask me why I was following them. I studied in Berlin at the technical high school, where I was arrested for the first time after having cut locks of hair from several girls. My family brought me first to the Maison de Santé, one of the hospitals in the neighborhood of Berlin, and then to Dr. Colla's Buchheide Sanatorium, in Stettin, where attempts were made to cure me through hypnotism, but without success. Then I started my studies at the technical high school in Brunswick. I was arrested for the second time for having snipped several locks of hair while on a stay in Hamburg. Now I was brought to the asylum, Friedrichsberg, in Hamburg and then to the Kurhaus Westend near Berlin where I was treated with baths, massages, and gymnastic exercises. Afterwards I returned to Brunswick, accompanied by my mother, and remained there until the summer of 1910 when I took my last examination as an engineer. After a short time as assistant to a professor of that school, I came to the Argentine Republic.'

"S. himself describes the phenomenon of his aberration: '*After I have cut the lock, I go home and kiss the charming hair again and again, I press it to my nose and cheeks, and breathe in the precious fragrance of it.'* Merely reading the confession of S. is enough to show that it is a form of erotic fetishism. . . . Should all such cases of fetishism be regarded as abnormalities? Certainly not! To a certain extent, with the exercise of some moderation, the deification of the hand or foot, the hair or voice, is only a quite individual symbolic form of our love which limits its ideal to a particular element, a part of human beauty, and we may say the same of the common habit of idealizing objects which are used by the beloved person. Psychiatry concedes this right to lovers, as otherwise all humans would be marked with the stigma of the pathological, and also does not interfere in the practice of keeping personal tokens and intimate objects, which may be classed as an exaggerated sentimentality when a handkerchief or a picture has attached to it the *representative* value of the beloved person.

"Besides this deification, at whose basis is always the person himself, there is still the pathological fetishism, which is irreconcilable with normality, and in which either the person plays a secondary rôle, or none at all. In the first case the attraction is exercised partly or entirely through a certain part of the body of the beloved person, which, to a certain extent, monopolizes the representation of the whole body. In the other case, it is love for the object, which happens to belong to the person, as, for example, the case of the shoes of Celestina which Mirabeau describes. Tanzi distinguishes these two forms of fetishism as paraphysiological and antiphysiological fetishism, and calls the latter of these loves *extra-corporeal*, a love outside the realm of the body, which he terms the most extreme form of idolistic love known

to science. According to this classification, we can then
diagnose this case as follows: St. is a hereditarily burdened degenerate, whose aberration manifests itself as
a paraphysiological fetishism of an advanced type. There
still remains, after this diagnosis, the matter of the cure
for Mr. St. We feel justified in ordering his commitment.
It is not to be denied that despite his sexual perversion,
St. has a quite remarkable intelligence; nonetheless,
since he cannot control his passion, he is unfit as a useful
member of society. *This lack of power to resist his passion, which he declares is unconquerable, has destroyed
his name, his career, and his position,* and caused twenty
failures up to the time of his imprisonment, which came
after he had cut twenty-one locks of hair. Thus his rever-
sions point definitely to repetition and make an intelligent man useless for life. Only confinement and careful
medical attention can restore him to society, or at least
ameliorate his present condition of perversion. With this
thought, and in agreement with his own wishes, we
ordered his commitment to the Hospicio de las Mer-
cedes.''

On the occasion of this and similar cases, the question
has been raised whether the hair-despoiler was guilty
of a theft, property damage, assault, or insult. The guilt
of theft and property damage was denied by the famous
criminologist, Wulffen, because the lock of hair, as a part
of the body, was not a movable chattel in the accepted
sense of the law, but guilt was confirmed as to assault
and insult, even in the sense of the statute act dealing
with dangerous weapons, since the lock of hair must be
cut with a knife or scissors.

Not only in the case of the hair-despoiler, but also as
a fetish in love life, the type of hairdress has an im-

portant position. Many years ago an old lady consulted me who, since the awakening of her sex life, was set into erotic raptures purely by a part in the middle of the head. Despite the pleasure she derived from this, she considered the constantly recurring thought of it a painful compulsion of the imagination, of which she was ashamed.

To many prostitutes, but by no means only to them, there is a great attraction in hair which is glued down tight to the forehead. The "soupbowl" haircut, as it is commonly termed when the hair is shaved high on the neck, has for a long time served as a strong means of erotic charm in all the large cities, where it is made use of by the apaches, pimps, and others low in the social scale. The "artistic" haircut exercises the same attraction upon another feminine group to which belong a large number of prostitutes. Many men make collections of hairs from the necks of women to whom they have been erotically related. Often these collections are made up of pubic hairs. For some people, especially men of effeminate make-up, short-cropped hair in a woman has a fetishistic effect, but to others, the majority, its effect is anti-erotic. *False* hair is often an object of fetishistic hate, and to such a degree that it can form a serious obstacle in marriage. In one suit for annulment of a marriage, the man testified that after the marriage his young wife suddenly took off her magnificent hair, in the beauty of which the groom had always taken particular pleasure. She had entered the marital bed almost completely bald-headed, and as he had had no idea that she wore a wig, he had thrust her out of his sight, startled and horrified. His penis, which had been aroused, crumpled up, and from then on every possibility of sexual intercourse was out of the question. He contested, successfully, the validity of the marriage on the grounds of the silence about the false hair.

The hair *color* has a great selective significance, it being now quite light blond hair, now deep black, now chestnut brown hair which excites, be it attractingly or negatively. One man among my cases, a Galician merchant, was obsessed with a sadistic hatred for *red* hair. Nevertheless, he finally married a woman with glaring red hair. In justification, he gave two reasons: he believed that through living with her he would be able to "break the habit" of his hatred, and moreover his wife was so wealthy that he had been willing to accept this physical defect into the bargain, especially since every one whom he had asked had considered the fiery hair more beautiful than hateful. He consulted me to have his loathing cured by hypnotism. I proposed to his wife that she have her hair dyed. She refused vigorously. She considered this antipathy of her husband's as a personal insult, or at best a whim which he would get over "if he really loved her." Such impressions arise only too frequently through ignorance and underestimating of fetishistic compulsions. The marriage was broken up. Even hair which is white, or sprinkled with gray, appears as a fetish. I had one patient who would put a white wig on his wife at intercourse. The fashion of white and powdered wigs may have arisen, as in the origin of most fashions, not without a certain fetishistic influence.

Almost as great as the effect of the feminine hairdress upon the man, is the effect of the male beard hair upon the woman. A "beautiful beard" often assumes the character of an overestimated idea, whereby the visual impression is not a little increased through the tactile effects of feeling. The close-cropped moustache, the so-called "toothbrush," is likewise a rather widespread fetish, and the *beard-down fluff,* not only on the male but even on the female face. Almost every type of beard has its admirers, though least of all the full beard, which, on the other hand, plays a large rôle as an antifetish.

Quite a rare case, which Krafft-Ebing also mentions, is that of one man who was attracted by women with full beards. When his first wife, a well-known bearded woman, died, he did not rest until he had married another woman with a magnificent full beard. This is, without doubt, a rarity, as is also the reverse case, the love of some women for men of feminine, thus negative, facial hair types, a much more usual phenomenon. The present fashion of men not wearing beards is in accord with the great spread of this latter fetishism which has been regarded, and not without good reason, as a sign that the two sexes have come much closer together, not only in a physiognomic, but also in a psychological respect. Indeed, *the type of beard which is the prevailing mode at any time is of a significance not to be underestimated as a gauge for the accentuation of sex in the period.*

A fetish which, because of the pigmentation correspondence, usually parallels hair fetishism and is connected with it, is the eye. The connection which usually exists is that blond hair usually accompanies blue eyes, and in the same way brown or black hair color is usually in harmony with the color of the iris. Dark eyes with light hair, or blue eyes with dark hair, on account of the rarity of this, have a particular charm which often has a very strong fetishistical effect. There are also people for whom the eye has *no erotic significance at all,* but they are exceptions and are far outnumbered by those to whom the eye is attractive not only as the "mirror of the soul," but even acquires a fetishistic signifi-

84

cance going far beyond this. It is not only the eye color which is concerned in this, but every single characteristic of the eye, the size of the pupils, the brightness and gleam of the eye which depends upon the secretions of the tear glands, the eyelashes and eyebrows—thus eyebrows which grow together are often a fetish, but also often an antifetish—finally the eyelids, the slitting of the lid, and the form of the eye as a whole. What *subjective* delusions the fetish magic can cause, was shown me some time ago by the answer made in court by a witness who had fallen into the hands of blackmailers: "How could I believe," he said, "that a person with such good, frank, blue eyes could be so bad!" For many men women's tears are an irresistible fetish. Even defects of the eye, such as flecks on the cornea, twisted or uncommonly narrow or wide eye openings, goggle-eyes, extreme shortsightedness, even blindness can be a fetish. Thus a short time ago I was consulted by a twenty-four-year-old man who had been blinded in the war, and an unusually beautiful nineteen-year-old girl who had fallen in love with him and for that reason broken her engagement with a well-to-do older man. The girl said that she had always been particularly fascinated by blind people with their peculiar helplessness. The quiet brave manner in which they tried to overcome their misfortune had "something endlessly stirring." This grave young man—he was a musician by profession —was one and all to her. If her parents should succeed in their plan to break up their relationship, they were determined to both put an end to their lives. They consulted me, asking that I should try to convince the parents of the indissolubility of their bond, the result of which was already evident in the shape of a three months' pregnancy.

In comparison with the eye fetishist, the *nose* fetishist
is rare; at any rate this form of fetishism is not so widespread as one might gather from the number of defiant,
jutting "facial peninsulars." Often there is connected
with the fetishistic prepossession for large noses a more
or less unconscious phallic cult, as the old folk belief,
which is in no way organically founded, that the size of
the nose is indicative of the size of the male organ (and
similarly, that a relationship exists between the size of
the mouth and that of the female organ). Next to the size,
the shape of the nose is also of special fetishistic attraction, whether it be Grecian, or a hooked or aquiline nose,
or the snub-nose. There is also a special fetishism for the
nostrils and the wings of the nose. In Berlin there was
one man who used to stuff the nasal opening at night or
put in clothespins to widen the nostrils. He was also
infatuated with large nostrils in other people, to which
he paid more attention than to any other part of the
body. His quite active sexual passions were centered
on this idea. He used to draw sketches of women's heads
with nostrils so wide that they would permit immissio
penis. One day on a bus he caught sight of a girl whose
nose was close to his idea. He followed her home, asked
her to marry him at once, was rejected and kept insisting and insisting until he was arrested. The man had
never had sexual intercourse.

Also the color of the nose, red or blue, the nasal
secretions, even the ozena has now a fetishistic, now an
antifetishistic effect.

Krafft-Ebing cites cases of mouth fetishism, one of
those which he describes having come later under my
care. It concerned a jurist whose exclusive sexual activity, usque ad ejaculationem, consisted of mutual pressing together of the lips, of kissing. Thick, pouting lips

86

attracted him to such an extent that, whether they be of the male or female sex, they were the whole concern of his sexual passion. Only the lips of the colored races, where it was a distinct racial characteristic that is, left him cold. Of almost greater significance than the form or color of the lips, can be the teeth visible between the parting of the lips, of which the psychological power of attraction can in pathological circumstances increase to the highest degree of fetishism. Different organs of sense take part in mouth fetishism. As the eye feasts on the variations in form and color of the lips, so the ear rejoices in the sound of the kiss, and the sense of feeling in the mutual contact of the countless tactile buds covering the delicate mucous membrane. The senses of smell and taste are also not excluded. Thus with many women the odor of tobacco, even the alcoholic breath of a man, can have a very exciting effect, though also, at times, an antifetishistic effect. The movements of the mouth are also of great fetishistic significance, as the pouting mouth, the speaking, singing, chewing, and above all the smiling and laughing mouth. Many men are absolutely helpless before the melodious laughter of a woman— "the lovely magic of her laugh."

It would far exceed the space permitted us to be thorough, going from one part of the body to the other, treating of all the fetish attractions of the entire human bodily surface. In what follows, then, we must limit ourselves to listing briefly the individual fetish points, one after the other, and only occasionally to illustrate the particular fetishism by a *typical example*.

In the face, outside of the already mentioned fetishisms, there is still the *ear* fetishism. There are fetishistic effects resulting from the shape of the ear, the color, thick fleshy ears or thin delicate ones, large outstanding

ears or, more generally, small ones; also swollen lobes
to the ears, little bumps in the rim of the ear, movable
ears, and ears pierced for earrings. I had one case in
which a person suffered from a desire to grasp hold of
women's ears, to pull at the auricle, and to push a finger
into the outer ear channel. The patient had repeatedly
gotten into trouble through the execution of this obsession which dominated and compelled him. For many fetishists, the ear opening, just as the mouth and nose openings, belongs among the sexually stimulating openings
of the bodily surface.

Then there is *cheek and chin* fetishism. Here also the
matter of shape enters before all others, the round,
strong, broad chin, the chubby face, and hollow cheeks,
even the neatly circumscribed spots of red on the faces
of consumptives, "graveyard roses" as the expression
goes, find their passionate admirers. One of the chief
fetishes of these parts of the body, however, is the dimple
resting in the places lacking fat; both the dimples in the
cheeks and in the chin. The majority of the dimple fetishists are of a physiological sort, but there are also such
as are ruled wholly by their passion, in a pathological
manner.

A few words also about the fetishistic significance of
the facial secretions. There is often a strong fetishistic
efficacy in the secretions of the tear glands. There are
men, and by no means only the sadistically inclined ones,
who intentionally drive their women to tears in order,
from the sight of their tears, to stir their own libido. The
fluidity of the oral cavity, on the contrary, has more
often an antifetishistic than a fetishistic effect. But without doubt there are also saliva fetishists who desire to
have some beloved person spit into their mouths. In
many cases of my own observation, women were at-

88

tracted by men who "spat powerfully." The secretions of the ear and nose are overwhelmingly antitropic, but here also it can always lead to an excessive passion, where something basically repulsive attracts in the sense of an antifetishistic-fetishism.

Torso Fetishism

The three points of the greatest fetishistic attraction on the torso are the breasts, hips, and genitals. But even aside from these regions the torso is just as rich in fetishes as the face. To list them, they are: *neck* fetishism; both the short, thick neck and the long, swanlike neck have their admirers; thus the open neck of the sailors and the same with the feminine décolleté. I had one patient, a teacher, who had an urge for letting his hand slide down the open necks of girls wearing sailor blouses. He was finally charged with assault as a result of this strong and compelling urge. Another patient of mine was fascinated by the seventh cervical vertebra. This rise in the flesh drew his eyes whenever it was at all visible. This curious prepossession loses some of its strangeness when one considers the fact that *every bump and depression* of the bodily surface seems to have a special inherent erotic magnetism. Thus it is with the Adam's apple on the front side of the neck from which often proceeds a considerable power of attraction. The function of this "organ" enchants even more than its structure, probably the only case in which this word is used not in its anatomical sense but in its physiological sense, the voice. The number of voice fetishists is very large. Many unnecessary telephone conversations are actually the result of *acoustical fetish hunger*. When

89

Alexandre Dumas in his novel "La Maison de Vent," describes a woman who was unfaithful to her husband because she lost her heart to the voice of a tenor, and Binet says that many marriages contracted with singers could be traced back to the fetish magic of their voices, then this coincides fully with the scientific results of sexual research in more recent times.

From the larynx we pass over the "round" shoulders of the women and the "strong" necks of the men, to the breasts of both sexes. For many women the first consideration here is the hairy breast of the man, and contrariwise, for many men the female breast with its many details—the erectile breast nipples, the region of the nipple, now somewhat brownish in color, now somewhat more rosy, together with the Montgomery glands—even as a secondary sexual characteristic, outweighs all other sexual attractions. Even the fine breast hairs can cause a fetishistic feeling of desire. Just as the female breasts can be so attractive in the mind of the man, can affect his senses of sight and feeling, so there can also be an antitropic aversion, as the case, which was described earlier, of fetish hate of the doctor toward the female breast.

Flabby breasts, as well as the flabby stomach and the double chin, as, usually, all hypertrophic abnormalities, have an antifetishistic effect, although occasionally also a fetishistic effect. A specific form of intercourse of the breast fetishists is coitus inter mammalis, between the pressed together mammary glands. For the region between the chest and the pelvic girdle, there are many fetishists for every single part, especially for the region of the waist. The navel often exercises an antifetishistic influence. I have had many cases in my practice in which the sight of the female navel would sicken men to the

90

point of absolute nausea. A strong body is more frequently a fetish with women than with men. To prove
that what may have a fetishistic influence far exceeds
everything one would imagine, is the fact that even the
intestinal gases can have an attracting effect. Thus in a
Montmartre nightclub in Paris I saw a girl appear who
called herself "la femme pétomane" and her large audi-
ence was in part amused and in part excited because
from to time, amidst witty remarks, she produced flatus,
of varied strength and length. Those who wished to
derive the full pleasure of the odor sat in the front
rows, those who were content with the acoustical charm
sat in the other rows.

Hip fetishism is also very widespread, and it is both
the very broad and the very slim hips, with the corresponding firm or soft buttocks, which attract men who
for their part are either metastrophically or effeminately
organized, while hips of *medium* girth seem to attract
the so-called normal man the most of all. There is a
special role played by the very prominent buttocks, the
rump-fat, the steatopygia, usually found among the
people of the Orient and the wild African tribes, which
gives the impression of a natural bustle, very different,
it is true, from the ideal which the Hellenic sculptor
portrayed in his goddess of love, the "Venus callipy-
gos."

Besides the buttocks, the dimples in a buttock—one
also not rarely finds them in effeminate men—act as
spots of fetishistic attraction; many people consider
the facial dimples of little aesthetic worth by comparison.
On the back there is still also the hollow between the
shoulderblades, on which are focused several fetishes.
Not without significance is the shape of the back as a
whole, each with its own curves, which attracts much

and weighty consideration; even the crooked backs, and the hunchbacks have their lovers and admirers.

GENITAL FETISHISM

We come now to *genital* fetishism. By this, naturally, is not meant the steps of reflexes leading to the final sexual act, the quite normal compulsions to the genital organs as a sexual goal, but the primary and almost exclusive fascination for the male or female genital organs. Any sort of genital fetishism is considered by some people, including Krafft-Ebing, to be very rare, indeed its appearance is almost denied, while others, as Bloch, and Hirth, are of the opposite opinion, and Weininger even goes so far as to say: "For the woman, the man exists merely as a sexual part, and in contrast to this, all other characteristics step wholly into the background. The woman, to be sure, does not consider the penis beautiful, or even pretty, but it exercises, as did the head of Medusa on the men of antiquity, a hypnotizing, fascinating, and captivating influence." Goethe also, in the Paralipomena to the first part of "Faust" (Weimar ed. Vol. XIV, p. 307) seems to have the devil support a similar conclusion.

On the basis of my studies and observations, I consider the one opinion in this case as incorrect as the other. Doubtless the normal woman has a lively interest in the male organ, as is manifested in the phallus and lingam cult, but it is scarcely stronger than the interest of the normal man in the female pudendum, and in no way occurs as the rule, but only exceptionally, as the primary object of sexual attraction; if it should occur, then it is usually as a fetishistic aggravation. Even

92

among men there are penis fetishists, as among women
there are vagina and vulva fetishists. The immediate
assumption is that such men are homosexual, but experience shows that in its generality this assumption is
erroneous. Thus a few years ago—and this is no unique
case—I was consulted by a man from southern Germany who would stay in the lavatories for hours at a
time in order to catch sight of a man's organ, especially
an erect one. He carried with him a small auger, in
order, after the manner of a voyeur, to be able to bore
peepholes in the partitions between the toilets in the
public places, or, when the partition did not reach quite
to the floor, he would sprinkle the floor so that the genitals would be mirrored in the liquid. This man, who was
very unhappy over this urge, which cost him a great deal
of time, lived a harmonious married life, with several
children, and was far from having homosexual tendencies. I was consulted more recently by a pastor, a married man, father of three children, who made the trip
from his village to Berlin several times a year, driven
by the urge to seek around as a phallus voyeur. He emphasized the fact that the mere thought of sexual intercourse with a man filled him with loathing, but on the
other hand the thought of a male member, developed as
strongly as possible, *obsessed him constantly in an absolutely demonic way.* Even the fetish hate which is
directed against the genitals of the opposite sex is not always thoroughly attributable to homosexual inclinations.
Men constantly consult me who are drawn to women
in every respect, and then are repulsed by an aversion,
to them as inexplicable as it is unconquerable, for the
vulva and vaginal opening; they say that contact with
this part is as repulsive to them as if with some "slimy
beast."

93

With women there is also, frequently, a strong fear of contact with the phallus. Thus a man consulted me a short time ago, who had separated from his wife and was contemplating a divorce because she absolutely would not touch his member. When accompanied by otherwise quite normal inclinations, it is quite possible to treat such cases by hypnotic treatment or other psychotherapeutic means.

There still remains among the sub-species of genital fetishism, testicle fetishism. For many women the swinging testicles are a "toy" which attracts them irresistibly. Further there is the foreskin fetishism; one urning declares that for him every proceeding is rendered impossible by the free-lying glans penis, terming the appearance of a penis not covered by the foreskin as "impertinent." Fetishism for the clitoris, the large and small labia, especially in somewhat hypertrophic cases, is quite common. The majority of clitoris fetishists are adherents of cunnilinctus. About twenty years ago I observed one rare case of hermaphrodite fetishism. I owe introduction to more than one case of hermaphroditism to the fetishistic sagacity of this man. I have in my collection a photograph in which this patient was taken sitting upon the body of a woman, so that the upper part of his body seems to be merged into the lower part of the woman's body, through which is evoked the illusion that he is a pseudohermaphrodite.

Genital fetishism is connected not only with the first and fifth organs of sense, but often also with the third and fourth; the strong exhalations of the sexual organs of both sexes, especially, are by some persons perceived with an almost fetishistic desire, and by others with an antitropic aversion. The participation of the olfactory sense is also true in the last form of torso fetishism, the *anal* fetishism. The fetishist for anal odors, which he seeks to find even in the pieces of clothing which have been in contact with his favorite region, suffers from this affection even more because, apart from this inclination, he is usually an exceptionally fastidious person in other things. A person's fetish for the regio analis can become so great that even though he knows the abnormality of his urge, this will not hinder him from passionately licking with the tongue at this spot. There are expressions in the erotic vocabulary of every language for this practice, which gives proof of its strength and wide spread.

I will close this section with a professional opinion I had to give on a genital fetishist who had been convicted as an abortionist. His motive was not to earn money or to be of assistance, but a *compelling urge to examine and finger the genitals of women of the better class.* This desire he thought he would be best able to satisfy if he promised the women that he would remove pregnancy.

The manufacturer Karl Sch; born in X. December 7, 1867, has with but short interruptions been under observation and treatment at the Institute of Sexual Science for a long time. At his wish we make the following report which is based on the report of Professor Pfister of July 29, 1919, besides our own observations. The man has been accused three times of assistance and attempted assistance at abortions which are supposed to have occurred in the year 19—. He says that in every case the idea of an *abortion was far from his mind,* and that he usually made the women believe this only that he might attain certain sexual ends with them, namely *examining and fingering their genitals.* In every case he had made

95

use of an instrument absolutely unsuited to the purpose, and moreover had used this in such a way as could not possibly result in an abortion; and in two of the cases named the women were not pregnant at all. In the third case there may have been an abortion, but not through his manipulations, because the syringe, which was absolutely useless, had been only held to the vagina, and even after that he could not empty its contents, which were a twentieth part of a quart of pure water, because he had clasped the syringe with his right hand while his left had been lying on the body of the woman. The fundamental point in his statements is the fact that in all three cases the means used, and in two cases even the occasion for its use, could not possibly have brought about an abortion. In no case had he any idea of an abortion, or any intention of such, and especially no regular systematic proceeding for the accomplishment of this intention, but he had tricked the women, by saying that he would help them in an abortion, with a clear consciousness that he neither could nor wanted to do this. He had practiced this deception in order that *without their knowing of it he could make the women compliant to his sexual wishes.* These sexual wishes were of a particular sort: they consisted exclusively in *examining, fingering, and manipulating the female genitals.* He attained his end in every case: *every time there was a seminal discharge.* In normal sexual intercourse he was *completely impotent. He neither required nor took money from any of the women for his manipulations.*

It must be emphasized that Sch's testimony, which goes into all details and has been repeated by him several times in exactly the same way, does not lack plausibility. He says that the court termed him a professional and dangerous; were that disproven, and the uselessness of

96

the instrument to be established, then the grounds for the decision would be proven false in this respect, and the punishment objected to. On this ground the medical report deems it best to submit to a new test the facts of the attempt at abortion, with expert testimony as to the fitness of the instrument used in this criminal attempt.

Also the basic motive which Sch. claims for his actions, according to our professional opinions, presents a new factual circumstance of such incisive significance that it seems in conformity with the legal aspects of the case to ask for resumption of the procedure, insofar as medical opinion constitutes a judgment of the situation which can be legally estimated only on the assumption of expert testimony. The man has been silent as to his motive before the court because of shame before the women present. This seems quite probable in view of the collected findings of the experts observing Sch. As regards this observation, we can only agree, in the whole and in detail, with the previous report of Professor Pfister. We refer to this opinion and refrain from repeating our own individual observations of this case. We sum up its conclusion: Sch. is a *feeble-minded and psychopathic personality,* heavily burdened from birth. The morbid inclination of his feelings and desires extends even to the most varied of his habits and desires. It influences also his sex life. There is impotency with the normal sex act, accompanied by a high degree of excitable weakness of the nervous system. Since the so-called involution period of the man this has grown to some degree. *There came again into the foreground at the same time the characteristics of a perverse sexual life of an infantile sort, which had been present since puberty, but had been suppressed during the years of powerful manhood.* This consisted in a fetishistic urge to

97

examine and handle, which was directed to the female genitals. This urge was the direct motive of the proceedings leading to the trial for attempted abortion.

The question should not be raised at this point of how far Sch. was responsible for his actions. It should be reserved for later. For the time, it is sufficient to establish the fact that, according to our professional opinions, those circumstances which the psychological expert was called upon to determine, were not present, those circumstances from which are to be constructed the psychic preliminary stipulations to the attempt at abortion. There is present, according to our opinions, a new factual circumstance which is of significance in the judicial conception of the proceeding.

We summarize our opinion thus: The proceedings for which Sch. has been sentenced do *not* arise from motives which permit a decision of actual intent at abortion or attempted abortion. Establishment of the motives of Sch.'s actions, in view of his morbid psychic condition, is a matter for the expert's opinion. This opinion characterizes Sch.'s manner of procedure as a form of perverse sexual activity, and, indeed, as a particular form of *genital fetishism* in a psychopathic individual.

FETISHISM OF THE LIMBS

The arms as well as the legs contain a great number of the most highly important fixation points for fetishists. Of main importance here are the hands on the upper extremities, and the calves on the lower extremities. Next to be mentioned is the swollen upper arm of the woman which forms as much of an attraction as does, for many women, the strong flexing of the upper arm musculature

98

of the man, the biceps. Elbows and the lower arm appear rarely as fetishes, but very often the *hand* and especially the finger. One patient writes: "I have an unbounded passion for beautiful, slim, well-formed, not fleshy hands, which are of delicate lines, well tended and clean. I have an unconquerable desire to caress such hands. *The touch of a hand which is fascinating to me brings a great relief, compared to intercourse after which I feel very fatigued.*" In some cases it is the delicate, narrow, fine, soft, "transparent" hand which attracts, and at other times the heavy, coarse, bony hand. Accordingly, also, now the light gentle pressure of the hand, and now the firm clasp is found more erotically stirring. Fingers also become fetishes, the unadorned as well as the richly embellished. I had a case in which some one had an indescribable aversion to finger rings as well as thimbles. *He could not bring himself to marry because, mainly, of the fear of putting engagement and marriage rings on himself and his wife.* Again on the fingers there are the nails which, with all their details, form a fetishistic chapter. Some years ago I was visited by a foreigner who loved nothing so violently as dirty fingernails. Finally he fell a sacrifice to this abnormal passion which drove him, a distinguished aristocrat, into the lowest sorts of places, when he was murdered by a girl of the streets and her protector.

Next, on the leg, comes the upper thigh whose overskin, as that of the knee, has many tactile bodies, contact with which releases sexual sensations. There is a large number of men and women for whom the upper thigh is the absolute center of their sexual conceptions of lust.

A short time ago I was visited by a man who had a fetish for the hollow of the knee, who sought to achieve his satisfaction through kissing and feeling of this part of the female body, and whenever possible by bringing his genitals into severe contact with the woman's knee.

The fetishistic significance of women's calves and shanks is extraordinarily great. There are men who will follow women for long distances in bad weather in the hope that they will gather up their dresses and thus expose their calves to the greedy gaze of their followers. It should be said on this point that this sight seems to attract particularly the *exhibitionists*. I have often heard it said during my court experience that for exhibitionists the exterior motive usually came from the calves of half-mature girls. In the section on exhibitionism there are more details on this.

In comparison to hand fetishism, *foot fetishism* is rare. That it is usually the bare hand that attracts, and the clothed foot may be traced to the fact that in youth the first is usually bare and the latter, on the other hand, is usually seen clothed. But there are a great number of foot fetishists, and even the number of ankle fetishists is not inconsiderable. Although experience shows that the naked foot has more often an antifetishistic effect—I knew one man whose libido completely disappeared the moment a woman took off her shoes and stockings—this depends to a great extent upon the *positive fetishistic* effect of the leg coverings, about which we will be more thorough later. A fetish of the highest degree is the movement of the extremities, the gesture, and especially the manner of walking. To many men the tripping walk of the woman is just as fascinating as the sturdy walk of the man to the woman. I was in The Hague during the war, and the streets were full of thousands of English soldiers in their handsome uniforms, who particularly attracted attention by their brisk and springy walk.

100

When I spoke about this to my guide, an old Dutch scholar, he said, "Already several hundred Dutch girls have become mothers through this walk."

This fetish magic appears in its most intensive form in the dance. In almost all the larger dance halls the observant and understanding person has the chance to notice the dance voyeurs, who are to be recognized by the fact that they themselves rarely dance, but they never take their eyes off the dancing couples. They are usually older men and women, whose attention is focused either upon the male or female partner, rarely on both equally, although I remember one dance fetishist who was wholly fascinated by the difference between the heavy men's shoes and the dainty shoes of the women, so that he would follow the play of their movements for hours until he finally achieved an orgastic sexual relief. The two-step and fox-trot particularly attracted this man, as almost every sort of dance, from the ballet and the quadrille to the solo dance, from the quiet waltz to the wildest gallop has its fetishistic admirers whose organs of distant sense, sight, hearing, and smell, find their greatest satisfaction in this way.

COHERENT AND ADHERENT FETISHISM

Before we pass on to clothing or adherent fetishism, there are still a few things to be said about coherent fetishism. By this is to be understood the attraction which is exercised, for many people far more than is normal, by stuffs, and objects which are not donned or thrown over the body as clothing, but are brought into immediate contact with the bodily surface. Among these are pigments which are rubbed into the skin, or painted

101

or etched into it, as cosmetics, powder, or tattooing inks; also there are the little plaster patches which were so popular in the rococo period, and many metals and jewels which, as rings, chains, or buckles, are put through the ears, nose, and lips, over the fingers, arms and legs, around the neck, or fastened into the hair. In this field are also the artificial aids to the fetishistically attractive parts of the body, such as false hair, artificial calves, breasts and hips, bustles, false teeth and gold fillings. In the majority of cases, to be sure, these have an anti-fetishistic effect. Repeatedly, and to my mind with justice, it has been claimed as grounds for divorce that some characteristic in which the groom had taken particular pleasure, had, upon closer acquaintance, turned out to be false. There should also be mentioned the various devices for strengthening the organs of sense, as spectacles and ear trumpets. Different kinds of spectacles evoke now an erotic, and now an anti-erotic effect. In "The Natural Laws of Love" I mentioned one case of spectacle fetishism; another which I observed more recently extended only to the rimless pince-nez. Glasses generally have more of an antifetishistic effect, while the pince-nez is usually more attracting in men, and even in women. Many people have a fetish hate against glasses on women, but several years ago I was assured by a woman of the demimonde who always wore a monocle, that it was through this that she always had so large a following of men. It is well known that many dandies wear the monocle as a fetishistic attraction. A whole chapter could be written on the fetishistic significance of canes and umbrellas. I knew one woman to whom any man who carried an umbrella was "sexually impossible," her fetish hate toward crooked sticks was almost as strong, while the clattering of a sabre on a military man would set her

102

into the highest sexual ecstasies. Among the many forms of coherent fetishism is perfume fetishism. Many perfumes sell exclusively because of their sensuous attraction. *There are people who lose every bit of sexual self-control at the perception of certain odors.* Thus I knew several women who were so excited by the smell of the stables on a man that they were incapable of sexual resistance. With others there is an erotic effect from the smell of beer or carbolic acid, with still others the sight and smell of certain decorative flowers in the hair, the buttonhole, or the belt of a man or woman.

The large group to which we now turn, shows that fetishism, in the many and unendingly varied forms we observe, cannot possibly be inborn as such, but only a certain capacity for reaction can be inborn. This group does not extend to living parts of the human body, but to *lifeless* adherent things which are only destined as coverings or clothing for certain parts of the body. Whether these garments originally appeared as protection, as adornment, or through a sense of shame, one thing at least is certain: in the beginnings of time and the primitive impulses of man, they were unknown. For thousands of years the unclothed bodies of men and women strove toward each other, and the physiological, and from that the pathological, sexual joy in the colors, forms, and materials of clothing developed as an immediate result of the clothing which was gradually adopted and which is still today changing constantly. The will to please appears quite plainly in this, whether the individual taste of the person or the ideas of another are decisive in the choice of the clothing, and especially in the case of the vanity of an essentially narcissistic person, the significance of pieces of clothing is as a means of charm. At any rate one cannot doubt from the fluid char-

103

acter of fashion and its individual variations that in clothing fetishism we have to do with a disturbance in passion, in which *as in sex life, a constitutional point of excitement must, as an endogenous hypothesis of exogenous validity, correspond to the specific sensitivity.*

STILL LIFE FETISHISM

As with body fetishism, so now also with the fetishism for inanimate objects, for which Chevalier coined the phrase "amour azoophilique," it is the task of the exact inquirer and describer to go through the clothing from head to toe, or rather from the peak of the hat to the tip of the shoe, in order to show that there is no *one* of these pieces which is *without fetishistic significance,* though to be sure in varying degree. Contrary to the naked body, with the clothed body it is not the head with all its details, but the legs which form the main points of attraction.

If, now, we should here list in order several of the leading fetishisms, it would be as follows: in the field of head-coverings there are cap fetishists, fetishists for large and small hats, for all sorts of caps, from the elegant uniform cap and the expensive fur cap to the nightcap, and the set of the cap also, whether it be cocked or straight, or forward on the forehead, also plays a rôle. Immediately after the revolution in Berlin a great number of women became fetishistically attracted by the red cockades, which fetishism reached from the circles of the prostitutes to the highest court circles. One finds fetishists for top hats, felt hats, panama hats and other straw hats with ribbons of all imaginable arrangements and colors, fetishists for all kinds of

104

women's hats, with or without veils, from the most magnificent plumed hats to the most simple mannish riding hat. But all of these can also be antifetishes. Thus I had one patient to whom a hat with a veil was an unbearable sight, and another had the same fetish hate against caps without a vizor from whose wearers he turned away with a sense of horror. Charcot and Magnan report one typical case of cap fetishism in the *Archives de Neurologie*, 1882:

A man who was of an eccentric family had his first erection at the age of five, when he saw a thirty-year-old relative, who was sleeping in the same room, put on a nightcap. There was a similar result when shortly thereafter he watched an old female servant tying on her nightcap. Through contact with a nightcap, the erection increased to the point of seminal discharge. Patient refrained from masturbation, and also did not have intercourse until at the age of twenty-one he married a beautiful girl of twenty-four. On the bridal night he was sexually impotent, and also the following night, until in this strait he imagined at intercourse, in the place of his beautiful young wife, an old lady with a nightcap. Through this he was capable of copulation. He has been married for five years and since this time has always made use of this stimulus. He suffers physically under the idea which is as burdensome to him as it is necessary to cohabitation, and which, as he says, profanes his wife and his marriage.

Next to be considered is the neck clothing, including neck cloths of all kinds. I have already given notes concerning a fetishist for silken neck cloths on old men, and there are also fetishists for the highest possible sorts of

105

collars. Further there are fetishists of both sexes for soft collars, for dirty collars, for sailor collars, and for "Lord Byron" collars. I have already commented on fetishists for sailor collars, who approached girls wearing these collars in a suspicious manner. One homosexual fetishist concerning whom I had to testify during the war was especially attracted by the cravats of the soldiers, and next to that by the little pouches which they wore on cords around their necks as sort of amulets.

An exceedingly strange case in my observations concerned a woman who suffered from a fetishism for collar buttons. The basic feeling was one of an intense fetish hate for this article of the toilet, the sight of which on the neck, and especially the slight mark it left pressed into the neck, irritated her strongly. On some people, however, usually men of the world, the mirrors of fashion, they awakened in her a strong sexual desire, and then what was formerly an aversion coupled with a fear of contact, turned into a strong desire to gaze at the formerly repulsive object, and to take it into her mouth and if possible destroy it. There are numerous examples for this change of feeling from a negative to a positive tropism, and vice versa. A common antifetishism arises from rubber collars; indeed rubber seems to be the first of the antifetishistic materials to the human body. For many people contact with this material is unbearable, while on the other hand I have known of cases in which the smell of rubber and the touch of it works as an aphrodisiac, without the presence of which it is impossible for the person concerned to attain potency.

In cravat fetishism, besides the stuff itself, as silk or satin, the manner of tying also plays a great rôle. While there is often a strong attraction exercised by the

106

loosely wound artist's tie, the sailor's knot, and the long narrow ready-tied cravats with all sorts of pins, which correspond closely to the brooches of the women, yet many women feel nothing but a strong aversion to this ready-made tie, as to the detachable cuffs and shirt fronts, in which they see symbols of a bourgeois mediocrity.

We come now to the manifold fetishism for underclothing and personal linen. These pieces of intimate clothing play no mean rôle as fetishes. To the query as to whether the naked, half-clothed, or fully-dressed body was the more attracting, of more than one thousand people, forty per cent answered giving preference to the half-clothed, thirty-five per cent to the fully nude, and twenty-five per cent to the fully-clothed figure. Corresponding to their attracting significance, almost all prostitutes lay great store by elegant linens, and in this respect the men of fashion are in no way behind them. The usual fetishes are shirts with men and lacy things with women, though also the stiffly-starched shirt on men, as silk underwear on women, is regarded by many with a passion far overstepping the average. I will introduce here a few cases from my own practice which are pertinent. In one divorce proceeding the woman testified that from the beginning of the marriage the man had insisted that at intercourse she put on flannel underdrawers. She had acceded to this wish, but with ill grace and had considered it a humiliation to her. "If he had at least demanded silk drawers," she said, "but such a common thing as flannel." Because the man had already consulted me before the marriage concerning this peculiar fixation on flannel, and his wife had learned of it, I was called in on the case as an expert. The marriage was finally annulled. The following extracts are from the interesting testimony given by the woman as evidence in the trial:

"After my confinement, everything went along in the usual way for several weeks, until one day my husband asked me to put on a soft pair of flannel underdrawers or underskirt during intercourse, and if I had none, to buy myself some. In the house in which we were living there was a store which displayed such things in the window. I naturally asked why and wherefore, to which my husband answered that they were so wonderfully soft. I answered with a shrug of the shoulders and said that I did not understand. At the time I was unable to understand his ill temper. I know now that *only my refusal to this demand of his could have been the cause.* Then one day he himself brought home just such a soft pair of women's flannel drawers, and these I was supposed to put on at intercourse. I did not see it that way, and so my husband put them on himself. This went on for about a year. I continually expressed to him my feeling about this strange urge of his. He was continually in a bad temper because of what I had to say about it. Finally one day I saw to it that this piece of clothing simply disappeared. He made a terrible face when I told him about it, but at the time I didn't realize why. The next occurrence was that at Christmas I received as a present some flannel material for dresses, which my husband bought me himself. I thought no more of it, thinking that my husband had done this because of the cold weather, and only thought it curious that he should have bought it himself. What the aim of the present was I learned later, for one evening he asked me to put on the underskirt I was making and to wear it to bed, and what seemed even more strange to me, he was constantly

108

asking me how long I was making the bed jacket which I was making of this material. I should make it down to the knees he thought, to which I laughingly replied that I couldn't possibly make a bed jacket that long. *Also I was to wear the bed jacket to bed.* Now I must say that at one time when it was very cold I did wear this jacket to bed. Our bedroom is on a sleeping porch, and I could not heat it; and my linen nightdresses were often too cold. When I saw what this led to, I naturally did not wear it at night any longer. During the next three years, always at sexual intercourse, there arose the question of the underskirt, and it was now with this skirt as it had previously been with the drawers. Then, as before, I made known my dislike of this, but he was always offended whenever I said anything. Finally I saw to it that this piece of clothing disappeared also. When I returned home after a six weeks' stay at my mother's home in Hamburg, I found a large flannel spread on my husband's bed, which, in itself, was certainly nothing to look at. I believed at the time that his mother, who had been visiting him in the meanwhile, had forgotten it there. When I asked him, he said that he had bought it himself. Quite superfluous, since he already had two woolen spreads, but naturally they were not so soft as the flannel. Again, soon after my return, another pair of underdrawers and underskirt were bought me, for the purpose known. I would like to say now that my husband always made the strange request that he be allowed to take the woman's position at intercourse, and said that his physician had told him to do this. I acceded once to his wish, but in the morning I was so tired out that I could neither sit nor stand. At this time my husband bought me a brightly-colored flannel dressing gown. This I was to wear to bed and always around the house. My husband told me that since he was a little boy the touch of flannel had always given him great pleasure, and that *his mother knew of this circumstance.* When the Christmas presents were distributed, the servant girl was also given the same sort of flannel underskirts, which were placed on the same table. My husband told me that when he was living alone he had had intercourse with the servant girl at the house, who had always worn such things at the time. As before, I refused to put the things on, and so he put them on himself. This was in October. By Christmas the things were no longer soft enough, and there had to be new ones. One evening while we were passing by a store where such flannel things were usually hanging in the window, my husband expressed a wish that I should give him some for Christmas. *He had only to see the things to shake all over his body.* I acted as though I had not heard, and busied myself with the baby. On Christmas Eve while I was still making preparations, he begged again. I naturally did nothing about it, paid absolutely no attention; on the contrary I was particularly attentive to him that evening, and ignored his ill temper, although I knew well what was the cause of it. Soon after Christmas my husband brought home still another flannel bedspread which I was to spread over my bed, because he liked to be able to feel it there. I did not like this, because I felt that any advances he made to me were really made to this thing and not to me. *I always felt nothing but misery, from the beginning of my marriage to the end, from marital intercourse.* Such misery that I was constantly running from one doctor to another, but they always said, 'It's just nerves.' Finally one doctor asked me if I were happily married. From the beginning of our marriage I had always had the feeling

110

during intercourse, whenever this stuff was not present, that my husband was thinking of something else, and I even said this to him when I told him that I thought that he must have some other woman, because he did not have his thoughts on me.

"We have not had intercourse together since the ninth of December, 1914. In February, 1915, we agreed that as soon as the war was over we would get a divorce. And I took it for granted that we would not again resume our marital intercourse. Then in April of this year my husband approached me with his claims as a husband; I was speechless, and asked him what had happened to our agreement. He replied that he did not want to bother me, but *would I just allow him to sleep beside me.* I said that that was absolute nonsense, and refused. Then my husband approached me with his claims for the second time in April of this year, and I refused him for the second time. I often noticed that my husband spent a lot of time in the mornings in the unlighted hallway. One morning I wanted to find out what the reason for this was, and I saw that he was busy at the closet in which my clothes hung. *Now he had only to feel the material,* and that satisfied him. Is it not then quite explicable that I always opposed his wish? I think that in the circumstances it is impossible for my young boy to remain to be educated under such an influence."

This whole testimony is indicative throughout of the naïve lack of understanding with which most women oppose the relatively harmless fetishisms of their husbands, and through this opposition work against their own marital happiness. In the divorce proceedings the woman testified that doctors had advised her that to cure her husband of this unnatural inclination, she had to

111

remove every single piece of flannel from the house.
Should such advice have been given, which I doubt, it is
absolutely the worst imaginable. *On the contrary, married life would have been very harmonious for both
parties if the wife had met her husband halfway in regard to his fetishistic peculiarity.*

Another and very severe case was one of *underclothes
fetishism,* involving an employee of the railroad. This
man was apprehended when he broke into the house of
a police official to steal some women's chemises. He testified that at regular intervals of time he wandered around
through the streets of the town in which he was living,
at night, in order that through a crack in the curtains
he might somewhere espy some piece of underclothing
of some married woman who was undressing. Then later
he would sneak back again to steal this and he would
wear it on his own body while working. This case differed
from a partial transvestitism in that the articles of clothing concerned could never be ones which had not been
worn. In the trial I advanced the viewpoint that in the
case of this man who was hereditarily very heavily burdened the freedom of decision could not in the slightest
degree be affirmed, as the law required. The expert for
the prosecution, a university professor, made the claim
to the court that in judging a case of theft it was absolutely immaterial whether the culprit wished to enrich
himself or to satisfy himself sexually; in both cases he
was only acting to his own advantage. The court supported this theory, and sentenced the man for house-
breaking without ameliorating circumstances. A few
days later the man was found dead in his cell. He had
hanged himself.

Handkerchief fetishists are almost always regarded in
a false light. They are regarded as pickpockets. I had to

give expert opinion on one man who had been a student at Jena. He had already been punished four times on the charge of pocket-picketing. He had never dared to mention the real reason, and also had thought with good reason that it would not be believed. Now finally, on the fifth occasion, he gave the real reason for his actions. I was summoned therefore as an expert. The court agreed with the final conclusion of my opinion, "doubt as to the freedom of decision," and freed him. With handkerchief fetishism, as with nearly all fetishes for personal linen, the sense of smell is usually the main organ of sense involved. I have repeatedly seen fetishists who were attracted only to women's perfumed handkerchiefs.

Commonly there are fetishists for men's underdrawers; women's underdrawers have more often an antifetishistic than a fetishistic effect, while tights, especially flesh-colored ones, belong to the fetishes of the first order. I knew one bisexual artist whom nothing aroused so greatly sexually as women's underdrawers on men and men's shirts on women.

There belongs finally to the clothing fetishisms of the torso, corset fetishism. For people suffering from this anomaly, the display of the elegant corset shops form the epitome of all that is beautiful, the contemplation of which necessitates the overcoming of many restraints of shame. I have also, however, seen cases of intense corset hate; several people objectivized this idiosyncrasy, which was really rooted in sex, by opposing the idea of the laced-up body as the most injurious sort of martyrdom imaginable to the body. As an example, I wish to add the testimony I gave regarding one corset fetishist of the most advanced type; it was in a suit for divorce of a married couple living in Paris.

113

I repeat here the main points of the testimony, the applicability of which will be obvious: Of importance for the divorce regarding the question of whether or not the husband R. suffers from a pathological fetishism, are the letters of the French physician, Dr. P., who observed and treated the man for a long time. It appears from the first letter of October thirty-first, that the new specialist, Dr. V., whom R. also consulted, shared the opinion of his colleague. In the two letters of Dr. P. of October thirtieth and thirty-first, this doctor terms R. as a sick man and speaks of his illness as an "obsession morbide." There is no doubt that this does not have to do with a mere neurasthenia, which was also there and probably still is present, but the physician also meant the *obsession which R. connected with the sexual act.* The expression "obsession morbide," a morbid compulsion, is used here to denote a morbid fetishism. The German specialist, it is true, does not generally connect the sexual anomaly with this term, but in and of itself fetishism is just this sort of compulsion, and it is particularly to be mentioned that physicians in France often classify the sexual anomaly simply as a form of morbid obsession. While, however, the French physicians who observed and treated R. classified as a morbid obsession his peculiar desire for his wife's waist to be slim, they do say that this had nothing to do with the normal desire for this characteristic, but was a characteristic pathological anomaly of the fetishism.

Dr. W. also, who was well acquainted with the family and who had a closer view into the relationship of the couple, terms R.'s desire for the slim waist an "idée fixe." From the opening of this letter where the doctor speaks of the sexual impotency of R., the conclusion may be drawn that this impotency was connected with his fetishism, i.e.: *that he was potent only when his wife's waist was as slim as was possible.* In the wife's letters the conduct of the man is so described as to point to a characteristic fetishism of a pathological sort. Mrs. R. says that her husband always demanded that she should lace herself up as tightly as possible, that his love-making seemed to be centered around her corset, and that he always concentrated his attention to her waist.

In the letter of April thirtieth, 1906, to her husband, she writes one sentence which in a few words completely describes the sexual anomaly of her husband and shows that this sexual anomaly was present: "As long as you are sick." This expression, in the mouth of a woman who certainly knows little of sexual anomalies and has studied no medical books on the subject, bears the stamp of truth, and it is unthinkable that she is not simply repeating the impressions which she has received from sexual intercourse with her husband.

This condition of impotency unless there is the lacing-up of the waist, shows clearly, however, that the slim waist is the conditio sine qua non for R.'s libido, which thus presupposes an actual fetishism.

Even the letters of R. himself confirm this assumption. *As do so many people, he seeks to gloss over and explain his sexual anomaly through all sorts of aesthetic and even hygienic motives.* In and of itself, he admits his pre-possession, his passion for the slim waist; in the letter of the thirty-first of October he acknowledges that the problem of the waist has occupied him completely, and that he wanted to renounce it. But he considered his morbid inclination as natural. In the letter of October twenty-seventh, he says himself that he had advised his wife to lace up her body tightly, but that this was only as a good hygienic measure. In his writings of the eighteenth of November, he himself seems to feel his anomaly as abnormal. In the letter of April twenty-first, he admits his sexual impotency, and from the following sentence, "il est de mets qu'on aime" (there are foods which one loves), that his potency is dependent upon the thing which he loves, that is, the narrow waist and lacings. In the same letter he tries to convince his wife, by telling her the remarks of Dr. U. on his case, that she should meet him halfway in his fetishism, because he says to her that according to the opinion of Dr. U., as well as according to his own opinion, which was constant, sexual intercourse was possible to him only in the way in which he wished it; that is, in the fetishistic morbid way which R. considered as normal. The letter of May seventh reveals *the anxiety of R. lest his wife become fat,* and at the close he says clearly that it was this of which his illness consisted, that he could not possibly bear to see his wife in a physical state—a heavy-waisted state, that is—which was unpleasing to him. This dislike is not just the normal aesthetic dislike, but as the letter of June sixth says also, the thicker waist prevents his finding his wife worthy, sexually, of his affection. It can be seen from the letters of June sixth and eleventh how already everything in sexual intercourse was concentrated upon the slim waist, and indeed in the letter replying to his wife's letter of June first, from the fact that he declares quite impossible the conditions she sets upon which their future life together depended, that he should in writing and in all sincerity declare that in the future he would be indifferent to this question of waists. Finally in a letter of April first to Dr. U. he admits his "idée fixe," his fetishism, and doubts whether he can be cured of it. Even the less important letters to other members of the family show that the family generally had come to the realiza-

116

tion that there was some sexual anomaly centered about the waist of Mrs. R., as far as R. was concerned. The sexual anomaly with which R. is burdened is not recognized by him as something morbid, at least not in all the letters. But whether the sexual anomaly is externally the most or the least noticeable, it is apparent that there are still other morbid symptoms present in R., especially of a neurasthenic sort.

In no case, however, can the sexual anomaly be denied on the ground that in other respects R. is an intelligent person, even perhaps, in certain regards, gifted, or because there is no actual insanity about him. For as a matter of fact sexual anomalies have nothing at all to do with psychosis in the correct sense of the word; *they almost never lead to insanity; it is even found in intellectually highly gifted persons, in spite of which anomalies such as the fetishism in question form a morbid phenomenon.* For this anomaly, in and for itself, R. cannot be held responsible. It has nothing to do with a whim, *a search for a new sensation, a characteristic which can be laid aside at will, but more with a peculiar and ineradicable urge.* So it is a matter of no importance whether one considers it congenital or the result of some compelling association in early youth. At all events this fetishism is ineradicable in R. and has probably been so for some time. That an anomaly of this sort may be voluntary and have arisen as the result of excesses, a question which has been studied and investigated thoroughly now, is considered impossible by scientific investigators. It follows from the nature and inclination of R. that he is an incurable case.

It was only to be expected that R. was not cured through the treatment of the physicians P. and V. The contrary would be surprising. Brom, Baeder, and such

117

men might bring it about that R. would wish to sleep less often with his wife. But this course of treatment would not affect R.'s necessity for having the slim waist present at sexual intercourse. If, even without this requisite, be it through the mere imagining of the presence of the woman with the slim waist—an idea which would, in contrast to the reality, be easily robbed of its efficacy— be it through manipulation to erection ejaculation, he should be able to bring about potency, yet this would never afford him an adequate satisfaction, and in the long run would scarcely satisfy him at all. *He simply had to have his fetish present for sexual intercourse.* It hardly needs to be mentioned that intercourse in this manner can hardly be expected of any woman.

Concerning the responsibility of R. for his sexual anomaly, a differentiation must be made between the existence of the anomaly and its manifestation. R. cannot be held responsible for the existence of the anomaly. It did not arise from any characteristic dependent upon his own will, but is an ineradicable sort of feeling which manifests itself despite all will and reason. And so there is no doubt in my mind that the anomaly did not arise first in R. since his marriage, but was implanted in his nature before, and probably a long time before. In one passage of the correspondence there is a direct indication that R. has thought in this sexually anomalous manner for a long time now; he speaks there of having since youth the ideal of *aesthetic,* slim women, an ideal with which R. was not content to remain an ideal such as one finds in many aesthetically sensitive men, but, as shown by his relations with his wife, exhibited itself as a degenerate ideal in sexual fetishism. There is basically little hope for results with R. from therapeutic treatments, because it can be seen from his letters that he

118

flatly rejected his wife's demand that he give up his "corset and waist ideas," so that he is already psychically in an unfavorable state of obstinacy against any counter suggestion.

As concerns the rest: the question of whether or not R. is responsible for the sexual actions arising from his anomaly, the presence of an anomalous urge does not in itself relieve the person concerned of the responsibility for the manifestation of this urge. Moreover, it could be very well argued that R. could attempt to make intercourse with his wife possible through imagining a woman with a slim waist, without burdening his wife with the pains and pressures of a corset and laces. Perhaps his responsibility can even be asserted to the extent that rather than subject his wife to such painful sexual intercourse, he should renounce it completely.

His opposition to renouncing this idea, however, is comprehensible since R. felt real sexual satisfaction only through the tightest possible lacing up of his wife's waist, and without this he was either completely impotent, or else could undertake intercourse only as a sort of masturbational act. But it is also understandable that a woman would not agree to suffer under this anomaly, and endure intercourse with her husband in such painful circumstances. *It hardly needs to be stressed that the fetishism and the actual anomaly with which R. is burdened is really the lack of a personal property, namely sexual normality and the capacity for behaving in normal sexual manner. That the woman would have refrained from entering into this marriage if she had known of this lack, there is no doubt,* even as R.'s refraining from marriage in this case would have arisen from an *appreciation of the nature of marriage.*

The final question is: could the wife come to know

gradually and after medical observation, of the anomaly of her husband, for the first time? To this we must answer yes.

A woman like the plaintiff, who is completely without knowledge of this sexual phase, could not possibly recognize the perverse and morbid aspect of such an urge in itself, and especially since in the beginning her own waist was still slim, and the demands her husband made were not so outrageous. Such was the case for the first time when the defendant visited her at her parents' home in January and April 1906, when it came out that, despite the treatment of Dr. P. in Paris, the old illness was present again.

I sum up my report as follows:

I. On the basis of the written evidence which I have seen I am convinced that Mr. R. is burdened with a severe, either incurable or at least hard to cure, sexual failing, namely a highly developed form of fetishism whose presence has affected the marriage in such a way that one cannot consent to its continuance, if he recognizes this perversity as such.

II. From the written evidence and from the nature of the illness, it is to be concluded that the failing was present at the time of the entrance into the marriage.

III. In accordance with the peculiar nature of the illness and her capability for recognizing it, the bride could not realize her error until six months after entrance into the marriage. This could happen quite *gradually,* and indeed the illness might not be recognized as such until after years of living together.

An analogous case of waist fetishism came to my attention recently which was peculiar in that it was directed exclusively towards *blood relatives.* This erotic fixation on relatives, especially the widespread love for cousins, usually has its roots in a narcissistic-fetishistic complex, a prepossession for certain family characteristics of a physical, but more often of a psychic variety. Accompanying this there is usually a weakening of the sexual aggressiveness, if not an absolute inversion of aggressiveness.

Patient, a thirty-year-old officer in the Marines, writes:

"Up to my fifteenth year I noticed nothing at all of my peculiar make-up. At that time my aunt once spoke scornfully of the 'wasp-waist' of my sister. At that I observed my sister, and found her waist heavenly. From that hour on I always got an erection whenever my sister put on her corset, especially if I were able to help her at it. At this time however, I was not yet acquainted with a sexual urge. At the age of sixteen, when I went away to sea, this inclination disappeared for years. At the age of twenty-seven I married my pretty, slim cousin. A few years after my marriage, about ten years ago, my prepossession for very slim people, with quite narrow waists, came again strongly to the fore. This urge has remained with me since then. If I see such a person, especially if the person be elegantly dressed, I have an immediate sensation of pleasure. In intercourse with my wife, who is an excellent, good-hearted, and practical woman, I content myself with the idea that *she is quite tightly laced up,* for I would be terribly sorry to hurt her, which would be the case if she should learn of my desire. I absolutely believe that she would leave at once with our young boy. For this reason I have not dared to conduct any perverse intercourse with her. What now forces me to take strong steps against my sexual desire, and the reason I have turned to you, is the lust which has seized me since June

121

for my fifteen-year-old niece. When I had my furlough in June, I saw this girl for the first time in a long while, dressed exactly as my ideal; I was so enchanted that I fell in love at once. I constantly tried to be alone with the girl, and daily, if I were in her presence but a quarter of an hour, I had a seminal discharge. With the utmost energy I succeeded in controlling myself and did nothing that would have been disastrous. The picture which I acquired of my secret love now serves me to arouse myself to self-satisfaction. Otherwise I am as healthy as can be; my friends who have not seen me for some time all say that I am in the pink of health. And yet . . ."

Corset fetishists are also girdle and especially garter fetishists, and pay the greatest attention to the garter of their sweethearts as a symbol and relique. Stockings are of erotic meaning, from the finest sheer stockings which reach far over the knees to the short woolen socks. One doctor with whom I am acquainted says that for him a woman loses all her charm when she takes off her stockings. How common this fetishism is, may be indicated by the great popularity enjoyed by even the photographs which depict women clothed in nothing but long black stockings, often also in shoes. For many fetishists these two fetishes, shoes and stockings, make a whole, though by no means for all. Spiral puttees, because of the way in which they so neatly fitted the shanks of the wearers, and which were spread through all countries during the war, in a short time attained a high fetishistic significance for many women, and the same was true, in no less a degree, with the leather puttees.

Next to the button fetishist, in lay circles the shoe worshiper is the best known type of fetishist, and indeed he represents the *most common form of clothing fetishism.* There is no sort of shoe, and there is no single spot on these shoes, which cannot fetishistically excite and arouse. Now it is the heels, now the folds at the ankle, now the bootlaces, the instep, the leg, the soles, and now the shoe buckles which arise as the fixation point. The shape of the shoe is very often considered. Some react only to low shoes, some to ridingboots, others again to elastic-sided pull-ons, topboots, buckles or laced boots, for many the shoe cannot be too elegant and dainty, for others it cannot be heavy and shapeless enough. The same differences of taste, rising to the point of fetishism, are also true as regards the material of which the shoes are made. For many people cloth shoes are an antifetish, whereas patent leather shoes, again, lie on the fetish side. Between lie shoes of calf, neat, buck, and all other sorts of leathers. A young woman who was wholly without knowledge of sexual matters was instituting divorce proceedings against her husband, an officer, after a one-year marriage. The following passages are from her testimony: "My shoes had always to be black, with very high legs and high heels, and had also to have small, round, shiny, black buttons against which he liked to press his face. Stockings and underdrawers had to be black. He liked me to be very tightly laced up, and even put the girdle on me and pulled the laces himself. *At intercourse I always had to have on a corset, high boots and stockings, otherwise he was unable to conduct intercourse.* He always lay at the bottom at intercourse. Before he came to me, I had to wind a small bootlace around his member for him, and massage it with eau de cologne, and then *tread on it with the heels of my shoes.* This seemed to me to be going a bit too far, and I finally confided in my mother who was also very indignant about it." Here is very clearly shown the metastrophic significance of foot-coverings. *To love the shoe, means to wish to be inferior,* in which case the remarkable thing is that, as in the case last mentioned, the shoe worshiper expressly exercises compulsion in order that a compulsion be exercised against him . . . one of the sado-masochistic overcomings of contradictions which is so characteristic of love life.

There are fetishists who become violently aroused in hotels at night by the shoes and boots which the guests have put out in front of the doors to be cleaned. One man said that he indulged in onanism whenever he saw a pair of large heavy men's shoes, preferably soldiers' boots with spurs, standing next to a pair of dainty women's shoes before a hotel door. In the dark of the night he would steal up to the four shoes in order to stroke them, smell them, and kiss them. This man—he was a clergyman—had repeatedly bribed the hotel servants to allow him to clean the shoes of the guests early in the mornings. Although this condition was a source of constant pain to him, he could not overcome his passion. On Pera Street in Constantinople an old, earnest, and very excellent shoe-shiner was pointed out to me, who was at one time supposed to have lived as a distinguished and wealthy man in his native English city. Then, several decades ago, he suddenly emigrated to Turkey in order there to be able, unknown and unhindered, to indulge his strange inclination for boots. So what the elegant ladies of the Levant thought was a painstaking care in shining and polishing, was in reality an erotic caressing of their shoes. One of my patients suffered exceedingly from a passion for high curved heels. He left his small home town, where he lived as a very respected citizen in public position, once every month to go to the metropolis. There he would search for hours for the highest pair of

124

heels he could find on a woman and then induce the woman—it always was a prostitute who was concerned —to belabor his body with the heels until an ejaculation resulted. A famous painter was found murdered in London some years ago whose entire body was covered with fresh wounds and old scars which seemed to have been caused by spurs. Investigation revealed that his last visitor was a cavalryman. The unfortunate man belonged to the class mentioned of *ridingboot fetishists*. In my practice I have repeatedly been able to establish these scars on the bodies of spur fetishists. But one case some years ago in which I had to act as an expert showed that there is also at times an antifetishistic reaction in this realm. A man was charged with destruction of property because a guest in one of the leading hotels in the capital had caught him in the act of cutting a pair of yellow shoes with a knife. Generally, in cases of apparently purposeless destruction of property, as for example destruction of certain kinds of fabrics by spraying it with some corroding acid, there is more often than one realizes an antifetishistic motive at the bottom.

The following report, which reached me many years ago from a simple man in southern Germany, shows how ridingboot fetishism can extend not only to the rider alone, but also to the horse, and thus borders on *zoophily*.

He writes: "My fetishism is concerned with ridingboots. Other kinds of shoes leave me indifferent, even the ordinary boot whose sides are of two pieces. This perversion is inborn in me. My earliest recollections concerned with this go very far back. My first recollection is: I was scarcely five years old, and I still remember quite well getting into a pair of my father's high boots, and that even at that time I had a strange sensation of

125

pleasure and at the same time an erection of the penis; my mother came in then and asked, 'What are you doing, anyway?' . . . This has remained indelibly in my mind. Once, for no good reason, but driven by some unknown urge, I was looking for an old pair of my brother's boots which had been thrown away, and was unable to find them, so I inquired about the boots. My mother was busy in the kitchen and my father also was in there at the moment. My parents asked what I wanted to do with the old boots, and whatever was I thinking of, and so on. I did not find the boots, and forgot about them for the time. I was then just about seven. I believe that if I had found the boots I would have simply put them on.

"Once I was allowed to be measured for a pair of boots. I was very happy and thought that the shoemaker would make me a regular pair of boots, like ridingboots, but he only made me double-stitched, high-sided boots, and on this account I felt as though I had been cheated greatly. When they were quite new, however, they excited me somewhat, and I touched them with my erected penis. I was about nine years old at the time. Once, when I was about fourteen and a half years old, I was talking to a friend about sexual matters, and I said, 'Also I get a great pleasure out of ridingboots.' He said, 'How in the world did you happen to get interested in ridingboots?' I answered, 'I don't know.' He meant that he also got pleasure from them, but then I soon spoke of something else, and I considered it a very stupid remark of mine. In the future *I never again openly expressed myself about ridingboots*. Once, when I was fifteen and a half, an older brother who was a butcher got a new pair of ridingboots. I had a great deal of pleasure when I was able to be alone with them; I pressed them tight to me, put them on, and masturbated in them (already

126

had a seminal discharge at this). During the time I was apprenticed to my brother I had only a few chances to be alone with the boots; I put them on every time and masturbated in them, but on the whole during this time I did not have the chance to come into contact with ridingboots, and I wanted to drive these 'stupid ideas' out of my head.

"When I was seventeen I went to Tuebingen, and there despite my resolutions my attention was again attracted to ridingboots. The students, with their high ridingboots, pleased me mightily. I myself would always have been glad to wear ridingboots, but this was impossible, because I did not need them, and wearing them only to indulge this silly pleasure in the boots I considered still more stupid, no matter how much I wished to have the boots.

"I attempted to eradicate this inclination for ridingboots. During my stay in Tuebingen I never had an opportunity to indulge my desire for them; only that once, when I was home for a short visit, I had the chance to get hold of the boots of an artilleryman who was a friend of mine. He had taken them off while doing some gymnastic exercises; I took them, put them on, and walked up and down in them as though for a joke, and masturbated in them. From then on, on this account, he thought that I was just plain crazy. It has always been just as it then was. Now, as before, I look secretly at men in ridingboots; they seem to me in their boots *so manly and worth associating with.*

"With this fetishism there is also connected my bestial passion, which centers about horses. I remember the following incident as the first indication of its origin: I was about thirteen years old, and was still going to school. While delivering newspapers, I happened to go

127

to a drayman who was in his stable. On the way home the thought came to me of how wonderful it would be if I could stroke his horse. This desire did not disturb me overly much and I soon forgot it again, but whenever I brought the man his weekly paper, the desire would recur, to be able to stroke and pet his horse, but I scarcely once found courage to stroke the horse.

"Starting with the time of puberty, this remarkable love of horses became more and more pronounced. I would have liked very much to be able to caress, stroke, and kiss them. But first of all I never had the opportunity to come into contact with a horse, and secondly I have never encouraged these desires, but rather tried to suppress them. Often since maturity I have had sexual dreams, and often about horses, but most often about ridingboots. I have never yet dreamed of having intercourse with a horse. When finally I found the explanation of my psychically feminine nature and my fetishism, I assumed that this exceptional love of horses was also something abnormal. I first read about the actual condition of morbid bestialism about a half year ago in a book by Professor Krafft-Ebing. The cases mentioned there, however, were also apparently morally degenerate people, and I do not believe that one can term me morally degenerate.

"With horses I love equally the male, female, or gelding. I could, with the greatest of pleasure have coitus with a mare (would rather die on the other hand than have intercourse with a human female). At the same time manipulation of the sexual parts of a stallion would give me the same pleasure, especially if at the time I should be wearing high ridingboots.

"I *never* have actualized my love of horses, and also do not believe that it will *ever* come to that. In the first

128

place, I still have a certain moral scruple which will restrain me; secondly, I have had thus far no opportunity; thirdly, I am restrained by fear of coming into conflict with the law; and finally, above all else, there is my fear of the animal. I have no extraordinary love for other animals, though, indeed, I am a great friend of animals.

"Riding has a special appeal for me. I believe that after a long ride at a trot, I would have an ejaculation in the saddle. Up to now, however, I have had just one session of riding, and that recently.

"My love for horses can scarcely be termed immoral, since so far I have not actualized it sexually. The horse is to me absolutely the noblest and the most beautiful of all animals, and it also deserves the greatest sympathy, for it is the slave of mankind; work is its lot, and ingratitude its reward. In patience and resignation it is marvelous, for *it suffers without complaint*. It makes me unspeakably sad when I see how roughly and inconsiderately horses are handled. As far as concerns my sexual pleasure in horses, I do not believe that it will be very hard for me to refrain from criminal intercourse with horses, firstly for the reasons already given, and secondly because it would give me sufficient joy and pleasure if I might take care of horses, might ride and drive them, and, naturally, wear at the time a dashing pair of ridingboots.

"I have now bought myself several pairs of ridingboots, and also riding-breeches, and have often worn ridingboots in spite of the fact that I, a timid common fellow, have always felt very bashful about appearing in ridingboots. However, I would feel an absolutely different man if I could wear ridingboots, unembarrassed, and also when possible, leather, or leather-trimmed ridingbreeches.

129

"Previously my only wish was always to join the cavalry, and though I am exempt from military service on account of a weak heart, yet I would still be very glad to be in the cavalry. How a man of my poor weak spirit would fare, I do not know, but I do not believe that I would be treated more ignominiously than by my employers, and all in all I would have not a little pride and joy in being a cavalryman. The object which fascinates me most of all is a fine strapping rider, with dashing boots, and a beautiful horse. For this reason *I have a prepossession for all riding occupations,* especially and before all for officers and the cavalry; for example, the regiment of the cuirassiers is my favorite, although I know them only through pictures.

"In the last analysis, my whole perverse nature is an insoluble riddle. Why I am this way, I do not know; but this I know certainly, that I am innocent of my condition, and that I have simply been made the way I am by inscrutable Mother Nature. I am often not quite clear about myself, and many times stand in absolute contradiction to myself. On the one hand I would like to lead a clean and ideal life, would like to be a decent, educated person with good morals and associate with educated people; on the other hand, I often catch myself at the lowest of thoughts, would like for example to be a stableboy or a stud-groom, and the *lowest sort of work about horses would be a pleasure to me.*

"I would like also to mention, as an attempt at explanation of my fetishism, that both my father and grandfather were tanners, and so had always to handle leather. My grandfather, however, was a tanner against his will, and my father had to give up the tannery because business was so poor. As another and perhaps better explanation, I wondered whether perhaps my mother

130

might have been influenced just before my birth by a ridingboot, a horse, or a rider upon a horse, or have thought of or seen something of this kind. Be that as it may, however, I am as I am, and cannot alter myself, but I wish to be able to command myself in this matter.''

Some time after this confession came into my hands, I received a report that the writer ''had committed suicide because of a disappointment in love.''

In the category of the fetishists for leg-coverings, a minor group is formed by the retroussé fetishists, men who watch with eagerness when a woman raises her skirt and thus allows a glimpse of otherwise covered parts, elegant gaiters, fine sheer stockings, ''light clouds of white laciness, or even the colored silk of a petticoat.'' Bloch (Part 2, ''Ætiology of Psychopathia Sexualis'') says that ''Paris has always been the paradise of the retroussé fetishists.'' If this is true—and in general all assumptions of national peculiarities in the realm of sex are to be accepted with the greatest of caution—then it must have its basis in the fact that in Paris more than anywhere else women have the habit of raising their dresses exposing the calf without its being considered shocking. For many women, also, there is a fetishistic effect whenever a man pulls his trousers high, as when he sits down with his legs crossed, and thereby exposes the part of his shoes which is usually covered, and a glimpse of his socks and even at times his underdrawers. For the most part the retroussé fetishists are also fetishistically interested in disrobing, and find their whole sexual pleasure in the sight of a woman undressing. In one French novel a woman says to such a fetishist, ''What a marvelous lady's-maid you would have been.''

From the bed also there arises a fetishistic attraction.

By this is not meant the everyday sensation, that a person lying in bed seems especially desirable to a person of the opposite sex. It was more in the realm of fetishism when, as happened in a Bavarian village where the Passion Play was being given, an American woman offered a large sum of money to the portrayer of the rôle of the Christ to be allowed to sleep, alone of course, for one night in his bed. Here it is a moot question whether the matter is not one of religious fetishism, or fanaticism. Another case which I observed is less ambiguous, in which a person took a position working in a hotel in order that, in the heights of sexual ecstasy, he might throw himself upon the beds in which still remained the linen used by some beautiful woman or other, and thus gain sexual relief. A short time ago I was consulted by a merchant from western Germany who was interested solely in sleeping women. Only such women charmed him as were lying and resting; if they were standing or walking, they left him indifferent, whereas he had a fetish hate toward sitting women. Investigation also revealed that in addition to this, there was another peculiarity: that whenever he rebuked or scolded any of the girls working with him in his office, he had an unaccountable erection. The connecting link between these two anomalies and the explanation for them may be sought in an embryonic sadism, erotization with the feeling of the defenselessness of the women as the arouser from passivity.

We must still regard briefly the two upper layers of clothing, the suit and its street covering, the overcoat. I wish to mention a few examples of costume fetishism, a very widespread phenomenon, which I have observed. I had patients who were only capable of sexual intercourse with women who wore black clothes, preferably

132

with widow's veils. Others became so excited at the sight of women in bridal clothes with myrtle wreaths and bridal veils, that even without any onanistic assistance they would come to an ejaculation. Among the many apparently curious people who throng the steps of the churches and courthouses to watch the bridal couple enter and depart, there are many *erotic voyeurs* with fetishistic, triolistic, hypererotic, and other sexual complexes. Garnier ("Les Fétishistes," p. 59) speaks of one young man who spent a great part of his time in the Bois de Boulogne in front of the restaurants in which wedding feasts usually were held. There is often a fetishistic prepossession for the dress of nurses and nuns. There are prostitutes who even go out on the streets in this sort of clothing in order to attract men. Girls in the clothes of children's nurses, governesses, and cooks often have a hypererotic effect while the same effect is had by long, trailing dresses, ball dresses, riding clothes, all sorts of national costumes, old modes, such as crinolines. During the war women in men's positions had many admirers, just as women's clothes with a slightly masculine air generally will attract metastrophic men.

Of no small importance is the color of the pieces of clothing; thus to many people blue suits are especially exciting, to others white clothes, but also green, gray, and black, so that in the end every color can have a fetishistic or an antifetishistic significance. A senior master in a school writes: "I am set, through looking at chrome yellow and lilac gray colors, into a condition of sexual intoxication. I masturbate with these colors, and dream of them whenever I have a pollution." I remember the case of a lady who was quite carried away by the red braid on uniforms, even the cord to her husband's trousers set her into ecstasies. Sexually, as far as women

133

are concerned, the uniform of the soldiers, the military profession, stands at the head of the list. This *uniform fetishism* can reach such a degree that the affection of many women can change into a strong dislike if the man whom they loved while he was a soldier, should one day appear in civilian clothes. In this regard, I have had the opportunity to observe several very remarkable cases. All sorts of uniforms come into consideration here, but especially, perhaps, those of the cavalry and the marines. The sailor's uniform fascinates homosexuals, but also very often normal people. Thus I had to give expert opinion on one married man who had given offense through having tried to make sexual advances to several girls in sailor's dress. The patient's wife, and also his twelve-year-old daughter and eleven-year-old son, always had to wear sailor's dress. The man's dress clothes, swallow-tailed coat, stiff shirt, etc., can affect just as frequently fetishistically as antifetishistically. There is a novel, "Fetish-hate," in which is described from life how a woman draws a knife against her lover when one evening immediately after sexual intercourse, he appears dressed in the evening clothes which she hates so much. The garb of the clergy, the robe of the judge, as almost every professional and working habit, can become fetishes.

There are, not rarely, cases in which a strong fetish hate is concentrated upon the overcoat. Thus, for one Berlin society lady, every man with a topcoat, hat and stick was the object of the strongest aversion, though it is more often the case that both the woman's coat and the man's become a considerable fetish. I had one patient who was particularly excited by the Havelock, another who was fascinated by the boldly flung officer's cape. Among the women's coats every shape and color,

134

every cut and material has its fetishistic admirers, especially and above all, however, the *fur coat,* and that not only since Sacher-Masoch glorified it in "Venus in Furs." Krafft-Ebing treated the fetishism for fur in common with that for leather, silk and satin, as a stuff fetishism, and doubtless the stuff is the predominately attracting medium, but not so much so that it should form a separate group of its own. It belongs to the category of clothing fetishism, in the different varieties of which, including personal linens, next to the color and shape the stuff plays a certain rôle.

Of especial interest is the fetishism for animal peltries, such as fur and leather, insofar as it enlightens our understanding of a sexual anomaly which now falls in the field of forensic medicine and which has since olden times given rise to many strange conjectures and superstitious beliefs, such as the belief that sphinxes, centaurs, and such creatures could arise through the union of humans with beasts.

If Krafft-Ebing deals with zoophily, which has also been called by others sodomy and bestiality, in connection with fetishism, and even terms it directly animal fetishism, so this point of view seems to me to have more in its favor than that of Paul Garnier, who in his great work, "Onanism," evaluated intercourse undertaken between humans and beasts as merely a special form of onanism, because in this intercourse only a sensual stimulation, without spiritual participation, can enter into the question. However this does not correspond to the facts altogether. It is, in the main, true, that these acts are not seldom undertaken by persons who have a lot to do with animals as a sort of substitute proceeding, which does not in any way disprove its fetishistic character, however. Thus during the war I had to give expert

135

testimony concerning a Bavarian sergeant-major who in Rumania had coitus with a sow. The men had noticed how he would repeatedly sneak into the pigsty and close himself in there. The suspicious soldiers bored little peep-holes through the door and established the fact, to their amazement, that their superior was conducting with the sow coitus absolutely according to rules. Arrested on their information, he said as his justification: The *light skin* of the pig had always reminded him so much of the *delicate skin of his wife*. It was two years since he had last seen his wife, to whom he was most devoted and who had presented him with seven blooming children; and in order to be true to her, he had had dealing with the animal. Despite this excuse which was frankly brought forward, and which arose from a not inconsiderable psychic weakness of the accused, despite exemplary conduct in service and many war honors, the man was condemned by the court martial to a considerable term of imprisonment. The naïve manner in which the accused explained his criminal action, is strangely common in such occurrences, and is significant of the weak-mindedness of the man. Thus a farmer who was accused of similar conduct with a sow, when asked by the judge how he came to do such a thing, made the laconic answer, "My wife is away on a trip." Another testified in his own justification: "The sow always followed him around and looked at him so pleadingly, so he did what it wanted him to."

The exaggerated love for animals by many people, particularly single and childless men and women, is a realized and inherent erotic characteristic. I have made many inquiries of veterinaries concerning the attitude of the owners toward the animals, and it has confirmed me in this to a most far-reaching degree. Particularly,

136

one specialist in Berlin for dogs' illnesses related to me many examples of the affection and caresses exceeding all imagination which many dog owners lavish upon their animals, people of whom Wulffen has already said that they give their servants inferior food, while they serve cutlets and beefsteaks to their dogs. Many years ago I was called in by a woman whose husband had just died of a paralytic stroke. When I told her of her husband's death, she said, "Oh, Doctor, what haven't I had to go through this year; in April our dog died, in the summer my canary bird, and now my husband also." In another case a woman desired me as a witness to the effect that it was necessary that her cat sleep with her in bed; as a reason, she spoke of her severe rheumatic pains which could only be appeased through the warmth of living catskin. In reality, however, it was a sexual fixation with the unusually large and beautiful tomcat which she introduced to me. The landlord and the tenants had insisted on the removal of this animal, which disturbed their sleep; despite the prevailing shortage of homes, the woman would rather give up her comfortable home than part from her beloved beast.

Though in this case of cat love it was doubtful whether the woman who owned the cat was fully enlightened as to the erotic character of her violent passion; just so, many women, in the gushing affection which they bestow on their lapdogs, do not realize or will not admit this sensual factor. Yet in another case, which was submitted to me, the motive was quite obvious. A beautiful, healthy, twenty-five-year-old girl broke her engagement with a very excellent man, an architect, *through love for her canary bird*. She could not share her love for the bird with another. When she caressed the soft feathers of the bird with her hands and lips, she received

137

a sensual excitation which rose to the utmost grati-
fication. On the other hand, in caressing her fiancé she
remained utterly cold. Rohleder reports a similar case.
Only in this case the object of the ardent love of a thirty-
year-old maiden was a male parrot; she would have it
crawl and tickle at her head, chin, and breast until she
was aroused into a state of the highest sexual excitement.

In the majority of cases the contacts here described
would not suffice to bring about a sexual relief, but it
would depend far more upon dealings around the sexual parts. Here one must distinguish between such actions as men might undertake on animals, and such as
women would allow animals to undertake on them. Male
zoophiles prefer female animals, usually, and females
prefer the males. The first is more common in the country; women with such inclinations are usually found in
the cities. On the other hand, there are also the acts of
homosexuals with animals; thus there was, according
to Merzbach: a homosexual landowner would be mounted
from behind by a trained dog and dealt with per anum.
The most common form of activity of woman zoophiles
is the passive lambitus; they have their genitals stroked
cum lingua by the animals, of which dogs are most frequently concerned; among men this is more rare. Still
I had to give expert testimony in a case in which a
butcher was in the habit of having calves suck at his
member until a seminal discharge resulted. He brought
cattle from the country to the central cattle-yard in
Berlin, and had this performed in the trains until he
was finally discovered and brought to court. More common among those cases which have come to the courts
are those in which men have forced into the vagina, anus,
or cloaca of animals.

138

In the special literature on this subject one finds mentioned especially the following animals with which dealings of this sort are undertaken:

Horses: When it was reported one day in Potsdam to Old Fritz that a cavalryman of the garrison there had been surprised at sexual intercourse with a mare, instead of the expected severe sentence of imprisonment, he wrote curtly under the evidence: "Transfer the swine to the infantry."

Cows, with which for the most part as with mares a stool is used, goats (of which it is said that particularly in the East and in Italy strangers have often reported being approached by pimps on the streets), swine, sheep, dogs, which are particularly used by women who suffer from pruritus vulvae. Feathered beasts like hens, ducks, geese, turkeys and pigeons are not seldom put to improper use by men who insert their member into the cloaca and at the same time strangle the beast or cut its head off, whereby, through the convulsive death agonies of the animal, an ejaculation is brought about. There are analogous zoo-sadistic proceedings with still other animals and the conjecture arises that at the basis of the intense interest which many women and men take in the slaughtering of animals, bull-fights, and similar horrors where blood is shed, there is really a sexual desire, though it may be for the most part unknowingly.

Thoinot, in his "Perversions du Sens Génital" tells of one man who occupied himself in a Parisian brothel in this way: a girl had to hold a small dog whose stomach he slit open. While he was digging his hands into bloody intestines of the animal, he got his satisfaction. In the Gross *Archiv fuer Kriminalanthropologie* is reported a still more horrible case of triolism; a man was accused with having trained a large dog to have coitus with his wife. He would hold the weeping and struggling woman down by force, strip the clothes from her body, and insert the dog's penis into her vagina. The dog understood what was wanted and would go through with the cohabitation while the man would look on. The accused, who had repeatedly carried through this criminal act, was sentenced for "sodomy and forcible lechery against his wife."

According to Mantegazza and Krauss, both asses and she-asses have at times been turned into sexual objects in southern countries. Krauss also tells of having once observed a Chrowotin woman, who fully naked, had intercourse with a tomcat. She was worked up through this into a thoroughly violent orgasm. It still remains to be established whether or not the many strange stories of women having intercourse with monkeys, and men with female monkeys, are true. At any rate it is worthy of note that according to an old Peruvian saying syphilis was originally a disease of the monkeys, from whom it was transmitted through sodomistic acts to men.

It is certainly possible that diseases such as erysipelas, anthrax, and tetanus can be contracted through sexual acts with animals, although we find scarcely anything to this effect in literature. One of the best known and most common diseases which humans can acquire through caressing, and especially through kissing animals is echinococcus. I observed one case of an echinococcus swelling in the liver which was later successfully operated upon. The patient, a thoroughly effeminate man, had been infected by his male dog Nero, who played a large rôle in all his thoughts and actions, without actual sexual intercourse having taken place.

It is naturally also conceivable that men infect animals. Although cases of this sort have not been made

140

known, a brief indication of it is that the curious superstition is rife with many people, that one can cure sexual
diseases through intercourse with an animal—the southern Slavs prefer hens for this. To fill out the list of
the animals coming into this question, it should be remarked that the ancient Egyptians are said to have had
coitus with female crocodiles, while respectable Roman
ladies kept favorite snakes which they took to bed with
them for the purpose of sexual stimulation. A woman
snake-dancer told me that her passionate affection for
snakes was not free from erotic sensations. Thus the
worship of the holy ram in ancient Egypt resulted, on
the women's side, in sexual union.

In his clear and unbiased treatment of these questions,
Forel was quite right in expressing the opinion that from
a eugenic point of view it would be far better for an
idiot or a weak-minded person to violate a cow than to
impregnate a human female. At all events sodomy is to
be considered one of the least harmful forms of pathological perversion of the sexual urge, because no one
suffers any harm from it. For this reason in the latest
draft for the German statute book, as in most other
countries, lechery between man and beast has been left
exempt from punishment, in contrast to earlier times
when people were burned at the stake who had had improper dealings with animals, as, for example, women
with dogs. This was probably through the mistaken
notion that issue could arise from such intercourse. This
belief is still persisted in, as I can perceive from the
inquiries which are often submitted to me. A few years
ago a rumor arose which circulated through Charlotten-
burg with great determination, even giving the name
and address, of a woman who had brought five dogs into
the world. It is biologically *absolutely* impossible for

141

animal semen to unite with the feminine ovulum, just as also it is impossible for the male spermatozoa to force their way to the animal eggs.

Can plants, as animals, become objects of sexual attention? This question I would answer in the affirmative. Here also there is present a bridge from the physiological to the pathological fetishism. It is the not rare flower fetishism. A flower in the hair or belt of the woman, in the buttonhole of the man, and usually some particular flower, is a fetish for the visual or olfactory sense. And even the tenderness which many single ladies and effeminate men bestow upon their flowers does not seem to be free from an erotic touch, even if it be unbeknown to the flower-lover himself.

The example brought forward by Bloch seems to teach that dendrophily can extend to trees, when he tells of Xerxes who rendered to a plane tree in Lydia the reverence and honors of a woman, spent time with it as with a sweetheart, and heaped it richly with jewels and other presents.

A few years ago a man confided in me who was having an "affair" with an old oak tree in Machnow near Berlin. He had, as he said, an idolatrous veneration for it, and often in the darkness, when he felt quite safe from observation, he would press his naked member against the "venerable trunk," until an ejaculation resulted.

From the love which in antiquity was directed to trees personified as dryads and naiads, it is only a short step to the erotic fixation upon probionts and inanimate objects such as crystals, diamonds, pearls, and other precious stones. In my "Natural Laws of Love" I have already described in detail a case of crystal fetishism observed by Koerber and me.

The case concerns a young girl who had fallen in love

142

with a large crystal bowl. She went daily to the show window in which the bowl stood to feast her eyes on the sight of it. One day it disappeared, a buyer from some other country had acquired it. To the girl, however, it was as though some one had died, and for a long time she suffered from a longing which she could scarcely master. The case seemed to me so remarkable that I should also like to take room here for the account from the letters of the young lady which show that towards humans she had no erotic feelings.

"Even in my earliest childhood," she writes me, "I surrendered myself to the ecstasies of the crystal. How this love awoke in me and through what agency, I cannot say; before it directed itself to the crystal objects in our home, it had already brought about marvelous dreams of crystal palaces, which must exist somewhere on this earth. Then later I sat for hours over pictures which I found in books, where grottos of ice and fantastic formations enchanted me, and I lost myself in the dazzle of the play of light in the crystal formations. The cruets with the vinegar and oil were for me, for a long time, the most beautiful things on the table. During luncheon I took particular pleasure in the preserves, because they were served from crystal dishes . . . and when I finally had it before me, I could scarcely eat from excitement, for there was something so incomprehensible, the refraction of the light, and the strange border of light which the jam produced where it touched the plate. . . . For many tastes in many things, edible as well as potable, crystal always had a great deal of influence, and there are many things which I can enjoy only from crystal.

"Once I found on the lawn of our house, rolled up in a piece of paper, a prism from a chandelier. When I un-

143

rolled the paper, and the sun's rays broke up, sparkling, in the crystal, I was exceedingly aroused and masturbated. . . . With a chandelier with crystal prisms, I always become absorbed again in the breaking up of the light and am infatuated with the chromatrope. . . . I studied the prism through the different periods of light in the day; I knew when the sun would be caught in it, and I never neglected to make my visit to it at that hour. The streaming light, which was diffused to all sides, afforded me an extraordinary pleasure . . . it was as though fine grains of gold-dust were oozing through my blood . . . I felt it hotly *going through my whole body until I was exhausted.*

"Often I would go into stores and ask the price of different crystal bowls, glasses, carafes and so on, only for the reason that I might be able to take the different things into my hands, come into *contact* with them, be able to stroke over the smooth surface, but most of all to be able to feel its weight; the weight of expensive crystal gave me a quite special joy. . . . When I was twenty years old, I discovered in the show window of a shop a crystal bowl of extraordinary beauty. It seemed to me to muffle the diversity of light with a quite special and mysterious veil in order through this to attract more alluringly. I had to go to this window once every day to gaze on this wonder.

"I dreamed of rooms in which it could stand, of particular little tables with a salver of precious stones as a stand for it, of colored silks on which it would rest and which would set it off with its subdued colors. Preferably I thought of it, though, on a salver of dark silver, simple and quiet, where no other color would interfere with its own play of colors. Then I would imagine it in the middle of a room on a high, narrow

144

stand. It must be semi-dark there, with only a few wax tapers on the walls. Then I would pour in oil . . . an oil as clear as water, but thick, and heavy flowing, so that the peculiar light would shimmer on the smooth surface, and below it would gleam as though stars were in the bowl. Then I would throw a ruby into the oil, and I could not do enough in my dreams about this wonderful thing which was to reveal everything to me.

"I went into the store and asked the price. . . . I knew in advance that it was absolutely beyond my means . . . but this might give me an opportunity to take the precious thing in my hands and feel its weight. I reckoned in every way how I might still be able to attain possession of it . . . one day the bowl had disappeared from the window, and I was sure that it had been sold. I went in and asked after it again, and at confirmation of my fear was terribly afflicted. . . ."

Among the stones and metals that have incidental erotic-fetishistic effects, is marble and bronze. For this reason people conclude that in statue love also, Pygmalionism, there is a form of fetishism. Other authors have established this anomaly more as related to the love of dead bodies, to necrophilia. Both forms of these disturbances have in common an increased sexual excitability, which, going beyond the living, extends to imitative and inanimate bodies. I will return to these sexual extravagances and ecstasies in the next chapter which deals of hypereroticism. Let it just be mentioned here that a connection similar to that between fur fetishism and zoophily connects the erotic fixation upon stones and marbles with that strange inclination which extends to statues and corpses.

HYPEREROTICISM

THE fetishism dealt with in the preceding chapter leads over to the quantitative variations of the sexual urge to which we will devote our attention in the next two chapters, the equally extensive plus and minus groups of the sexual function, hyper- and hypoeroticism, the aggravation of the libido and impotency. On the *positive* side, a sensuous perception can evoke a passion far exceeding every normal degree; on the negative side, a total of personal characteristics can be so repulsing that every desire and ability for sexual intercourse is extinguished. To be sure, these exogenous reasons are not alone responsible for the *strength of the desire;* of even greater importance is the endogenous factor, the degree of the strength of eroticism limited by the inner secretions, and dependent therefrom the heights of reaction and effect of sexual attraction and aversion.

In this chapter the discussion will be of sexual excess. In order to recognize it as such, it is necessary that one be perfectly clear as to what constitutes a measure in sexual life. In this respect there is in no way a unanimity of opinion; 150 cohabitations a year, three a week, which to one writer seems too much, seems to another moderate during the bloom of human life, or at least not immoderate. The *strength* of the desire is in and of itself, as well among men as among women, uncommonly differing, to such a degree that here, as always in the realm of sex, it is only under very great difficulties that a norm can be established, to which the physiological belongs and where the pathological begins.

There are persons who have absolutely no, or quite little, necessity for sexual activity. But at least as frequently there are individuals of both sexes with whom the barely satisfied desire is ever freshly reawakening. Just a short time ago a woman complained to me that in the eight years of her marriage, aside from a very short lapse of time in between, her husband had completed the sexual act with her four or five times every day; in another case an unmarried man, who is to be believed, told me that in the space of a year he had had intercourse in the normal way over one thousand times. In a court proceeding at which I was present a short time ago, the husband testified in the presence of his wife that during their honeymoon they had had intercourse on the average of eighteen times in twenty-four hours.

The well known lovers and courtesans of history, whose names have become bywords, as the Casanovas, Don Juans, Phryne, and Messalina, stand in one wing; men like Immanuel Kant and the painter Menzel, of whom it was said that he knew neither love nor sexual intercourse, and women like Cornelia Goethe, of whom her brother Wolfgang said that in her nature there was no trace of sensuousness, are on the other side. *Between these two bounds there are all imaginable different degrees.* The *individual* strength of these desires maintains itself, aside from certain definite exceptions and fluctuations, at a fairly constant pitch for several decades.

147

In other words, frigid men and women continue at a lower degree, and temperamental people at a higher degree of libido than is normal to their sexual temperament. The direction of the desire as such has nothing to do with the strength of the desire. Thus people attracted to the same sex as well as the heterosexual people can be uncommonly passionate, or possess only a weakly developed sexual urge. In the case of the bisexual people, the degree to which they are attracted to the one sex or the other is usually widely different; the patient himself often expresses this numerically, such as that he is attracted about ninety per cent to the feminine sex and ten per cent to the masculine, or vice versa.

For the question of the *ability to control the urge,* investigation of the strength of the urge is of considerable importance in individual cases. Here certainly the erotization of the blood stream and the brain centers by the mass of incretory sexual hormones which feed them, plays a decisive rôle. Only here we have no means or method by which objectively to measure the *degree of erotization,* especially in relation to the *degree of ability to withstand,* a relationship which naturally changes considerably in accord with the degree of attraction proceeding from the sexual object.

The expert before the court is not seldom asked whether in a concrete case the sexual urge was controllable or not. In such cases I have always taken care to analyze that, when the accused entered into his dealings with the sexual object possibly there was only an effort to be satisfied with the mere being together which was made so much more enjoyable through the desire, without there having been any intention of the criminal action, the deception, which the prosecutors and the judges usually see in the mere approaching of one per-

148

son to another. The excitement could have risen gradually through the involuntary workings of proximate
attraction until finally a moment came when the judgment relaxed, and the person concerned, without being
able any longer to think of the consequences of his
actions, without free determination of the will, has gone
through with the deed which was originally not planned
and finally over the extent and result of which he is no
longer absolutely clear.

I bring in an example here of a doctor, twenty-five
years in practice, who reported to me that he met a girl
who had attracted him sexually to a great extent and
went with him into his home. There he noticed some suspicious flecks on her body which he thought to be syphilitic. For that reason he refrained from coitus and only
joked with her; but after a few hours of this chaffing he
had become so aroused that, although he still realized the
danger of infection, went through coitus with her and
actually was infected. Similar cases in which hypererotic
men have intercourse with women whom they know as
gonorrheal or syphilitic, are not at all rare; these examples are a conclusive proof of the occasional power
of the sexual drive.

It is by no means a rare thing for the sexual urge to
maintain itself after the peak of life even until after
the fiftieth year at a considerable height. I have in my
files a great number of women, especially widows, who
still complain many years after change of life of an exceedingly excitable sexual condition. With men also there
usually appears a pronounced old age libido. Thus in
Rome I saw a German painter of over eighty-five who
assured me that he still had intercourse every week with
girls, even though with a half-dormant member. Like
many old people, in agreement with the Biblical story

149

of King David who slept with Abishag the Shunammite, he was of the opinion that a magnetic fluid, a sort of power of youth, streamed forth from the youthful body which renewed his own youth. In another case an old man consulted me who, at the age of seventy-two, had just been infected with gonorrhea. Krafft-Ebing has classed this libido sexualis senilis, or postclimacterica, with the sexual desires which appear before puberty, and terms them both *sexual paradoxes.* I consider this common classification a very unhappy one. The prepubic sexual desire falls into the class of *precocity,* whereas the *postclimacteric,* to my way of thinking, can be called pathological only if it is unusually strong.

There is no question of the fact that with the female sex the inner secretions in no way correspond to the outer. The examples of George Eliot, who at the age of sixty married a man thirty years younger than herself, and of Ninon, with whom three generations fell in love, she responding to their love, are not isolated cases. At the age of thirty-four Ninon seduced, so it is authentically reported, M. de Sévigné; at fifty, his son; and at seventy-six, his grandson. This last affair she had shortly after the great tragedy of her life, which came about when a young nobleman became enamored of the great courtesan. Unfortunately, as had happened in the case of Oedipus, it had been concealed from him that she was his mother. When Ninon, frightened by his passion, revealed to him the mystery of his birth, he stabbed himself before her eyes.

With men also there has been an attempt to establish a time of relaxation corresponding to the woman's change of life, after the fifth decade, with an accompanying cessation of the necessity for sex. Organically there is usually at this time a characteristic enlargement of the prostate, which seems to be caused by a stoppage of the secretion, or to be bound up with it. Should this be correct, then the decreased secretion of the prostate juices could explain the decreased excitability of the sexual centers. We assume that in the secretion of the prostate, of which Fuerbringer has already shown that "in a specific manner it can release the dormant life in the numb spermatozoa," there is contained a synergetic component for the substance called *andrase,* which is of decisive significance of the vivification at the time of maturity of the developing sexual characters.

The involution of the prostate, which is by no means always hyper- but also not rarely hypotrophic, in many cases does not appear, and even where it does, we see that *libido as well as potency* often remain relatively uninfluenced by it. The duration of these two characteristics, the desire and the ability, are subject to just as great variations in the male sex as in the female. Loewenfeld thinks, on the basis of his experiences, that in the male potency is usually extinguished between the ages of sixty and seventy, mostly after sixty, but that cases are not rare "in which sexual desires and potency are manifest even in the seventieth year." I have already mentioned that I have met a number of persons between seventy and eighty who say "that a beautiful woman has today the same effect as she always did." Here also, as among the women, there are not lacking historical examples of famous men. Thus Goethe is to be remembered who was violently in love when past eighty. Rubens was far past his fifties when, in 1630, he married Helene Fourment who bore him five children in the ten years before his death. Not long ago there was reported from Heidelberg a famous professor of law,

151

who, in his eighty-fourth year, had married a famous beauty.

The *Zeitschrift fuer Sexualwissenschaft* reports another case:

A man, eighty years old, brought suit against his forty-four-year-old wife for divorce on grounds of obstinate refusal of her marital duties. The wife explained in a convincing manner that her husband, who gives the impression of being sixty, was sexually potent and desirous to such an extent that he demanded cohabitation of his wife *daily,* and despite his advanced age was actually able to go through with coitus in a thoroughly normal manner. The wife refused her marital duty because the man was unpleasant and unlovable, but especially because she was afraid of becoming pregnant, because he refused to use any precautionary measures. The woman also asserted that the man was accustomed to satisfy his sexual urge in no other than the normal way, without perverse actions of any sort whatsoever.

From what we know of the peculiarities of fetishistic inclinations, it is possible that such people could be desired just for their age alone. Thus some years ago there was living in Munich a young woman who had the nickname "the corpse's sweetheart" because she was only seen with very old men, most of whom had already passed seventy. "Others," she said, "are out of the question."

In general, the *sexual impressionability lasts longer than the possibility of sexual expression*. The age at which the germ cells and sexual centers start and end their function, both through the same chemical stimulation, which also awakens and enfeebles the other sex-

152

ual characteristics which until maturity are present only in the preliminary forms, differs with humans to a not inconsiderable extent according to climate, race, family, surroundings and mode of living. On the average in our latitudes the awakening of the sexual urges for both sexes occurs a little before the middle of the second decade of life. This point of time, next to that of conception, is the most important in an individual's life, more significant perhaps even than birth which, regarded from a purely biological viewpoint, is scarcely anything other than a change of environment.

In a consideration of the strength of the urge, *sexual rhythm* is of an importance not to be underestimated. We observe in men and women periodically a regular rise and fall of the urge in an alternation comparable in this function to the rest and activity of the other bodily functions. A healthy organism cannot remain in a state of complete rest for a long time without an irresistible urge for activity. Thus, our heart works half of our life and rests the other half; our brain and nerves sleep a third of our lives and are active two-thirds; hunger and satisfaction of hunger, need for air and pauses in breathing—all succeed one another; in short, as a rhythmic change rules everything in man and in nature, so also the otherwise uninfluenced sexual urge is subject to a rhythmic increase and decrease, particularly from the ebb and flood of the sexual hormones. The occasional influences on the strength of the urge are, aside from sexual relief, dependent upon the strength of the attempt; whoever wishes to renounce all sexual excitations and attractions must withdraw into solitude, and even here he runs the danger during the periodic swellings of his desire, of being "tempted" by sexual imaginings.

153

Other influences upon the strength of the urge are, like foods, pleasures, and medicine, only passing and effective indirectly; either they lead like alcohol to a lessening of resistance, or as different drugs (caffein) to an increase of the general nervous sensitivity, or like asparagin they arouse the nervi erigentes by a diuretic action. In general one can say: the stronger the effect of the chemical inner stimulus upon the sexual centers, the less of an external nerve stimulus is needed for its excitement; and vice versa, the less the erotic effect of the chemism, the more intensive must be the external stimulus. From this point of view one cannot deny a theoretical justification to the organic therapy which is now being experimented with so much; to a certain extent it constitutes a sort of modern homopathy by the introduction into the blood stream of the same products as the body would throw off, for the attainment of those characteristics in the blood which are lacking in the particular person under treatment. Whether the actual result really corresponds to the theoretic consideration in the way planned, and whether, even when the desired result follows, it may not even there be explained through suggestion, is undecided. It is to be assumed that symptoms of a deficiency could be eliminated with greater probability if the transplantation of living organic tissues of the same species could be applied in such cases.

If we use what has been said above concerning the curve of sexual fluctuation as our basic average measure, then we can regard as excess or as hypereroticism every degree of libido in which the desire for sexual activity awakens immediately or very shortly after there has been a satisfaction—in the sense, more or less, of the line

154

from "Faust": "And in pleasure, I languished for desire."

In the literature on this subject there are expressions for this heightened sexual desire, which, from an exact scientific viewpoint, seem rather extravagant. Among these I consider the expression erotomania, which has been in no way uniformly defined by the different authors. Thus Féré sees in it a sort of andromania, or nymphomania, a chase after a husband or for the possession of a person of the other sex, when, according to his opinion, there is often a sort of hysteria causing severe psychic sufferings with feelings of anxiety, which can rise to a psychosis and lead to suicide. Esquirolin, 1838, described erotomania as a love-frenzy which can be directed as well to living beings and inanimate objects, in which the erotomaniac degenerates into a "plaything of his imaginings." Garnier again calls the erotomaniac, "un psychique, qui plane dans les régions idéales de l'amour mystique." German authors now conceive of erotomania as a general search for sexual activity, and now more as an *extravagant fixation* upon one particular person. With men such erotomanic condition, particularly when it is not limited to the passion but is transformed into excesses in action, is called *satyriasis*, with women it is called *nymphomania*. The satyr, half beast and half man, was represented in the old mythology as a very ruttish creature who was constantly pursuing and seducing the nymphs and dryads.

Nymphomania derives its name less directly than indirectly from these antique nymphs; the small lips of the feminine vulva are also called nymphs, and with the woman a highly increased libido is often accompanied by local symptoms at the genitals. Priapism and vaginismus are not to be confused with satyriasis and nym-

155

phomania. Priapism, with which we will deal later, signifies frequently appearing and long lasting erections which often have nothing to do with sexual desires, while vaginismus, with which we will deal in the discussion of sexual neurosis, is a reflex contraction of the vaginal musculature. So, as these last named terms represent still undefined conceptions, it would be best on the grounds of scientific clarity to drop the expressions satyriasis, nymphomania, and erotomania, and introduce for all these conceptions the expression *hypereroticism* which falls into a number of minor classifications.

We start with a division of *hypereroticism* into its *polygamous* and *monogamous forms, polyeroticism,* and *superfixation.*

POLYEROTICISM

The polygamous hypererotic lives almost exclusively in the sexual sphere. One can say that his organism and particularly his psyche are just appendages to the genital central point; he is, so to speak, not a man with a sexual organ, but a sexual organ with a man. And corresponding to this, he is unceasingly on the hunt after the objects of his boundless libido. He never stops until he had made his own the person who had attracted him. He usually has sexual intercourse daily for decades, often even several times a day.

A short time ago a married couple consulted me. The woman bitterly complained that her husband, an officer in the cavalry, had for years "used" her daily and as often as eight times in a day. If she should refuse, he would go out into the streets in a high rage, and, having found some prostitute, would go through coitus with her in the wife's presence.

156

Such men, besides cohabitation or instead of it, usually undertake still other acts. The first of these is active and passive oral genital action, lambitus, to which such people are often almost forced.

One patient writes:

"I have a peculiar urge toward lambitus, which I must fight with all my strength not to undertake with my wife."

In the range of sexual polypragmasy there are all sorts of other degenerate species down to, what is almost inconceivable to the normal human, the person who swallows down all sorts of excretions. Thus a short time ago I had to be the expert for a noted psychopathic case whose dandified, thoroughly fastidious appearance was in strange contrast to his passion, reported by two witnesses, of eating feces.

It should be remarked that the organic condition of these persons' health suffers relatively little, aside from the high pitch of sexual neurosis and sexual infections which in the long run can scarcely be avoided.

Although the still widespread opinion that severe illnesses of the nervous system, especially spinal consumption and softening of the brain, can appear as the results of sexual excesses, may not be in accordance with the facts; yet I cannot rid myself of the impression that metaluetic illnesses are more common with persons who, their nerves having become less capable of resistance through syphilis, have too often incurred the risk of sexual ecstasies. The professional efficiency of the hypererotic is almost always considerably diminished, despite the fact that there are often among them very talented, particularly artistically talented, people. Many of them

157

incline as well to other extravagances than sexual ones, such as gambling and all sorts of drinking.

With polyeroticists there often arise serious social conflicts, as for example several women believe at the same time that they are loved by the man or have claims on him, through which there often arises between the parties concerned very bitter dramas of jealousy. This becomes even more serious when hypererotic men marry.

Thus a woman once consulted me in the following case:

Her husband, the son of a very rich manufacturer, had married her for love when she was a poor factory girl, against the strong opposition of his parents, when she was eighteen years old. In four years she bore him four sons. Then he was taken ill with some abdominal complaint which resulted in a strong sexual cooling on the side of the man. She suffered very much from her husband's neglect, until one day it was revealed that, in the time when he was not living with his wife, he had had an affair with a second woman who already had three children by him. He had promised to marry this woman. His wife brought suit for divorce, in the course of which it came to light that these two women were both sharing the same fate because the man's strongest affections at the moment were directed to a third woman who already had two children by him. The father cared for all the children with the same devotedness.

The reason which brought this woman to me was not the marital disunion, but the fate and future of her children. They were between the ages of fourteen to eighteen years, and were already leading active sexual lives. The two oldest and the youngest had their regular girl friends; and the youngest at the time was infected

158

with gonorrhea. The next to the youngest, a very effeminate youth, had homosexual relations with a friend of
the same age and disposition.

With the feminine sex there is frequently an analogous condition of aroused sexual excitability. If the girls
are of a poor or not very well-to-do family then it almost
always leads to prostitution, which is also true even of
girls of better standing if an unbridled libido drives
them polygamously to try as many men as they can.
More than one woman of good social standing consults
me in the course of a year whose daughter for this reason
has fallen to prostitution. Thus a short time ago there
was a very highly intelligent woman who had given herself the greatest trouble to take her child out of a brothel
in Hamburg, the girl claiming that only in that erotic
atmosphere could she feel at all comfortable. Other nym-
phomaniac women walk on the streets and give themselves with neither choice nor resistance to any man
who accosts them. A short time ago a business man consulted me about his sister-in-law, a handsome Jewish
girl, who had several times been taken advantage of by
soldiers home on leave. "To a soldier with spurred boots
I can make no resistance," she said. Further examination revealed that the patient was quite weak-minded;
she had no idea of what countries Germany was fighting
with and against in the war, and was completely careless about her dress and hair. With many men and
women of the polygamous group of the hypererotics
one finds imbecilic traits, whereas those with the monogamous fixation are very seldom weak-minded, but are
often hysterical, strongly neuropathic or maniacal.

Although *true* exhibitionism, of which we will deal
in a later section of this volume, is very seldom found

159

with women, yet with such as suffer from this hyper-erotic condition, one often finds the urge to attract men through immodest gestures, such as exposure of the sexual parts, revealing the breasts, the buttocks, movements of the hips, fast rubbing of the tongue over the upper lip. And with that is coupled obscene talk.

Krafft-Ebing's observation:

That sexual miseries with women often arise from nothing but sheer lack of restraint is taught by the historical examples of antiquity, as that of Messalina who was called "Invicta" when she "arose from the embraces of fourteen young athletes," or Cleopatra, of whom Marc Antony writes to his physician Soranus that she had intercourse in a house of prostitution with one hundred and six men.

Similarly, there came to me in 1917 the fame of a woman of Lodz in Poland, who in one single day completed sexual intercourse with "two companies at full war strength." The Roman ladies followed the examples of Cleopatra, Agrippina, Livia, and Pappaea when at the feasts of Bona Dea, of Priapus and of Saturn, they could not have enough of sexual excesses. Also belonging in this group and, at the same time, significant of the change of attitude and customs in this field, is the report of Herodotus that the pyramid of Cheops was built with the gold "which the daughter of this king had received from her lovers in return for countless times giving her body."

In rare cases, with women, an unsatisfied hypereroticism can rise to a *coitus hallucination*. There are almost always highly hysterical women who in their violent ecstasies actually believe that they are copulating and

160

their uterus throbs and convulses, and they actually excrete mucous with orgastic sensations. Such paroxysms occur during sleep or intoxication, in hypnotic and narcotic conditions. They not rarely have as their object immoral contacts or even rape, toward physicians, so that experienced practitioners have made it a point never to hypnotize or give narcotics to hysterical women except in the presence of witnesses. Often even perverse actions are claimed. Actually with most hypererotics the peculiarities which the ancients described, often pictorially, as the "figurae veneris," play a large rôle.

I wish to give a brief extract from a divorce proceeding: in this case a woman from the court circles in Berlin, shortly before the war, gave this description of the sexual demands her husband made of her:

"Up to now my feeling of shame has not allowed me to speak of the perverse sexual inclinations of my husband, which are the *main reasons for my wanting a divorce*. Continuance of the marriage is impossible for me as a healthy woman, because I feel an insuperable aversion and disgust at the abnormal wishes of my husband, a feeling of opposition which in the course of years has risen to a point no longer to be borne. During the early part of our marriage even, my husband would make me, while bathing, soap his member well, in order that he might be able to have intercourse with me the more easily.

"He expressed great displeasure because I did not wish to bring a mirror to the bedroom which would make it possible *for him to watch while he was having intercourse with me*. Then he arranged a small hand-mirror, which was the only one handy, in such a way on the bed that he could see both our bodies in it. He was surprised

161

that I could get no pleasure from that. He would often ask me whether I would not bring some friend of mine, *because intercourse with three was so much better,* because then the other woman could take part by licking at my sexual parts. Perhaps his greatest pleasure was when he commanded me to repeat the names of different men at the very moment when his intercourse with me had reached the high point. If I did not do as he wished, his motions became so violent that he caused me severe pains.

"He also often demanded that I kiss his member, and would stand up before me completely undressed, in a state of the highest excitement, and ask me to admire his member. He would also often prolong intercourse while he kissed my sexual parts and wanted me to take his member into my mouth at the same time. Even in daily life his conversation was full of obscenities. He would demand of me indecent descriptions, because these would excite him. He would often go purposely to the picture stores where there were pictures of naked women, to look at them and become excited. It can be well understood that I often thought of ways and means to avoid this intercourse with him. Thus I used my periods as an excuse and remained longer than necessary at my toilet only in order to put off this constant demand and pain which was an absolute martyrdom for me.

"It became gradually clear to me that the strange demands of my husband, regardless of whether they were morbid demands, as I thought them to be, or not, were a humiliation and a mortification to me, which with my family background and my position I had to consider as disgraceful. Now my disgust at these proceedings which I have described is so great that return to my husband is for me a physical and psychic impossibility.

162

I do not consider it possible for my husband to change, as I had hoped for a long time that he might, and furthermore consider that his first wife was unable to continue married life with him for the same reason as I."

Since 1900, in an incomprehensive misconstruction of marriage as a community of love, the conception was raised that "insuperable disinclination could suffice as grounds for divorce under certain suppositions," the divorce acts have disclosed to us, in the most cynical manner, details of married life about which people would formerly have kept silent; whereas now both parties vie with each other in raking up these mysteries of the bed— firstly, in order really to provoke a disagreement; and secondly, in order to transfer to the other the greater burden of the blame. As in the case mentioned above the woman complained of the man, so in the following, the man accuses the woman.

From the eighth of May to the thirteenth, Mr. M. F. came to me daily to ask me expert's testimony, and provided the material therefor.

After a six-weeks' marriage he was living apart from his wife, and was considering both divorce and contestation of the marriage. The reason for the divorce lay almost exclusively in the fact that his wife demanded of him an exaggeratedly perverse sort of sexual intercourse. She was not open to reasonable ideas, but flew into a fury at her husband's refusal to go through with the unrestrained ideas she demanded. She forced him to obey, through threats and force, so far that his health had finally become endangered through his wife's extravagant sexual demands.

The particulars follow:

In regard to sexual matters F. is a thoroughly normally constructed and feeling man, of normal sexual urge. However, he has decent feelings and a natural sense of shame, and he feels that the sexual demands which his wife has forced upon him are unworthy and painful to him since he is already forty-eight years old, the father of two grown children by his first marriage. Through this sexual behavior of his wife, which is so contrary to every reasonable idea, he has been robbed of his feeling of care and joy for his children and has become filled with indifference and even aversion. Only through a great power of control was he capable of giving the details of the sexual demands his wife made upon him. His wife (a woman of forty-three) had the characteristics of extraordinary sexual excitability and sexual desires, without however, as her husband said, being able to "get it over with" in the normal way, even after hours of sexual activity; that is, to attain to that physiological relaxation of the glandular and blood vessels of the sexual organs which is at once the goal and the result of sexual activity.

When the husband, after working hard all day, wished to rest, the wife would try in every possible way to arouse his sexual feelings, in which she did not hold back from anything, even from stimulation of his genital parts. She would force him to intercourse for hours at a time, and when, through constant loss of semen, this had become impossible for the husband, she would force him to continued activity hours longer with his fingers around her genitals, *until his arm was lame.* And then she would try afresh, even through the most shameful means, to re-arouse him sexually. She had not the slightest regard for his tiredness and natural need for rest; the man actually, during the six weeks of their married

164

life, would get at the most one hour of sleep—so that in the morning he would go to a hard day's work tired and weak from severe loss of semen, while his wife would then sleep until midday. Whenever the man refused her sexual demands, she would roll over on him, not let him sleep, and try against his will to arouse his sexual desires. She was absolutely not affected by reasoning and reproaching in the daytime. She claimed that it was her marital right to have satisfaction in the way she wished, and threatened to commit suicide. An attempt of the husband to take another bedroom for himself to get a bit of sleep and rest had resulted in her defeating him by stealing the key. So there was nothing left him but recourse to complete separation.

This man actually presents a condition of not inconsiderable nervousness, which may have been caused by his marital conflicts: an indication of how far these conflicts must have affected him. If what Mr. F. says is true, and there is no reason for doubting it, then the expert opinion must be that from a medical consideration, the continuance of the marriage cannot be without still further harm to the husband. I do not wish to give an opinion on what is not a purely medical problem, but from the great number of cases which I have had in my practice in which the woman has wished divorce or annulment on account of perverse actions or demands on the part of the man, I can assume that in such cases the marriage was held by the court as untenable, although these cases lacked a decisive incident, which the case just described furnishes in the highest degree, namely the possibility of fundamental endangering and injuring the husband through the unusual *hypereroticism* of the woman.

165

According to my opinion there is not the slightest doubt that this possibility is presented and would certainly be realized by longer continuance of the marriage. A permanent disturbance to rest and the nightly loss of semen several times, must without doubt be of fatal consequence for the nervous system and the general physical constitution of a man of his age. Even after a few months these consequences would appear in symptoms of general fatigue and a high degree of nervous oversensitivity coupled with an inability to work.

From a medical point of view I have arrived at the conviction that, assuming the truth of Mr. F.'s statements, continuance of the marriage, on account of the uncontrollable hypereroticism of the wife and the forms of its manifestations, would evoke an inevitable severe injury to the health and working ability of the husband.

In connection herewith, several things may be said concerning certain sexual forms of relief which, insofar as they fall into the realm of hypereroticism since they are excesses, vary from the normal forms of cohabitation. As it usually happens, they are interpreted as "perversities" or as "refinements," which is not in accord with their real nature which much more often is caused by some psychological compulsion. For the practicing sexual pathologist these peculiarities have their significance, because the question is often raised by married women as to what attitude they should take toward such demands on the part of their husbands. In divorce cases the desire of the husband to have coitus in other than the usual forms is often given as a very troubling fact.

When we except the commonly accepted divergences from cohabitation, as the side position, there still remain three sorts of varying from the normal which de-

166

mand our attention: coitus a posteriori, succubation, and coitus in statione. Coitus interruptus and prolongatus is not mentioned here, which indeed also differ from normal intercourse, not in the position, but only through the artificial interruption of the natural progression. It is even still a moot question whether or not this is a natural form. Man is the only creature known who accomplishes cohabitation belly to belly, in a position which for many, as fat and awkward people, makes the technique rather difficult, so that many cannot accomplish it.

With people whose urge varies from the norm anyway, and who therefore regard coitus with aversion and anxiety, the situation is in no way made more easy by this. In contrast to man almost all animals have intercourse in such a manner that the male party mounts the female from behind and as soon as he has gained this position he introduces his member into the vagina, which in this position is comfortably in a direct line, visible, and usually standing partly open. It is now maintained, and it seems to me not without justice, that this form "ritus bestiarum" is the one which most nearly corresponds to the genital and general bodily construction of both sexes.

Many years ago I came across a very learned work by a physician called Klotz, which dealt exclusively with this subject and brought forward many proofs that humans do not have intercourse in the proper manner; even the length of the woman's hair, by which the men should hold her, was called up as a proof. Though here also is some exaggeration, yet certainly the judgments springing from moral theology by which this act is interdicted, are unjust. I have repeatedly advised married couples who came to me in doubt because they could not succeed in coitus, to attempt the defloration and first cohabitation in this position, and achieved results with this advice.

In the conflict between false shame and marital happiness, the choice should not be difficult. Without doubt there are also men, such as the buttocks fetishists, who give the preference to this form, indeed even such as are obsessed with the idea of using a woman in this manner. In such a case there often seems to be a sadistic basis to the matter.

In one divorce case to which I was taken, the wife testified that from the beginning of their marriage her husband wanted to have intercourse with her only from behind, and she further deposed that he had even tried repeatedly to force into her anus, which he had at times succeeded in doing. The man contested this in the most positive manner. The vagina alone had been the goal of his wishes which, to be sure, he had sought to reach a posteriori, because he knew from experience how much "more comfortable and pleasant" this was. Finally he proved that his wife had tactile delusions in the network of neurons of the whole vaginal, perineal, and anal region.

Still more common than the above mentioned is the desire which arises through a psychological and purely voluntary urge: *incubation* in the woman, and *succubation* in the man. I have pointed out in the section on metastrophism that the more or less strong urge to have intercourse in this manner proceeds from an intersexual constitution, in the man from feminine components, in the woman from masculine components.

There are three minor divisions into which this act can be divided and this seems to be the extreme state of aggression-inversion: either both parties lie, the woman above and the man below; or both sit, the woman on

168

the lap of the man membrum situs in vagina sua habens, which usually takes place, for example, on benches in the parks in order to have the sexual enjoyment with the least possibility of being *observed* and without an express desire of succubation on the part of the man; while the third is that in which the man lies and the woman sits upon him, rides him so to say. This really belongs between the two other minor divisions, because the degree of aggression-inversion is not quite so strong as in the first of these, but yet is considerably greater than in the second of them.

A still greater variation of normal cohabitation, on the order of this last, is *coitus in statione*. Of this one can say that generally it is done "more obeying compulsion than of one's own free will," even though there are isolated individuals who have an express liking for it; as, occasionally, people are to be found who have a strong prepossession to have intercourse not in closed rooms but "in God's open air," especially in the fields and woods. Coitus while standing is very widespread among the lower prostitutes because it entails the least expense of place and time; a prop against which to lean one's back, such as a wall or a tree, is easily found without a great deal of time being spent. Also, in the open where she can shout for help, the prostitute is less endangered than she would be in some building. The execution of intercourse with little or no possibility of lying to rest inflicts greater strains upon the nervous systems of both sexes than cohabitation carried through in a prone position.

Although the variations of cohabitation which have been mentioned up to now are of no consequence from a *eugenic* standpoint, because the male sperm are dispatched to the place where they will be able to fulfill

169

their function of fertilizing the egg, this assumption does not hold good in the case of the following form of intercourse. Here other erogenous zones and organs take the place of the genitals, not only as preliminary but as fully satisfying equivalents for one or the other party. For men such sexual equivalent organs are usually the finger and the tongue, for the women, next to the hollow of the hand there is the oral cavity, as well as the cavum rectale, intermammale, and axillare. These points are predestined for this use or misuse not only because of their similarity to the penis and the vagina, but especially through their wealth of supersensitive nerve bodies.

Many people have an *instinctive* desire to bring these erogenous points into contact with each other, be they identical, as mouth to mouth, lips to lips, tongue to tongue, hand in hand, or, be they not corresponding points, in which case the main contact tendency is that of the tasse-bodies with the genitals. As long as these superficial aims are merely preliminary to or urging to coitus, they can be regarded as purely physiological steps, but not so when this act is used as a complete substitute leading to ejaculation.

In such cases they are usually psychically conditioned indications of incomplete psychic sexual sensitivity. At all events we are not justified in saying that these acts, called the figurae veneris by the ancients, and treated of with great detail and earnestness by several Indian and Grecian authors, are purely voluntarily assumed by every one; or even that they are to be looked at as obscenities, but rather we must go back to the curious psychological conditions of which they are the motory symptoms, of which the voluntary suppression is not always possible. On the other hand there is also their

170

voluntary adoption, against instinct, as for example in intercourse with the so-called demivirgins who wish to reserve their maidenhead for the proper deflorator on the bridal night, which is not rare.

As concerns *digitation* this is considered as a wholly satisfying act in the majority of cases only with such adults as bear the stamp of a greater or less *infantilism*.

I have often had the opportunity to see married couples who said that in a marriage of many years they have never completed the act of coitus, but have satisfied themselves purely through the man playing with the genitals of the woman with his fingers, also introducing his finger into her vagina, and the woman being excited in this way until she masturbated with him. Neither were able to give an actual reason for this sort of satisfaction. It did not seem to be fear of pregnancy, but the man was rather weakminded and the woman very childish. In another case there was a man who would use a similar form of activity only with prostitutes, a sort of primary effect on the end bones of the index fingers.

There is also at times a strong urge, actively as well as passively, both in homosexual and heterosexual intercourse, to bring the finger into contact with the anal region. Even the deep boring of one or two fingers through the sphincter ani is not rare. It happens that there is here a difference established between the finger and the penis. Thus the question was raised in a trial at which I was an expert witness. The defendant stated that he had bored two fingers into the anus of the other, while the plaintiff claimed that he had been pederastricized cum membro while sleeping. This point was of decisive importance since the use of the penis is punishable, and the use of the hand is not.

Of greater significance is the *oral* form of activity.

171

Here the first to be mentioned is *cunnilinctus,* the rhythmic stroking of the clitoris and other sensual regions of the vulva and vagina by the tongue of a man or also of a virile woman. In addition to fetishistic cases, it seems that here a metastrophic urge to submissiveness plays a rôle, but the ultimate cause of this form of sexual relief is in no way explained. As I have seen from divorce proceedings, many women consider the desire for and exercise of this act as humiliation to their persons, while on the contrary there are many women, particularly among prostitutes, who strongly desire this act after they have once become acquainted with it. It is certain that with many women, after long cunnilinctus repeated several times, a full orgasm is brought about with mucus discharge. I have often been consulted by women who never came to an orgasm by cohabitation, but always quite readily with lambitus.

Just as common as the act undertaken cum ore hominis is that undertaken cum ore feminae, in which the tactile bodies of the lips are used more than those of the tongue. In this form of intercourse, which also appears between men with each other, it is questionable whether the introduction of the penis into the oral cavity is more an active or a passive affair. A short time ago an urning who was brought up before the court, who had intercourse exclusively in this manner, stated that he found in this intercourse an expression of his *femininism;* he would have preferred, he meant, by far to have been able to receive the phallus of the man he loved into a vagina. Only for lack of this would he allow himself to be the object of coitus usque ad ejaculationem in os. Doubtless with coitus oralis both positive and negative causes are involved; among the negative ones there is usually a genital frigidity, among the positive ones the

172

erogenous character of the mucous membrane is involved. Even the reciprocal lambitus, popularly termed by the figure 69, in which the position is taken so that the mouth and genitals of both people come into contact at the same time, is a form of intercourse not only found in the circles of prostitutes. Therefore, one cannot judge with mere moral indignation.

Lambitus of other erogenous regions is not only common occurrence in the sexual life of beasts, even in such places as there are excretions and which, according to general conceptions, are objectively repulsive. Exactly this spontaneous elimination and overcoming of all feelings of aversion show the presence of a feeling independent from the will. Even the anal zone, with the man as well as with the woman, is not only the goal of the tactile but also the taste buds which are so thickly scattered on the apex of the tongue. It may be mentioned that this region of the woman is by no means a noli me tangere for the membrum virile. The idea that pedicatio muliebris is only undertaken from prophylactic reasons, for prevention of pregnancy, does not correspond with the facts, as little as does the idea that it is a question of "calibre." There are far deeper reasons which fall in the realm of hypereroticism and sadism. That passive pederasty should be desired by a man from a woman, I would have considered very unlikely if my idea had not been changed by a case belonging to another doctor in which the patient, a very effeminate transvestist, had an irresistible desire to have his rather virile wife, by means of godmichés around her waist, perform pederasty with him.

SUPERFIXATION

Monogamous hypereroticism has in common with polygamous hypereroticism the sexual overemphasis, but

173

otherwise is quite different from it. *In the polygamous form the heightened libido extends to a type. In the monogamous form, to an individual.* With monogamous hypereroticism it is very much more difficult to draw the boundaries between physiological and pathological cases than it is with the polygamous form. It is of course absurd to regard strong cases of amorousness as morbid, as some foreign writers have done, who have simply termed love an illness, though doubtless there are cases in which the fixation of one person upon another far exceeds all measure and all arguments, so that the extent which was normal must be regarded as no longer maintained.

Let us take examples from life, and first of all one which is reminiscent of the flight of the last crown princess of Saxony, who caused so great a scandal. A woman in my practice, of a lively temperament, married a rather brutal man, addicted to alcohol, whom she scarcely liked but who always desired her strongly. They had four children from the marriage. She became pregnant with the fifth. A tutor was engaged for the eldest son, who was fluent in languages, unusually cultured in appearance and had a quiet, friendly manner. From the first day on the woman was completely under the spell of the tutor, whose presence became a necessity to her, a desire which she could not conquer. The husband, who could not but perceive this passion, wished to send the tutor away. The woman did not hesitate a moment between her husband and her lover. She fled with him, threw over everything in the way of children, her home, and social position, had no fear of convention and scandal, and increased his slender earnings by toilsome work with her own hands. As was probably the case with the above mentioned

174

Louise of Tuscany, there was here an erotic superfixation on a neurotic foundation, strengthened also perhaps by an antifetishistic feeling towards the alcoholism of the husband.

Superfixations of even as great intensity are not less common with the male sex. The following is one of the commonest cases: A young lad, past twenty, well-bred, but of neuropathic constitution, becomes acquainted with a girl who attracts him unusually. She is below him in social position, often older than he, but is not a prostitute. He cannot leave her. His life takes a completely new turn. He has no other thought than this woman, lives completely in her, offers her everything that he has; the protests of friends and pleas of parents have no effect. Though faced with the choice of living free of care in his parents' home or laden with care with the girl, he does not consider a moment but accepts all the other difficulties for his beloved's sake. More than one young man of good family has, through pathological love for a prostitute, turned into a pimp.

Because this fixation is usually not recognized by associates, parents, marital companions, and even physicians, for what it really is, namely, a spontaneous overfilling and overflowing of the brain with erotic stimuli because of exaggerated erotic impressions, it is more often regarded as an estrangement or infidelity which could be controlled, therefore it is imperative that a clear picture be given of the course and nature of a strong passion of love in its arising and development. First of all, every sensuous organ focuses upon the point of departure of the desired impressions. Because the whole bodily surface is physiologically a sense organ, equipped with millions of receiving stations of peculiar

175

sensitivity, there is scarcely a part of our body where this sexual stimulation cannot take place.

In the majority of cases with humans the eyes take the leading place. Now more from the personality as a whole, and now attracted more by some particular part, the organ of sight discovers ever new charms with every position and movement of the object, through the clothes and ornaments which are added, knowingly or unknowingly testing whether they will have as result an increasing or a lessening of the inner sense perception. With no less pleasure than the eye catches sight of the person, the ear hears the voice of the beloved. Its sound can be felt as so sympathetic that the meaning of the words can be wholly neglected over pleasure in the sound of the voice. Other sounds also which proceed from the person, his step, even discords like snoring, can be perceived as harmonies. The sense of smell follows closely behind the senses of sight and hearing. Often hypererotic persons touch with their hands various parts of the body which excrete strongly, breathe in the odor clinging to their hands, virtually intoxicating themselves through the odors which to others are unpleasantly repelling.

Not with the animal world only, but also with a great part of the humans sniffling and smelling, as an "olfactory kiss," plays a great rôle with the "tactile kiss." The sense of touch is erotically stimulated, positively, more strongly than all the other senses. The lover is ever anew seeking to make a contact of the delicate nerve bodies of the papillae of his skin with the bodily surface of the loved person; he pets her cheeks, strokes her hair, presses her hands, tries to bring a contact of the tactile buds, especially of his mouth, with those of hers, and through embracing tries to bring the greatest possible

176

skin area of the beloved person into immediate contact with himself. *From the sensory nerves the sexual excitement transfers reflectingly to the vasomotor nerves.* The effect of love on the blood circulation is so obvious that earlier observers placed the seat of love in the center of the circulatory system, the heart.

When the poet writes: *"flushed* he followed her footprints," or "with beating heart he waited her approach," in scientific idiom this is the change in the circulation and the appearance of congestion on a nervous-vasomotor basis which causes, as also in any general pleasure touching on skin hyperemia, a rush of blood to the corpora cavernosa of the man or woman. The part played by the heart appears also in the severe oppression of the heart and condition of anxiety which become most painfully noticeable in the case of an unrequited love.

Other organs of the body also, though not so apparently, are affected by the nerve influence of love. The exact physiologist is well rewarded for his trouble in examining people who are deeply in love, those who are happily so as well as those who are unhappily so, not with a mere physiological examination, but with the assistance of a physico-chemical analysis, to establish how the nerve alteration influences the digestive system, the respiratory system, the functions of the kidneys, and the composition of the blood. It is not absolutely impossible that more sensitive methods of examination may not at some time make it possible for us to objectively make a diagnosis of strong or weak love. The sensations of pleasure called forth through the sense of touch, which release both the lightest and the strongest of the vasomotor reflexes in the body, form the transition point at which usually the power of self-con-

177

trol and ability to resist the urges which were set under way by the sensuous perceptions, subsides.

With the erotic fixation there are, together with the physical sensations, a whole row of psychic sensations, the most important of which are the following: if the organs of sense for just a short time, a few days or even hours only, miss the impressions which are so pleasant to it and so satisfying, then the lover has set in depressions of the nervous center, similar to what occurs at the deprivation of some narcotic stimulant as morphine. The longing is in actual fact a condition of the nervous system closely related to the longing for morphine. In the one case as with the other the question is one of a deficiency sensation in the inner chemism.

We can hardly go wrong if we think of the working of the andrase and the gynase as quite similar to that of an opiate, one of those narcotics which arise in the organism, a delicately differentiated one which in accordance with its adequate or inadequate dissolution has a quieting effect or provokes discomfort and disquiet. The feeling of displeasure at separation is often the first manifestation of a great and true love; forcible separation can evoke frightful states of unbounded emptiness, nameless misery, and the most despairing desires, which draw the whole psyche into sympathetic accord and often lead even to a complete disgust with life. This strong longing is one real difference between real love and the usual sexual urge, in which case the longing for the person is usually extinguished after the actual sexual act.

With the desire to see, hear, and touch the passionately beloved person is coupled usually the wish to possess these pleasures *alone,* a wish that expresses itself in dissatisfaction and doubt in the strong psychic emotion of jealousy. In extreme cases this passion leads with

178

younger people, but also not seldom with older persons, to mutilation and killing of the beloved and of oneself.

With these two more *negative* feelings there are associated two positive feelings, which yet, as most positive things, are less realized than the negative ones. One is the great interest in the loved person for whose sake one will do anything possible. To true love belongs the willingness to sacrifice one's ambitions. Then also there is the great strengthening and elevation of one's own personality through love, whose mere presence brings the highest side of human feelings to expression. From the delights and happiness of a great love there streams into the nervous system a wealth of power from which springs with increased harmony and love of life a renewed desire to be busy and create. On the other side, however, unhappy love impairs to the highest degree the efficiency and joy of living. Who robs a man of his love, cripples him.

An excess of sexual passion on the aggressive side leads to an *increased activity* on the other side, to so great a degree of passivity, dependence, and submission that a person becomes as a weak tool in the hands of the person whom he loves. Such cases are often spoken of as *sexual bondage.* I cannot here agree that sexual bondage belongs in the field of masochism; rather I have reached the conviction that it is a question really of a quantitative excess, in which the devotion to the loved creature leads to a complete surrender of all one's own nature in the other personality. There has been much talk of suggestive or hypnotic influences with these strong fixations, and in many criminal cases where a person did some criminal act at the request of the other, suggestion has been supposed, whereas in reality there was nothing but sexual bondage.

179

I have repeatedly had to act as an expert in such cases. One of the most interesting was the case of a bank embezzler who, himself a very effeminate type, was quite under the spell of an energetic man whose submissive cat's paw he had become. Even while they were both sitting together on the bench in court one could see how the one hung on the words of the other, powerless and incapable of resistance. I had to appear in a quite similar case between two women, one of whom had stolen food-stuffs at the command of the other. In an extreme manner this bondage also came to light with a young woman who, coming from the best social class, made a show of herself with her young husband, before countless guests, about their most intimate sexual relations. At the trial of the suit which resulted from the public scandal created, when she was asked how it happened that she, a well-bred lady, should expose herself to the ridicule of strangers in this shameless way, she replied, *"Because I love my husband,"* and even when her husband was brought forward as the main witness she persisted in this explanation in order to eliminate all consideration of him. Apparently with both parties there was a *hypererotic complex,* with the man taking the form of an increasing of sexual activity almost to the point of sadism, and with the woman a passivity almost bordering on weakmindedness which practically crippled her sexual volition.

Usually such a receptivity to suggestive influences presupposes a more or less conscious erotic submissiveness, just as in the last of these reports, and the ease with which the person is influenced is much explained, but still the two phenomena of psychic bondage are not to be regarded as identical. It happens especially often that consorts of prostitutes suffer such a great weakening

180

of the will that they are absolutely "wax in their hands." Thus robberies during cohabitation are often executed at the orders of the mistress. Usually we find these sexual slaves among women, in their relationships to men, but there are also plenty of men who jump at the command of the wife whom they both love and fear, and hypersexual men and women also are in a state of slavery among each other. Thus a short time ago two women committed suicide together, the younger of whom, an actress of twenty, was completely under the influence of the older, a very virile homosexual of forty-five. The latter, a daring speculator such as one often finds in this group, had suffered heavy business losses and in addition was threatened with a criminal suit, so that she came to the decision that she would shoot herself. When her friend learned of her decision, she explained that she could not bear being separated from her beloved, and worried her with this so long that she agreed to the common death. This case is not by any means unique, but on the contrary my experience seems to indicate that sexual fixation is the first of the reasons for *suicide pacts*.

The following opinion on a divorce case, which I made with my colleague Kronfeld, will show what complicated and, for the layman, hardly understandable relations often appear. The explanation of the case which we came to resulted in reëstablishment and complete harmonization of the marriage which had been endangered by the intervention of a masculine type of woman.

Mrs. Anna M., thirty-five years old, has been under our medical observation since the tenth of November. She wishes of us an expert report on her psychic condition and her sexual inclinations which she wants to use in discharging the accusations, made by her husband, of a relationship hostile to their marriage. This report is based on the remarks and observations of the examined party as well as on the remarks of the witness in the case, Miss Eleonore A. The mother of Mrs. M. is nervous, suffers from hemicrania and gastrodynia; a sister of the mother has suffered for thirty years of hypochondria. There are no other signs of nerve strain. As a child the examined suffered from alcohol poisoning, was always a very delicate child, and was afflicted from the ages of five to nine with various nervous conditions. Thus she speaks of the so-called hysterical *micropsia and hyperaccusia,* everything within her range of vision was quite diminutive, all noises were penetratingly loud. Furthermore as a child she used to talk in her sleep and walk around with closed eyes; once she was found in this condition outside the house on the beach, another time on a balcony. She was very sensitive, fearful, had nightmares, chewed her fingernails, and especially, which has remained unchanged to the present day, she was *moonstruck.* During the nights of the full moon there appeared a languor, sleeplessness, and a marked decrease in efficiency and power of resistance, which extended to a *complete irresoluteness.*

Otherwise there is nothing sickly to be reported from the early history of the woman. She is a soft, sensitive, *impressionable* woman, *pliable to suggestion,* of an imaginative character, intense and unstable feelings, great weakness of will and lack of balance. She is in every respect a passive person and shows all the signs and weaknesses of such.

These peculiarities of her character make themselves manifest in her love and married life. Sexually aroused when very young, but without any knowledge of sexual

182

matters, the young girl indulged in phantastic imaginings in which she was the *subject or slave of a cruel king*. There is absolutely *no* sign of any homosexual inclination in her urges from the beginning on. She was married in 1909; at the start the marriage was happy, and the woman had two children. About her marriage she says: it was some harsh and brutal characteristic of her husband which, in a way, brought her under his spell. In the course of the marriage, however, she often suffered from her husband's lack of delicacy of feeling; her great longing for tenderness remained quite unsatisfied; and so in this way her husband diverted her sensual desires into a direction which originally was quite foreign to her. The manner in which he did this corresponds exactly to what the witness, Miss Eleonore A., testified later. Despite these slight clouds on the marital horizon, the marriage was a happy one. The woman trusted her husband blindly in all things; she was so much under the spell of the man, in accord with her passive and impressionable nature, that she did and accepted everything her husband said without delay or consideration. At times she gave an account of her inner dependence upon her husband, but with neither the power nor desire to change it. On the contrary, she derived a special pleasure from this submissiveness.

In March, 1916, the husband came to Warsaw; he remained there with an interruption of two days until June, 1917. In the meantime, in April, 1917, the examined became acquainted with Miss A. The latter, through her intellectually and humanly interesting and superior personality, made a great impression upon the rather lonely woman. It probably happened that Miss A. approached her in what was to Mrs. M. an unusually friendly manner, and was accepted. She believed, and probably correctly, that Miss A. had a deep affection for her, without however, considering this in the least as erotic. At the beginning of May she parted from Miss A. as from a new and very precious friend, to return home. On her side there was still not the slightest erotic note in this friendship; and also, except for one kiss, not the slightest thing had happened which was plainly erotic, or which could be understood by her as erotic. This changed when Miss A. as a result of an agreement, came to Berlin in the end of May, 1917, and looked up her new friend. Miss A.'s suppressed tenderness seemed somewhat remarkable to the examined, but still aroused no suspicions.

Then it happened that one evening Miss A. expressed her affection physically in an excessive manner, and it resulted in contact of a sexual sort to which the examined found herself brought by Miss A. The examined naturally did not have the slightest sexual feelings about the matter; on the other hand she enjoyed the tenderness and devotion to which she was not accustomed. She was wholly unconscious of the risk and criminal nature of the situation, and it is still even not quite clear to her that Miss A. had abnormal feelings in a sexual regard, and that it was a question of sexual devotion. In the confusion of the different feelings which were aroused, the weak-willed woman was able to become clear neither about herself nor her friend; she certainly did not come to the point of making any resistance against this friend, whom she felt as so much the stronger and dominating personality. Paradoxical as this may seem, yet it is not on that account less believable, that she endured the embraces of her friend for fear of hurting her by refusal.

Not until after the departure of her friend did it gradually become clear to her that the matter was not

one of mere friendship. She did not become clear about
the sexual side of her relationship, but about the erotic
coloring of Miss A.'s feelings towards her. She herself was so unconcerned in her own feelings about the
matter that she told her husband quite openly about her
experience with Miss A., and learned that the friendship
had become erotic. She had no more personal intercourse
with Miss A. It is significant, furthermore, that this
erotic relationship took place during the time of the full
moon at the end of May, the influence of which on the
nervous system and will power of the examined we have
already mentioned.

In this case the expert has the following questions to
decide:

1. Did the examined enter into this sexual relationship of her own free will or not?
2. Did she do it because of a perverse sexual desire?
3. Was she fully aware of the sexual character of this
affair and the fact of its being contrary to her marriage?

This *first* question we answer in the following way:
without doubt the examined is, on the whole, accountable
for her actions. However she is a psychopathic personality with unstable weakness of will, extraordinary impressionability, and a very emotional nature. Moreover
she is moonstruck. As for actions committed under the
influence of another, especially when these are not
planned and considered but rather an expression of her
emotional life, and when these actions are more endured
than performed, as in the preceding case, then in psychopathic consideration there is obviously a considerable
decrease and narrowing of her own free determination.
Added to this is the influence of the full moon which, in

185

people affected by it, always results in a heightening of
nervous excitability and a limitation of the intellectual
consciousness. Thus we are inclined to the opinion that
in the case in question the examined lacked free determination of the will to a considerable extent.

The *second* question has already been answered
through the description given of the case. On the whole
there is absolutely nothing to be found of a perverse
sexual inclination in the sense of a sexual oversensitive-
ness or homosexual inclination. The examined, on account of her long loneliness and separation from her
husband, as well as the days of the full moon, was in a
very critical period, especially under the influence of her
pliable emotional excitability; moreover she was at the
same time completely under the spell of the dominating
personality of her new friend, as was in accord with her
own quite weak-willed nature. That sexual episode was
the outgrowth of this situation alone.

Similar cases of *bondage* are often described in the
literature on this subject, without, even in the slightest,
any perverse sexual feelings entering the question. Thus
this very same year was described the forensic case of
a young woman who was in absolute bondage to a French
prisoner of war, whom, at his command, she concealed
for eight months in her room, and by whom she allowed
herself to be sexually abused in the most perverse manner; and as regards this perversity it was medically
established before the court that the woman concerned
was sexually frigid and felt nothing. The case in question is, in its psychological structure, completely analogous to the one cited. The psychic bases for the action
of the examined are sickly weakness of will and heightened suggestive impressionability, not perverse desires.

And with that is also answered the *third* question. To
186

our conviction Mrs. M., *even at the very time,* was not yet conscious of the sexual character of the actions under discussion. Her doubts first arose when reviewing them in retrospect. At the time of the action she found herself in a conflict with manifold feelings which had overtaken her just when she was particularly little able to resist. The main feature of this was the warm friendly admiration and devotion for Miss A. It was the actions of this friend which first plunged her into doubt as to the nature of her affection for her, which then led to the conviction that it was an erotic friendship. That the examined at the time of that sexual relationship actually *can* not have known that it had to do with a sexual act is substantiated not only by her description of her own inner experiences, but also by universal medical experience. We not rarely find it with women that they confuse the boundaries of the sexual and the general emotional beyond all recognition. Feelings of friendship and affection lead with them to violent physical amorousness and embraces which often exceed all limits, without these caresses being considered sexual or erotic at all. In ordinary life we find this usually in the so-called "boarding school crushes" of young girls.

Objectively, there is probably an erotic feeling at the basis of these stormy physical expressions, but the person concerned has no knowledge of it; and still less need that person be conscious of it who is merely the passive receiver of these caresses. At times we find the same thing true even of actual sexual actions; thus young girls masturbate for a long time, before they have any idea at all of the nature of sexuality, with all possible imaginings of an unsexual but exciting nature. The examined states that there was a similar condition with her. Thus as regards the third question we come to the conclusion

187

that at the time of this experience the examined *was wholly unconscious of the sexuality of her action or enduring.*

HYPEREROTIC DEVIATIONS

The sexually enslaved person often seeks purposely for a tyrannic person and gradually considers it more and more pleasant if he is under the thumb of the stronger person, humiliated and enslaved by him. Here occur all sorts of remarkable practices of abasement down to imitation of animals and inanimate objects, which I describe in the section on metastrophism, but there is an important difference whether these actions are by a woman towards a man or by a man towards a woman. In the last case there appears an aggression-inversion, because the man, in himself the superior, does not wish to be the active but rather the suffering party, and thus the submissive woman remains in her proper rôle, only that when it is excessively pronounced, it falls into the realm of hypereroticism.

Proof is found in endlessly many psychological and sociological facts that the sentence of Goethe, "Learn betimes to serve woman according to her command," together with the Shakespearean sentence, "She loved me for the dangers I had pass'd," run as leitmotiv through the history of woman's love from the earliest to the most recent times. In this erotic desire for submission is rooted also woman's former deprivation of economic, social, and political rights. Just in the last twenty years has the change been made, and clearly this change will result in the greater sexual freedom of the woman being accompanied by the attainment of equal rights in all fields. Yet the law of nature is still unaltered and valid that the woman, as the passive receiver and carrier of

188

the male seed has inherently a far greater organic dependence upon the other sex than has the man.

If, then, the increase of this basic urge is the form of hypereroticism peculiar to the woman, then as the analogous phenomenon in the man we have the reverse, a surplus of activity mounting to a sadistic brutality. First of all the question is one of quantity, then of the pain. Both can be dealt with in their pathological aspect only through tracing back to a preliminary physiological phase.

In taking possession of a woman, as in the copulation itself, there is a certain amount of violence, which expresses itself in grasping hold of, embracing, and holding fast the beloved body, in penetrating into the openings of the body, especially the vaginal opening which must first be forced through, placing the hands on the skin of the other person which often goes to pinching and scratching, and finally the love bite, which is not only found among wild animals but also among humans; all these and many more are indications of a psychophysiological lust for power which can only too easily assume a terrible, sadistic, tyrannic character. It is not at all necessary, with Lombroso, to draw in *atavistic* actions as an explanation, going back even to the protozoans who gobble up their partners out of love; it is much better to seek the founding of the phenomenon and the cause of sadism with Robert Miller *"in an unusual increase of inner secretion,"* called forth by some powerful impression on the sensorium. On this point Krafft-Ebing speaks correctly of a "waking of psychic dispositions through external provocations which for the normal persons would be meaningless and without effect." As the logical continuation of this train of thought Krafft-Ebing explains positively that the sadistic feeling is always in-

189

born, it could not be acquired during life, but only awakened. Schrenck-Notzing and Binet, on the contrary, assume associations in youth, eliminating the rôle of the sexual constitution.

This however, as we must suppose from the present status of sexual science, is directly dependent upon the activity of the sexual glands, through the inner secretions of which are determined not only the saturation of the central nervous system with eroticizing substances, and thus the *degree of the libido,* but also in accordance with the secretory relationship of the andrase and gynase, the more actively aggressive male or passively receptive female peculiarities of the sexual urge. We must therefore assume for a double reason, *quantitatively* and *qualitatively,* in the so-called sadism, an increased endogenous and even incretory virilism.

Wulffen goes even a good step further. He believes that almost all powerful interferences in the virtues proper to a man, and thus all crimes, are the result of disturbances of the inner secretions. He thus comes to a point of view which certainly has something in its favor, although in its generality it can scarcely be proven, at any rate lacks a convincing proof, namely that all sorts of force, corporal punishment, mortification, maltreatment, horrors in war and peace, even insults, extortions, incendiarism, property damage, cruelty to animals, and even their prosecution and punishment have their roots in the last analysis in sadism.

Comparing the *working of the sexual hormones with that of alcohol,* he says, "If sexual relief, as we have seen in biology, can be evoked by an inner secretion, then this can also work upon the individual latent criminality as an *intoxication.* This involves exactly the same psychophysiological occurrences as with alcohol poison-
190

ing, easier releasing of motion, strengthening of impulsive will, and, on the other hand, repression of psychic accomplishments. Similar intoxications are to be found with tuberculosis of the lungs and also, apparently, with epilepsy. *Human criminality is thus to be interpreted as the result of the sexual intoxication proceeding from the germ gland.* And when the much-abused Lombroso compared crime with epilepsy in its cause and working, aside from a certain extravagance of opinion, he was perhaps much closer to the truth than many of his opponents were able to realize.''

It will seem to us that this extravagance, which Wulffen observes in Lombroso's views on epilepsy, are to be found in his opinion of sadism as a criminal factor. For philosophizing theorists it is certainly of importance whether or not in the last analysis *all* characteristics and aims of all creatures including man have sexual roots, but not so much so for the practitioner who, if he does not wish to be lost in the maze, may not extend the concept of the sexual beyond the erotic consciousness. For a full comprehension of the sexual-pathological, knowledge of the physiological not only phenomenally but also ontogenetically and phylogenetically, is of value.

Thus, in order to understand sadistic hypereroticism, we must remember that in the very nature of the sexual attack there already lies something violent. The conquest of every woman involves a physiological bodily injury, the piercing of the hymen, and every further cohabitation represents a more or less forceful entry into the bodily opening, even the bodily emotions at cohabitation assume to a certain degree the character of a violent attack. To steal and forcibly deflower a wife was a general custom in the old days. The honeymoon may be a survival of this former custom of abduction. Even old

191

phraseology, such as that one could kill a person for love, that he loves her so much that he could eat her, are evidence of cognate primitive instincts.

In the animal world acts of violence are very common in love life. When the cock approaches the hen he often belabors her with violent pecking at her head and comb, and the tomcat in mounting the cat often sinks his teeth deep into her neck; even insects are often inclined to destroy their mates in frenzies of love.

"Like a madman," writes Boelsche, "the frog throws himself upon the female; he claws her so violently on the body that she not seldom dies of it; a carp is mounted so that the scales fly off."

Through all these observations one is led to perceive a sort of atavism in sadism, a reversion to primitive times and conditions. These sexual instincts of cruelty and violence have been overcome most of all through the development of restraining and sublimating mechanisms. The efficacy of these anti-erotic factors depends not so much upon their own strength, but far more upon the degree of erotization itself. Not only does the urge not run counter to an opposition of the will, but rather, and to a greater degree, the will to an opposition of the urge. Thus it happens that many men are conscious of how attractingly their brutality can work on women.

There was a story going the rounds during the war which, if not true, was at least based on good psychology. In many places the women and girls were advised not to allow themselves to be seen during the passing of the enemy troops, because otherwise they might be violated. So all the women had hidden themselves behind the doors and windows, but after the last of the hostile troops had left the town they all rushed forth, quite disillusioned, with the cry, "What about this rape, anyway?"

192

A man who has practiced law for twenty-five years showed me that no cases in the sexual field deserved to be considered with more distrust than the endlessly many brought forward by girls, even though pregnant, who claim to have been raped or forced. Even the objection that they were made unresisting or irresolute through corruption, is always to be accepted with a certain care. Those who know are united in the opinion that defloration or impregnation through the use of sheer physical force is exceedingly difficult, if not absolutely impossible, except in cases where the woman's arms and legs are held by another person or, as is supposed to have happened frequently in the last war, is tied down to a bed. The imagination is usually inclined to paint such cases in awful colors, and relatively trifling attacks are changed gradually into serious encroachments. In the realm of sex, rumors grow through exaggeration to something horrible, and at investigation one is amazed from what little cause the most extensive stories arise.

The claims of young girls that they were surprised in their sleep and raped rarely deserve belief, as also the not at all rare claims of young men that while they were sleeping a coitus in anum was executed against them and they only awoke when the ejaculation in recto resulted. During the campaigns there were many cases of this before the court martials in which the soldiers stuck fast to their story that they were misused in such a way while they were sleeping, by their officers or comrades. In reality an alcoholic excess usually preceded the affair, but in no way caused a loss of consciousness; the execution of anal intercourse always presupposes a certain degree of willingness on the side of the passive party. Psychic means of compulsion are in every case more likely than physical means; the main ones which come into consideration are the bending and elimination of the sexual will through hypnosis, through suggestion, threats, and narcotizing, especially through alcohol and chloroform.

A number of years ago I was consulted in a case in which a doctor had assaulted a patient in hypnosis, an occurrence frequently reported in the literature on this subject. The patient was a married woman who suffered of a very sensitive nervous weakness and hysterical convulsions. As is so often the case with hysterical women, she had an unbounded faith in the doctor, his voice exercised such a soothing effect upon her that it made her sleepy and after the doctor had talked to her for a long while, her eyes fell closed. On account of different neuralgias, cardialgia, and sleeplessness, an hypnotic cure was started by the doctor. The patient was an incomparable medium. When the doctor merely lowered his raised hand, it caused her eyes to close immediately.

In the legal proceeding which was instituted against the doctor at the instigation of the husband, the accused made a full confession. He described as follows the suggestions he gave, which the woman obeyed automatically: he commanded her to lift up her skirt, to lie down, spread her legs, to fetch out his penis, insert it into her vagina, and then to make the motions at coitus until there was an ejaculation on both sides, which resulted with her exactly as in coitus while conscious. The woman was silent.

The impotent husband, who had suspected the doctor for a long time, caused the arrest of the pair. The doctor testified that he had done this to the woman "on therapeutic grounds"; she had lived very unhappily with her husband, her depression had finally become so great that

194

she had been ready to make an end of her life; through sexual intercourse with him she was physically and psychically restored. The doctor was sentenced to one year in the penitentiary under the statute punishing any one who abuses a mentally ill person or one found in an unconscious or other state, into extramarital intercourse.

In such cases of subjugation of the will can we talk of hypereroticism? To this question I would like to answer no. On the whole these cases have to do as much with an unrestrained snatching of the opportunity presented as with an abnormally increased libido. This could be spoken of only if some one habitually indulged his lust through instruments pliable by hypnotic manipulation.

For certain sexual types artificial methods of lulling the person to sleep are unnecessary; it can be done through methodical suggestion, exhaustion of the will through pleading and begging, or all sorts of tricks of surprise, intimidation, deceit, all means which, used with sufficient cleverness, seldom fail in their effect upon the greater part of the female sex. Here we meet with the great lovers of the type of Casanova; the sphere of thoughts and feelings is filled exclusively with sexual conceptions, which they indulge in a manner completely debauched.

Of importance for an understanding of hypereroticism is the fact that many men must overcome some resistance in order to have an erection. The main attraction for them lies in the removal and suppression of resistance, without which, as they are accustomed to say themselves, the sexual act for them is scarcely different from the performance of other intimate needs and emissions. It is the doom of many marriages that women, in quiet humility and resignation, are always at the command of

195

their husbands. They are not exactly desired on account
of this willingness, because the man fancies himself only
in the pose of the sexual victor and hero.

One of the most common methods of overcoming resistance in sexual life is stupefying the will center, for
which purpose alcohol is the most used in Europe, and
in other places, also, the local means of intoxication. The
intoxicant does not increase the sexual desire, but its
real efficacy affects the deliberation, the criticism, which
the narcotic more or less eliminates so that the actual
bar to sexual impulse is removed. In my books, "Alcohol
and Sex-life," and "The Throat of Berlin," I have set
forth this fateful connection in detail. Also *exhaustion*
weakens the capacity for resistance in a similar way,
for example the tired feeling caused by dancing, whereby, however, the lust caused by the contact of the bodies
and the erotic influence of the music also play their own
parts.

From many unmarried pregnant girls and also from
many who have fallen into prostitution, one hears again
and again the same reasons for their fate: their intellect
which was befogged with music and alcohol no longer
had the strength to resist the caresses which became
more and more pressing. In a diagnosis the decision is
often difficult as to whether an excess of libido or too small
a degree of resistance capacity is to be made responsible
for the success of a sexual act.

We have to assume a heightened libido in a sadistic
sense when there is a desire to inflict physical abuse or
pains upon a woman at intercourse. There is a quite
gradual sequence here leading from the biting kiss,
pinching, choking, scratching, violent hugging, to direct
physical injury as sticking with needles and lancets,
cutting with a knife, inflicting burns and other wounds,

196

up to the so-called lust murder and sexual anthropophagy.

In very many cases, probably one can even say in the majority of cases, it goes no further than a sadisme imaginaire. Mere thoughts of cruel acts or the sight of them release sexual feelings which can rise to the point of erection and ejaculation. I have had the opportunity of seeing a number of people who reported that even in school the telling of the story of the Passion of Christ evoked an involuntary excitement of the genitals causing pollution, which they could not explain. Other people have the same effect from reading army reports or descriptions of massacres which so often come with war and revolution. The intoxication from these tales of horror leads only too easily to excesses when, for example, from one policeman being shot in a fight the mind voluntarily exaggerates this statement into sixty who are put up against the wall and horribly slaughtered. There are always people who describe minutely a happening in all details to excited groups, as they would have liked to have seen it themselves. I often ran across such people during the Berlin revolution.

When there was the great Spartacist disturbance in east Berlin some time ago, during which many hundreds of men and women lost their lives in the severe street fighting, a widow came to me whose son, whom I was observing because of an extraordinary criminal act he had committed while in a semiconscious condition, had not returned home from a visit at my house. I accompanied the woman to the morgue where we found her son shot through the head among several hundred partly mutilated and crippled bodies, some even with their throats cut wide open. There was an unbroken line of people, mostly women, passing before the still unidentified bodies. An attendant whom I knew called my attention to girls who for several days had kept coming into the line again and again because they could not tear themselves away from the sight of the men lying there completely naked, mostly sailors, soldiers, and Spartacists; their eyes were fixed on the hemorrhages and on the considerable putrefaction which had set in on the rather enlarged sexual parts of the dead.

There is no doubt for the specialist that sexual motives were in play here to a very high degree. I have seen similar facial expressions with women in Madrid and Sevilla when with a passionate eagerness they followed the dangers to which the bull-fighters exposed themselves. When I was present many years ago at the execution of a murderer, the wife of the public prosecutor was standing near me. She thoroughly followed every detail of the horrible execution. The man screamed and attacked the executioner, who was dragging him onto the scaffold, with his hands and feet. His quick breathing and moaning left an absolutely awesome impression. When the guillotine cut off his head, she acted as a woman in an orgasm.

Whether sadistic or masochistic feelings prevail here, more pleasure in the execution or endurance of the horrible, sympathy with the hanger or the hanged, malicious joy or pity, or both together, cannot be judged without a more thorough analysis of the woman. Sadistic fancies usually have the character of compulsions, which differ from other compulsions in that they are more clearly accompanied by erotic feelings; but on the other hand there is a thing they have in common, that almost without exception they have to do with proceedings of which the patient is quite especially afraid. "Couldn't it happen that our thoughts would be realized some day, and we should do the deeds that would bring ourselves and others into danger?'' is a question often asked by people of sadistic fancies, which, in the great majority of the cases, fortunately may be answered in the negative.

There is a long path from an idea to its execution, which is seldom traversed to the end. Not only because of the effectiveness of a counter-idea, but because, for the hypererotic, there are a great many preliminary and intermediate steps which come into the consideration which already afford a certain satisfaction.

To strengthen the *sexual day dream,* the hypererotic makes special use of three means: *speech, writing,* and *pictures.* The very common desire to talk about love stories or sexual proceedings in a more or less veiled manner, amounts, with many people, to an absolute desire to use indecent words and tell smutty jokes. There are people, though very reserved and sensitive, for whom the pronunciation of low expressions is a prerequisite for sexual excitement. I was once consulted by a woman who, in sexual ecstasies, implored her husband, a very decent and serious scholar, to utter obscene words to her. Often this sexual word intoxication affects the speaker still more strongly than the hearer. I had to give opinions in several cases in which men were accused of insult because they had shouted at women on the streets the prohibited terms for the male and female sexual parts and the sexual act. Careful investigation revealed that here it was usually a case of *exhibitionist equivalents.*

In one of the larger cities of eastern Germany there have been found in the schoolbags of the girl students of a high school, slips of paper on which were written obscene words and sentences. All attempts to discover who was responsible for this gross misdemeanor were in vain. Then one day it developed that the teacher of the class, who had played the biggest part in the investigation, and who seemed the most indignant about the affair, was himself the culprit. Investigation of his psychic condition revealed that he was a heavily burdened neuropathic case who suffered from many compulsions and complexes among which was this one, to shock girls through lasciviousness. Despite the fact that several experts agreed on his sick condition, which, though it did not exclude any free determination on his part, at least curtailed it somewhat, the formerly very esteemed teacher was not only discharged from his position without pension, but was also sentenced to rather a heavy term of imprisonment.

A justice in M. sent me the following relating to a similar case:

"In a criminal case which falls due on the calendar the eighth of February, I would like your advice. The accused, a married man of thirty-five, wrote a letter last fall to a thirteen-year-old girl, in which he asked her to have intercourse with him 'in the French manner.'

"The letter runs as follows:

" 'My darling! You will soon be coming out of school, and already you must have learned something. Have you ever heard of sexual intercourse, especially the French way? This way is entirely without danger for the girl. The man licks the sexual parts of the girl until the highest point, the pleasure, comes. It is a *heavenly* feeling for the girl. If you are willing, come tomorrow afternoon at four o'clock to the extension of —— Street at the corner of —— Alley. If you do not wish to come alone, bring a girl friend with you, but she must keep quiet.'

"The accused had this letter given to the thirteen-year-old girl in school by his own ten-year-old daughter. On this account charges were preferred against him for attempted corruption of a child to lewd practices.

"In answer to my question, he answered that he could give no explanation of how he had come to write the letter.

"In the inquiry proceedings a woman stated that she had often seen the accused unbutton his trousers in the arbor in his garden and handle his sexual parts so that she had to see them. He did this more often when she was looking at the garden from her window.

"The accused explained that he had a very strong sexual urge. When he arrived at a hotel as a traveler, often when the chambermaid entered, he had immediately shown her his sexual parts.

"I would be very grateful to you for a short report of whether to your mind there is any abnormality present which should be so considered as to justify leniency in punishment, and in what books I can find information about it."

In another case on which I had to report, a man of good position gave out slips of paper to decent women on which was written:

"I am at the command of ladies whose husbands are sick or absent, as well as spinster ladies. Satisfaction guaranteed without consequences."

These examples lead us to that graphic form of expression of hyperesthesia which Bloch called eroto-

graphomania, and Merzbach called pornographomania.
Bloch perceived in this inclination only a particular
variation of onanism, whereas the cases of this disturbance which have come to my attention usually make a
hypererotic impression of exhibitionistic coloring. To
understand this anomaly is thus of importance because
ignorant people not seldom see in such documents evidence of the first order; the notes which arise from a
heightened eroticism have usually enough become the
doom of their writers, because their assertions, the content of their letters and diaries where it is a matter of
pure invention, are incredible.

One of the cases of this sort, which I observed, concerned a sculptor of extremely artistic qualities who
committed suicide immediately after he had been convicted on the basis of this sort of self-confession. The
judge was not convinced that his written "Confessions"
really were nothing but sexual phantasies. The letters,
which were brought forward as evidence, were found in
his coat pocket by his landlady who read them and then
handed them over to the police.

The writer described in detail criminal actions which
he claimed to have committed with military cadets; for
example: "Do you remember, my dear Kurt, how you
lay in my bed and I put my arm around your sweet
body?" Then he went on to describe in detail all possible
sorts of sexual acts. The letters never reached the people
to whom they were addressed, and the cadets who were
summoned as witnesses testified that the accused had
only gone as far as light caresses; at the motion of the
prosecutor, however, their testimony was discounted on
the ground of their fear of being accused as accom-
plices.

202

Places where the erotic writing and drawing craze particularly manifests itself, are toilets. It is an ancient custom to give expression in these intimate places to one's most secret political and sexual ideas. There is no land in the world where one does not meet this primitive form of expression which (aside from its artistic value, or usually lack of value) affords a deep insight into the otherwise veiled psychic disturbances, and thus presents a wealth of material for the impartial investigator. What interests us here above all is that there are persons with whom this urge to cover the walls with phallic and other sexual symbols appears with an almost inconquerable force. Many abandon themselves to this desire in quiet closets also.

Some years ago a teacher had a stroke at his desk while he was drawing, in gay colors, pictures of cohabitation, of which thousands were later found in his drawers. The man, who was considered so much the pattern of modesty that no one dared to bring up sexual questions when he was present, had written on a piece of paper which lay on his briefcase, that through his whole life he had given himself over to no other form of sexual activity than self-satisfaction, and in this to a most excessive mannerism; when he had been alone, he had *always* played with his genitals with one hand.

It must still be stated that the presence of a second person is in no way a prerequisite for the operation of erotic states, but that at least as often it has to do with solitary debauchery. I have already pointed out, in the section on ipsation, that there are occasional cases, with both sexes, which far exceed every imaginable possi-

203

bility. One of the most appalling cases of this sort we find mentioned by Hammond.

A shepherd began to masturbate at the age of fifteen, roughly fifteen times a day. It often occurred that, because of excessive stimulation, there was a discharge of blood instead of sperm. Up to the age of twenty-six he masturbated only with his hands. Then he came to introducing twigs of wood into the urethra. He did this very often for sixteen years until the urethra became quite callous and without feeling. The patient had an unconquerable aversion to normal sexual intercourse. He was very despondent, neglected his work, and busied himself almost exclusively with how he could satisfy his sexual urge.

One day he began to make a small incision into the head of his penis with a small knife. This operation caused a joyous excitation with an ejaculation. From that time on he repeatedly made these cuts and with the same results. After the patient had repeated this self-mutilation about one hundred times his penis from head to root was split in two equal parts. The bleeding was checked because he tied his member tightly together with a band. After complete division of his penis he achieved further sexual excitation and ejaculation by rubbing the ducts ejaculatori with twigs.

After making use of this manipulation for about ten years, a twig happened to slip into the bladder. The great pain which this caused brought him to consulting a physician who did a laparotomy and removed the twig which had been in the bladder for three months. The patient died three months later.

There could be no doubt that in this case, as in many

204

other cases of excessive ipsation, the matter was one of serious psychopathic changes and usually with a high degree of debile hysteria.

There are also, however, many hypererotics of both sexes who have less inclination to express the obscene in word, writing, or pictures, who feel it a necessity to have it work upon them, to hear, see, read, or collect it. They pursue these things eagerly and find them; it is a false conclusion, and one which is often drawn, that reading or pictures have in and of itself an effect. All these creations, whether they be actively produced or passively consumed, never have a primary but always a secondary significance. I have known erotobibliophiles who have put their whole wealth into erotic literature, and others who would not hold back even from theft to come into the possession of sexually exciting books and pictures.

The erotic collection urge is inwardly closely related to the erotic urge to exhibit. There is also here, as in the last mentioned and nearly all sexual anomalies, an object of active direction, an *urge to show*. But this must not immediately be classed with exhibitionism which is only one particular and especially compulsory and pathological variation of the urge which is far more common and comprehensive. The urge to see corresponds to the urge to be seen, of which there are countless variants. If people as a whole wish to be seen, the real voyeur puts particular emphasis on the fact he is not to be seen while watching private proceedings; he wishes that the observed should not notice him at all and fears that there may be silent witnesses present when he indulges in these private functions.

Visionism, like every other sexual anomaly, has also

its physiological point of departure. Almost every person is involuntarily and unknowingly a *fetish voyeur,* because, as soon as the opportunity is given him, as for example on the street, he starts hunting for the characteristics and objects which are of the sort to awaken a feeling of pleasure in him; this happens especially when he is alone. This physiological phase of visionism may develop into a pathological phase. This is not to be recognized only through the intensity of the desire but also through the characteristics peculiar to the voyeur and the dominance of the urge. One man among my cases had ten half-matured girls walk up and down before him *with their dresses raised* until he had an ejaculation.

There are two main groups of voyeurs of which one group desires only excitation and satisfaction when they completely occupy themselves with secret things; while the other, particularly the *triolists,* have the desire to exhibit themselves. Here the urge to see and show are bound together. Between these two groups there is a large number of people who neither are unseen watchers nor active participators, but who derive their main pleasure from the sight of obscene and lascivious scenes at which they are present. To these belong the visitors to the *tableaux vivants* and similar presentations which are to be found not only in Naples and Paris, where travelers' reports place them, but in almost all of the larger cities.

Thus in Berlin, before the war, there was the Club Roland, mainly frequented by artistes and pimps, which presented nudities on the stage. Hours before the start of the presentation the habitués were there to be sure of seats in the front rows, to more closely observe, while in the highest degree of sexual tension, the sexual acts,

206

performed partly in natura, partly with artificial genitals.

Another case which belongs to this group, aroused particular attention because it had to do with a young married couple, an officer and his wife, who put on a show in their dwelling before a large group of spectators, men and women, of their acts of love. It seems that at the basis of this was not only a desire for financial, but also sexual recompense, whether it was in the sense of a sadistically colored hypereroticism to make a laughing stock of the sexually enslaved woman, or be it in the unknowing metastrophic feeling of personal humiliation.

The true voyeur likes to bore holes in the walls and doors of toilets, guest rooms, and dressing rooms, through which he can spy secretly on pairs of lovers and watch all their proceedings which are devoted to sexual enjoyment; and also other intimate actions, such as disrobing, urination, and moving the bowels, without the observed having any idea of how their motions and movements are followed. If the person watched should notice anything, the attraction for the watcher would disappear.

There is a very artistic novel by Barbusse in which the voyeur is very graphically described.

Of the many cases in this connection which I have had the opportunity of observing in my practice, a few may be cited: a physician, a very busy specialist in sexual diseases, consulted me because he had noticed an insuperable urge to visit public toilets to look through the peepholes which had almost always been bored already by other voyeurs, and see what was going on in the next toilet; it was particularly exciting to him when the person in the next toilet, not seeing him, should be busy handling his genitals in an onanistic manner, which, according to the agreeing testimony of voyeurs in public toilets, happens very frequently. The most remarkable part of the case is that the man who had the opportunity to see so many members professionally every day, was excited only by the sight of a phallus outside of his professional duties.

In another case a patient threw unused condoms over the partition into the next toilet and waited to see what the finder would do with them; he was excited most when the person would put them on over his own member.

Another case with which I was connected in court ran as follows: in one of the best hotels in Berlin, young married couples received, for quite a period of time, typewritten letters which described, in all details, proceedings of the most intimate nature occasioned by them on several preceding evenings. Several of the persons addressed turned indignantly to the hotel management, who notified the police. Despite their vigilance, it was impossible to locate the culprit, until one evening a guest, unexpectedly leaving his room, found a small man with a black mask and black tights caught between the double doors outside his room. This man was arrested and searched, and in his pocket were found boring instruments which immediately created the suspicion that he was the writer of the mysterious letters. The assumption was corroborated. In the subsequent trial for the offense, the forty-year-old man, who was hereditarily very heavily burdened, testified that he had always derived his satisfaction *only through the sight of sexual acts,* never through his own personal exercise of them.

208

In almost all the large cities there are favorite places for the voyeurs, for example, under the bridges on the canals and rivers or in the parks. Usually, they enter into an agreement with prostitutes that they bring their so-called wooers, soldiers, sailors, workers, and students, and that they will pay the girl if they may be allowed to stand by and watch. It seems that this proposition is far more often accepted than rejected. The sight of the moving buttocks, the member going in and out, overhearing the moaning man and the groaning woman, all this transports many voyeurs into hypererotic ecstasies.

Then there are those voyeurs who sneak up on a pair of lovers to surprise and frighten them. They often use a pocket flashlight for this purpose.

It is obvious that this feeling of pleasure in the pleasure of another, the urge to assist, or, in a stronger form, to be present at the sexual acts, causes such people to bring this about as their object. Thus there arises that desire for erotic arrangements which is commonly called matchmaking. Notwithstanding the fact that this is a particular instance in law (where it is a punishable offense to assist in what is otherwise not a criminal action, and assuming that there is no pecuniary reward for the third person, in the case of sexual intercourse), from the standpoint of sexual science no reason can be assigned that seems to justify considering the assistance of a third party in sexual relations as a crime. In many cases formerly the contrary was claimed. What interests us here above all is the fact that the customary matchmaking enters here as a *compulsory urge of pathological coloring*. Particularly is this the case with women.

Thus a woman wrote who turned to me for advice on marriage:

"I like very much to caress people who are agreeable to me, and can kiss and fondle them without aversion. But as soon as they demand more from me, there arises in me *a feeling of indignation* and *aversion* which is even to me *quite inexplicable,* and I am quite disconcerted that my caresses should be taken as a sign that I was seeking sexual pleasure. Is that hyperesthesia? But then sexual intercourse between two other people would of necessity seem to me unclean and revolting. That is absolutely not the case; on *the contrary I am so happy as a king if I have brought together two people who love one another, or can give them the opportunity of seeing each other undisturbed* (*a friend of mine calls it matchmaking craze*). To a certain extent it is a *psychic pleasure* for me to know: 'You have arranged a few hours of uninterrupted happiness for two people.' Often in my imagination I plan wonderful imaginative apartments for a pair of lovers where they can dream and enjoy themselves. But the idea of thinking of myself in there with a man seems crazy to me. Is it possible that a person can have a glowing soul and an ice-cold body?"

A still more remarkable case of the desire for matchmaking is the following:

Some time ago a lady from one of the large cities on the Rhine consulted me. She had been married for some years. Soon after the marriage her husband approached her with the following proposal to which she acceded after long resistance to his earnest pleas and entreaties. Her husband invited one of his foreign business friends to evening dinner. She had to receive him in a light seductive garment, and her husband made his excuses that he had been called away by a very urgent telegram. After an excellent meal, in which especial emphasis was laid on a good Moselle wine, she played to the guest on the piano, and made "advances" to him. The husband, who had really not gone away but was following the whole scene carefully through a crack in the door from a dark little room adjoining, wrote down a detailed account of all that happened. The main thing was that the stranger did *not have the slightest idea* of all this. Gradually both parties became amorous and it came finally to coitus on the divan which stood before the secret watcher. Then immediately the apparently agitated wife had to ask the guest to leave at once because it had become late and possibly her husband might be coming home. Scarcely was the house door locked after the visitor than the man burst out from his hiding place to have passionate intercourse with his wife. From this marriage there was a fifteen-year-old son. If she agreed to the demands of her husband, so the woman said, then he, a wealthy businessman, was the "best man in the world," if she did not, then her life was "hell on earth."

The wife, who suffered deeply psychically, wished to know, for she had come to me secretly for advice, whether the actions of her husband were based on some illness, and whether it was true that if it came to a divorce, which was scarcely possible for her as a pious Catholic, she could be considered the guilty party as an adulteress. The first of these questions must be answered in the affirmative, and the second in the negative.

All the sexual excesses already mentioned differ from the group to which we will now turn our attention in that whereas in the former the sexual opposition was overcome really psychically, in those still to be cited it

211

occurred through a physical forcing of the will. In this respect we already have shown that in the animal world this sort of proceeding is the rule and is very widespread. There is much that leads one to believe, we have only to remember the original form of stealing one's wife, that in human love life also, as in the beginning, capturing the wife by force was the usual form. Even now the overcoming of a certain amount of resistance, even though it be only simulated on the part of the woman, is to be expected as a natural circumstance. I have seen many men in my practice whose potency became weaker and weaker the less resistance they encountered and who, on this account, almost entirely neglected their wives. But on the contrary the more a woman struggled, the more their aggressiveness and potency increased. With many there appear the frenzies of love which are so similar to outbursts of rage, greed, or indignation as they all have to do with strong motor explosions of an emotional intoxication.

A short time ago I had to give expert testimony in a case in which a soldier had inflicted a severe cut on a woman with his sidearms while in a state of sexual excitement, so that he himself believed that he had killed her; the woman managed to live through it. In this case, which in the beginning was assumed to be a murder preceded by rape, it was as follows: the accused had received a furlough home after being stationed for two years at the front. He had been on the train for two and a half days, had scarcely eaten for twenty-four hours, when he reached Berlin to rest until the next morning and then to continue his journey to his home.

In the neighborhood of the railroad station the man,

212

anxious, not only for food, but also *sexually starved,* happened to go into a lively café in which the waitresses took almost all his ready cash for several bottles of poor wine. The hostess, who pleased him most of all, played with his genitals. But when he, going into another room, wished to sleep with her, she refused, as is usual in this sort of a place. Then, becoming enraged, he hit her over the head with his weapon; apparently his completely exhausted, not to mention alcohol-weakened, mind no longer had the strength to simply suppress the sexual desires awakened after two years of abstinence. Thus he came to this not *merely impulsive, but explosive* deed, which, despite all the arguments brought forward by us experts, resulted for him in a heavy sentence of imprisonment.

This case, as with many others of murder, especially when concerning prostitutes, was treated by the press as one of murder preceded by rape. Even the expert's report was considered by them to indicate this, though most cases of lust murder, after more careful consideration and examination, prove to be based on other than sexual lust motives. Mostly, there is an unintentional killing.

Thus Heider and Ritter, the boy murderers whom I had the opportunity of observing, assured me that when they entered into conversation with their victims they had not planned to kill them. While they were assaulting them, the boys had resisted and screamed. Consequently, in addition to their sexual excitement, were the emotions of anger and fear which became the chief consideration and they had acted almost by reflex action to prevent the danger of discovery and to achieve their

213

sexual urge by an explosion of force. They had, therefore, grasped their victims by the neck so hard that death by suffocation resulted. Even the dismemberment of the body, as was done in this and many similar cases, did not occur as the result of sexual desire, but rather had been for the purpose of assisting in the disposal of the body and hiding all traces of guilt.

These statements, almost exactly the same as those made by the murderer, whom I personally knew, of little Lucie Berlin, sound in no way unbelievable and often may correspond to the facts.

In another case a girl, whose identity was never established as no one reported her missing, was killed in the cabin of a river steamer by sailors who completed the sexual act with her. They tied the body of the dead girl up into a sack and threw it into the Spree. Here also a lust murder was assumed. The hearing, at which I was present as an expert, revealed however that here also was a case of an unforeseen accident; the girl suffered from heart disease, and was apparently so carried away by cohabitation with the one after the other that she had paralysis of the heart when a very brutal and robust sailor, whom she wished to refuse, pressed her mouth shut.

Such cases of *death in the throes of sexual emotion* are by no means rare, especially with the male sex. Dr. Lipa Bey of Cairo has collected together a great number of cases of this sort. One case which attracted a great deal of attention and was typical of its kind, took place several years ago in one of the larger German ports and involved the king of a northern country. As

reported to me by my colleague, who first saw the unknown dead man, the case ran as follows:

The old king left his hotel without escort, ostensibly
for some fresh air before going to sleep. In reality he
went into a brothel to pay homage to the two gods who
have, since ancient times, been coupled together: Venus
and Bacchus. In the midst of her caresses the girl noticed that the quiet old man was absolutely struck dumb.
In order that it might not seem that he had died in the
brothel, they carried the stranger, who had no papers
of identification on him, to the curbstone and leaned
him against a lamp-post. There the police found him
and brought him to the port hospital where he was given
a place in the morgue with the other corpses that had
been found. In the meanwhile the king's entourage was
waiting in vain at the hotel for his return; a search
was instituted and finally the next morning he was discovered among the unknown dead of the street.

In most cases in which death results from cohabitation, the reason is either arterial sclerosis or endocar-
ditis; the violent fluctuations of plethora cause apoplexy,
or a tearing and advancing of the terminal arteries.
Thus death enters, not through an absolute, but through
a relative hypereroticism, because the body, which has
been impaired in its elasticity through calcification, no
longer seems to expand with the general sexual excitement. A thorough knowledge of these cases is necessary
for the expert in order, when there is suspicion of death
through violence, to determine whether the blame should
be laid to some other circumstance.

Next to children and young people, it is usually the
female prostitutes who are murdered during or after

the sexual act, whereas for their part the male prostitutes not rarely kill persons by whom they have been
desired. Here, however, it is usually not murder for the
sake of heightening sexual desire, but *murder for the
purpose of robbery,* which is so greatly favored through
this intimate communion without witnesses!

On this question I have expressed myself in detail
in my book "Homosexuality of the Man and the
Woman" (page 874 ff) in regard to the different motives
which arise in this question. I refer to the exposition
which I gave in a murder trial to which I had been invited by the state prosecutor. I argued:

"Murder in connection with blackmailing seems improbable, because with the killing disappears the consideration which had always before been present, pressing money from the victim. There are, however, a great
number of cases of this sort. In relation to today's proceeding I have studied through the literature available,
and can cite about twenty cases pertinent here.

"In the last year in Berlin alone there were killed by
homosexuals a butter dealer E., a merchant L., one by
the name of B., a military convalescent R., a French
houseman Gaudin; in Paris, in February of this year,
a writer named Paul B. was murdered by two boys with
whom he had had homosexual intercourse.

"The motives which enter in with these and similar
crimes are the following: Either it has to do with a
murder for robbery, the blackmailer killing his victim
because he is not willing to give him any more. For this
reason, for example, the Italian Archangeli, in Triest,
killed the homosexual art historian Joh. Joach. Winckelmann. Another and more rare motive, which is not
pertinent according to the circumstances of the case be-

216

fore us, is the blackmailers' fear lest the victim hand him over to the authorities. Because of the secret character of the proceedings between the extortioner and his victim, there are seldom witnesses present at the murder who are to be feared.

"Therefore, there is greater probability that a murder will be unexpiated than a bodily injury. In reality, the murders of homosexuals *who live alone* are almost never solved. A third motive is *revenge,* in case the victim rejects further attentions. The fourth motive is the execution of a threat, while often outspoken, yet often almost autosuggestive. Thus several years ago, for example, a man, V., in Stockholm, received a bomb from a Berlin blackmailer which had actually been promised him. It is not very probable that a blackmailer should kill his victim through emotion, in a fury of sudden wrath or anger, because it is a mark of this sort of criminal that they proceed, corresponding to their whole manner of work, in a very well-considered fashion. Conversation between a blackmailer and his victim is usually relatively quiet, more like a sort of mutual bargaining. Each one attempts to impose upon the other through his apparent cold-bloodedness and fearlessness. Rather would I hold it as possible that the motive is *negligence* because the one threatened the other with a revolver and said, 'If you forsake me, if you refuse my demands, then I will shoot you!' and the weapon went off.

"For this last possibility, there is the testimony of B. that he had no idea of why he had the Browning pistol in his hand, and testimony of the witness that the accused bowed over the corpse and shouted, weeping, 'Frieda, you are not dead?' The difficult decision of whether, in the case of B., there was a criminal action and by whom it was performed, which I, as an expert, consider as

217

possible in the light of my experience and psychological knowledge of the relationships involved in this question, will have to be pronounced by the court on the basis of the evidence taken.''

There are also crimes which are to be considered partly as lust murders, and partly also as murders for the purpose of robbery. It happens, for example, that some one may kill his victim in a sexual frenzy, and rob him afterwards. Another type of murder, which doubtless also falls in the realm of hypereroticism, although it is not a murder of lust but rather of aversion, is murder through jealousy, revenge, or unrequited love. Here also I have had the opportunity to observe a great number of cases of this sort and to act as expert on them. Wulffen distinguishes as real *lust murders* only those in which the motive for the killing lies in a depraved sexual desire. It would be more exact to say, in which the sexual desire is satisfied or relieved through the bodily injury or killing of a person. Since these actions are usually done in a heat of emotion, they are not premeditated. Its whole psychological nature marks the deed far more as one not planned in advance, but as one committed in a sexual passion if not in a sexual intoxication, so that objectively it must be regarded as manslaughter.

Of great importance in crimes which are to be termed as lust murders is the *manner of the violations;* first of all there is mutilation of the sexual parts, as cutting them out, then slitting open the body, ripping out the intestines, thrusting sticks, umbrellas, and other objects into the vagina and anus, tearing out the hair, hacking off the breasts, pressing back the throat. Wulffen correctly emphasizes the fact that in a great number of cases of

218

lust murder analyzed by him the mere coitus, with its psychological and inherent pleasure and forceful activity, can release in the active party sadistic feelings which may lead to the killing of the victim. Especially does this pertain to degenerate weakminded people of low potency, with whom it can be as well wrath over their own incapability of erection as anger over the refractoriness of the victim, both of which in common make more difficult the execution of the act and gaining of the pleasure, which then arouses the fatal emotional storm.

This, according to Wulffen, was the claim of the lust murderer who was declared insane, the leather worker Paul Dietrich: that whenever he met a female on a lonely path, he was set in a great excitement. His heart began to beat so hard that he was scarcely able to breathe and to think clearly; he had a heavy outbreak of perspiration and a fitful feverishness, and this condition increased until it reached a state of absolute loss of consciousness if at the attainment of his goal, the sexual act, he met with any resistance whatsoever. In such cases he first regained his senses when his victim was lying dead before him.

In *a real lust murder the killing takes the place of coitus*. Thus it happens that *where sexual intercourse does not take place,* the sexual pleasure is more often evoked by chopping and mutilating the body, ripping open the abdomen and burrowing into the intestines, cutting out and carrying away the genitals, wringing the neck and sucking out the blood; these horrible atrocities, which even exceed the frightful outrages which men commit under the influence of war psychosis, form a pathological equivalent of coitus.

The majority of the lust murderers, like the Jack the

Ripper who from 1887 to 1889 mutilated according to reports at least eleven women in the most inhuman manner in a London suburb, have never been caught, despite the number and the foolhardiness of their crimes. This is even more astounding since, from those cases where observation was possible, it has been proved that only very severe psychopathic cases were capable of such crimes. Thus Lombroso gave the following description of Verzeni, who was guilty of four lust murders and who even roasted and ate parts of the flesh of his victims:

"Verzeni was microcephalic, had an asymetrical skull, enormously developed jawbones, squinted, was beardless, lacked one testicle, and the other was atrophied."

Apparently here also there was a severe variation from the normal in the inner secretions.

"Two uncles were cretins, a third microcephalic. The father suffered of hypochondria pellagrosa, and a cousin is an habitual thief. The whole family is horribly greedy, but very bigoted."

Wulffen claims that it is significant that the lust murderer usually leaves the corpse of the murdered person in the same exposed place where the deed was committed. This may, in the majority of cases, be correct; but if the author means by this that this feelingless and careless attitude bespeaks the frightful sadism because apparently the sight of the mutilated corpse may still awaken feelings of pleasure, then this may be hardly correct; rather is it to be assumed that after the criminal has committed his murderous attack in an unthinking state of

220

blood-intoxication, he ran away, without taking time or thought to conceal the nakedness or the wounds. As a better indication of sadism than the desertion of the body, is the chopping up of the body and scattering it in different places, which is very often done by lust murderers; but here also, in the majority of cases, the more probable motive is an attempt to prevent later recognition of the dead person.

Prosecutor Wulffen was correct when he, who is so competent a jurist in this field, said:

"It is clear that lust murderers and killers are more or less psychopathic."

Despite this, many of them have been executed, as Vacher who, between the ages of twenty-five and twenty-eight, committed no less than eleven lust murders.

The medical expert said:

"Vacher's crimes are those of an antisocial, bloodthirsty, and sadistic person who believes that because of his earlier madness and the fact that he was not then punished, he has a permit for the perpetration of his horrible deeds."

This report, as so many others, is based more upon moralistic than upon psychological and psychiatric principles. It was quite similar a case with the lust murderer Menesclou, whom three psychiatrists held was mentally sane. After his execution it was shown that both frontal lobes of his brain, the first and second temporal as well as a part of occipital convulsion, were abnormally changed.

The twenty-two-year-old printer Paul Mirow, an epileptic, who, in 1907, was in the asylum Herzberge on account of epilepsy, confessed that he had seriously wounded three small girls with knife slashes, from which one of them died, prior to his confinement to the asylum.

At first no one believed his confession, but they were finally convinced by the positiveness of his statements when he marshalled together a mass of details known only to the police and to those connected with the children. This case goes to prove, as do many others, that the two main points which are held by the judges as conclusive proof against a claimed mental disorder, *methodicalness* and the *possibility of remembrance,* by no means exclude a pathological condition.

The antagonism which so often arises in such cases between the jurists and the medical men, crops up clearly in the case of the epileptic lust murderer, Tessnow, who despite the exonerating reports of many psychiatrists, was condemned to death, but could not be executed because just as he was led to the block, he had an epileptic fit. I was not personally acquainted with Tessnow, but I have spoken at length with different colleagues who had been drawn into the case and who were thoroughly convinced that the *death penalty* was pronounced in reality *because of the severe illness,* a thing which occurs *all too frequently,* unfortunately, in the juristic history of all countries.

Occasionally here also with weakminded persons *sexual superstition* seems to play a not inconsiderable rôle. Thus, as happened in Dresden, a nineteen-year-old boy was found murdered, whose sexual parts were missing. The culprit was established as a twenty-nine-year-old

222

journeyman potter, who was reported by the experts to be an imbecile. The murderer stated that he was impotent and that he had heard that one could become sexually capable if he ate the testicles of a man, a folk superstition which is not without interest, particularly in regard to the teaching of Brown Sequard which had just arisen and was much spoken of at that time and which was the scientific beginning not only of organic therapy but also of the teachings of the inner secretions.

If we sum up what has to now been discovered and observed of a medical nature about lust murder, then it may well be established that these horrible outgrowths of sexual passion belong among the sexual acts which are rarely, or one can say never, committed by persons mentally sound. *All the lust murderers who have up to now been examined by real authorities were strongly degenerate psychopathic cases, and indeed for the most part epileptics or strongly imbecilic persons.* These wild horrors arise in the sick brains of these people, and the question arises only in individual cases whether or not these hereditarily burdened persons are in a position to exercise *sufficient control over their pathological impulses.* In the overwhelming majority of cases this question would have to be answered in the negative, so that these sexual criminals do not belong in jails and penitentiaries, to say nothing of lethal punishment. They are, indeed, a public menace and should undoubtedly be committed to the asylums for the criminal insane. In the lunatic asylum at Broadmore, not far from Reading, where England's great poet Oscar Wilde walked the treadmill, I saw quite a number of such murderers strolling in a garden enclosed by a high wall.

The *gravity* of the hypererotic disturbance is to a certain degree in no way fully dependent upon the degree of the restraints. There are many psychopathic sadists who, instead of deadly wounds, inflict upon their victims only more or less severe injuries such as burns, scratches, bites, and stabs; or give expression to their horrible desire through chaining the persons, tying them or fettering them, or imposing punishments upon them as humiliating them, enslaving them, scolding them, pushing, hitting, or confining them.

Here again, as generally in sexually pathological cases, the relative stereotyped nature is remarkable. Thus it will scarcely ever occur that a person who stabs with a knife will strike, or a scourger will stab. It seems as though the sadistic impulse arises constantly in the *motor grooves* along which it fits a course for its release and relief. Some authors classify almost all criminal actions as sadistic. In our opinion however only such criminal actions as are connected with sexual desire fall into the realm of sadism, in which connection it must be admitted, though, that there are sadistic inclinations and actions which do not come into the consciousness as erotic. Man is not only a sexual being, but has the still more powerful urge of self-preservation which comes to expression in forcible defensive instincts and usurpations, which likewise can increase to a pathological point. To call every horror sadism, every submission masochism, every inclination eroticism is a generalization which will not help to bring about clearness in the sexual field, but rather obscurity.

Incorrect is also the widespread idea that the real sadists, *aside from* the sexual sphere, are *brutal creatures of force,* "wild beasts with brutalized facial expressions," as the newspaper reporters' imaginations usually describe them; on the contrary, they are often persons who should rather be described as weaklings and

224

mollycoddles; at times they are surprisingly good-hearted, solid, pious people "whom no one would have thought capable of such actions." One is tempted here, for one reason or another, to adhere to the idea of *over-compensation,* whether there be an endeavor to compensate for the horrible sexual instincts through an exaggerated goodness outside the sexual sphere, or an attempt to equalize the weakness, which is felt as painful, through an excess of harshness. It also often happens that the brutality is followed by sympathy with the mishandled object, which then gives rise to tendernesses and caresses.

I have had the opportunity to observe *exactly the same contrast* in the perpetrators of religious and political outrages, as of the sexual ones. During the time of the Spartacus troubles I had to testify concerning several men, old and young, who had taken part in the armed assaults and looting of newspaper buildings. I had scarcely ever seen more dreamy and gentle people; voices, features, movements, all clearly betrayed to the expert the feminine components of their natures. Involuntarily I had to think of the anarchist Koschemann who several decades ago sent a bomb to the director of the police, and who in court set us all into astonishment through his maidenly appearance and bearing. A strange contradiction, and one comprehensible only to the deep student of psychology, especially of sexual psychology.

The sadistic tendency can also extend to dead objects, pictures, statues, pieces of clothing, and other things meant for human use. Here usually the urge to destroy is combined with an antifetishistic conception by which it is aroused. In this realm fall a number of curious cases of property damage and insults committed by persons who, for example, hack up patent leather boots with a

225

knife in hotels; cut holes in bedding which is laid out to sun; spray with acids or ink, urinate upon, or in some other way befoul light clothing of women, to the rage of the wearers.

Some years ago an eighteen-year-old journeyman potter was arrested when he threw soot over a woman's light-colored evening wrap; no less than twenty-five women were invited to the trial, all of whom had had pieces of their clothing treated in the same way. The culprit admitted the offense in only the one instance in which he had been surprised, but was sentenced to a half year's imprisonment.

In this realm also belong violence and vandalism, from erotic motives, toward sculpture. For the realization of this, usually antifetishistic impulses unite with sadistic ones, the *sexual conception of dislike* with the urge for its forcible elimination. Here, also, for the understanding of the negative sexual effects, a knowledge of the positive counterpart is necessary. Thus disfigurement and hate for pictures stand opposed to desire for pictures and stealing them, which is usually motivated positively through liking, though also at times negatively through aversion.

To be sure the nature of Pygmalionism does not exhaust itself in love of statues as such, but also in the artificial, and occasionally artistic, construction of a figure corresponding to the inner desire whose sight and contact, which may go so far as actions similar to cohabitation, bring about physical and psychic relief. Primitive persons and tribes, naturally, make use of more primitive representations than the artistically conscious and capable people of Greece. I have seen dolls which a prisoner made as a substitute for a woman. We are justified only to a certain extent in speaking of hypereroticism

226

in such makeshift intercourse, nevertheless, to the same
degree as Krafft-Ebing does this, of those persons to
whom statues have become the objects of orgastic desire,
that men and women may fondle or handle their genitals
(thus it happened that recently a woman of the best
social standing was discovered removing the figleaf from
an antique statue in a museum in order to cover with
kisses the sexual parts molded from plaster or marble),
or whether, on the contrary, they pour acids or inks over
the sexual parts through a love-hate.

The hypererotic excitation is evoked usually not only
through the similarity to humanity alone, but through
some special property of the statue, as its color or
temperature, especially with marble, much as the necro-
phile is attracted to the corpse by the cool skin, or it
may affect single spots as a fetish or antifetish, as the
breasts or genitals, and then by prepossession be destroyed or exposed to tenderness.

Many thefts of pictures have their roots, in the last
analysis, whether acknowledged or not, in sexual motives.
This may also hold true in the two cases of this sort
which have aroused public condemnation in the past few
years: the theft of Da Vinci's *Mona Lisa* from the
Louvre, in Paris, and the violence done to Rembrandt's
Night Watch in Amsterdam. In both cases an erotomanic
emotional condition seems to have been involved.

Of late years the cinematographic representations have
demanded attention in this regard. The stimulating effect
is naturally increased through the motion of the bodies.
Although the psychic feeling of pleasure which is evoked
in persons of particular tastes to which the picture may
correspond, cannot without further proofs be termed
as erotic, yet there are cases of such type as can occasion a thoroughly strong libido rising to erection and

227

spontaneous ejaculation. I have become acquainted with a series of cases in which female persons particularly go to the pictures night after night in order to become sexually excited at the sight of some certain man whose real person may be thousands of miles away in some other country so that the probability of ever meeting him in real life is very remote. A short time ago I had the opportunity of observing in a young lad a similar case of hyperfixation on an American film star, the sight of whom gave rise to absolutely hysterical exaltations.

Even a *dead person* may produce sexual feelings to certain people. The old saying, "Death is a brother of sleep," has a significance here insofar as a corpse is likened to a sleeping person. I have known of more than one *sleep fetishist* for whom only sleeping people had any sexual attraction. They were thus able to evoke fancies and feelings which are finally, more or less consciously, of an erotic nature. One of the most gruesome of the sexual anomalies, necrophilia, may well be based on this, in which again there are really fetishistic motives to be considered, arising particularly from the color and condition of the skin, but also from individual parts of the body as the breasts and genitals. In this regard the embalming room, as well as the morgue, plays a rôle not to be ignored. Besides the fetishism, occasionally a sadistic impulse seems to be involved to some extent. With some individuals there is an association of thought between death and killing.

Through the entire range of criminal history runs a great number of horrible cases of ghouls digging dead women and girls from their graves and mutilating them frightfully, slitting open their bodies, ripping out their intestines, and cutting out their sexual parts. Among the best known was the case of the French sergeant Ber-

228

trand, first described in 1849, in the *Union Medicale*, which was under the charge of Krafft-Ebing. This man, really very remarkable from the sexually pathological point of view, in his youth masturbated seven or eight times daily, while excited by the imaginative conception that he had mutilated girls' corpses and which he was then violating. The majority of necrophiles find their satisfaction in these purely imaginative conceptions. Bertrand, however, eventually began to hack up animal cadavers. While ripping out the intestines, he masturbated. Then he caught live dogs, and after he had killed them, ripped out their intestines. Later he dug up different female bodies and hacked them up in a horrible fashion, and finally degenerated to lecherous dealings with the body of a young girl.

"I cannot describe what I felt in that hour. But everything which I have enjoyed with a living woman was as nothing in comparison. I kissed the woman in all parts of her body, pressed her to my heart as though I wished to squeeze her to pieces, in short, I did everything with her which a passionate lover can do with his beloved. *After I had behaved for about a quarter of an hour with the body in an almost drunken fashion, I cut it into bits and ripped out the intestines as I had done with the other victims of my passion.*"

In such a fashion he violated a great number of female bodies. One day he was wounded on the battlefield and thus discovered. The court martial sentenced him to a year in jail.

While these cases of actual desecration of corpses usually involve severe psychopathics of the *imbecilic* type, one finds in the lighter cases, which belong less in the realm of actual necrostupratio than mere necrophilia, *eccentric hysterics*. If in the one case it is usually the bodies of unknown persons which are dug up, in the other it is usually the bodily remains of persons whom they have known in life, often persons whom they have loved or even killed through jealousy or love-hate, on which they lavish their tenderness.

Such cases have been differently represented in poetry. We remember Romeo and Juliet, or Don Jose who threw himself on the body of his stabbed sweetheart with the words, "Yes, I have killed her! Carmen, my promised wife, my life!" A historical example is Oscar Wilde's Salome when she received the head of John on a silver salver from the executioner with the words, "Oh, John! You would not let me kiss your mouth, now I will kiss it. I will *bite it with my teeth,* as one bites fresh fruit." And this she did to the horror of even the callous libertine Herod.

The *physical* hypereroticism allows conclusions as to the general physical powers of the individual even as little as does the purely psychic. It is erroneous to assume, as is often done, that long-enduring erections are an indication of an excessive libido or an overpowering sexual strength. On the contrary, athletes, like giants, are often impotent, and anemic, consumptive, sickly people are often *overpotent*. In general, it is very difficult to draw the bounds between *psychic* and *physical* hypereroticism; in a great number of cases the two go together; nevertheless there are some proceedings involving the sexual organs which stand out so strongly as *physical excesses* that they demand especial consideration and description. To these belong especially the *erections and ejaculations which far exceed the average,* particularly the *tenesmus penis,* usually called *priapism,*

230

and the apparently many-formed *polyspermy,* insofar as it comes to light as an *involuntary seminal discharge* in the form of *pollutions* and *spermatorrhea.*

As has already been dealt with in detail in my book on the nature of love, it is not always the sexual urge proceeding directly from the brain, set into motion through adequate external stimulus, which causes the swelling of the genitals and the seminal discharge; the preliminary conditions necessary to this can more often be brought about by quite other factors which have nothing whatever to do with a desire for love or cohabitation.

This is due to the fact that the center which leads to the dilation of the masculine and feminine corpora cavernosa, as well as the center, lying immediately over this, of the rhythmic muscular contractions, which under the feeling of orgasm brings about the discharge of semen with the man and the cervical contraction with the woman, has its seat, not in the brain but, as has been shown through clinical study of spinal disease and the experiments of Brachet, Cayrade, Goltz, and others, in the spinal cord; and indeed the erection center may lie in the sacral segment and the ejaculation center in the lumbar segment. This *intermediary* center, in which are connected the neurons arising in the sexual urge and in the sexual parts, can be set in action as well from the center as from the periphery, the stream can be conducted from within or without, above or below.

Thus it is practically without any real significance whether the ganglion cells which govern these reflexes lie in the lower part of the spinal cord, whose integrity, as was learned by many who were wounded in the war, is essential for erection and ejaculation, or whether, as has recently been proposed by L. R. Mueller on the basis of

231

experiments with animals and observation of humans, the real reflex center of the genital organs lies in the pelvic plexus of the sympathetic nerves whose ramifications meet the branches of the higher lying parts of the central nervous system in the terminal part of the spinal cord.

I shall return to the innervation conditions which still remain in this connection; here I should like first of all to introduce a number of examples which will show that the genital reflexes function also in many cases in which there can be no part played by the sexual urge. Thus the enlarging of the prostate gland, which is so common a sign of old age between sixty and seventy, exercises a peripheral stimulus of the nervi erigentes. Erections, the loss of which had long been regretted, set in with old men, which they welcome as a reawakening of their sexual urge, an error which not rarely induces them to enter into a new marriage to the discomfort of their adult children and grandchildren.

A similar paradidym are the erections which set in at the beginning of a *gonorrheal* infection. The developing inflammation has a reflectory stimulus on the nerve trains leading to the spinal cord. Ignorant of the threatening illness, the young people understand this to be a sexual excitement, to which, often enough, they yield and so spread the disease yet further.

Also the swelling of the member with which many men wake in the morning, has nothing to do with a sexual urge. It is caused for the most part by the pressure of a full bladder. A long time ago an invert consulted me who was married and had six children and was expecting a seventh. I asked the man how this was possible for him. Aside from purely psychic feelings, he had absolutely negative feelings towards his wife.

232

"But that is quite simple," he said, not without a certain pride, "I always made use of my morning erection."

Thus it was not a sexual urge, but their father's full bladder to which these children owed their lives. Also the reputation which various foods and drugs enjoy for the promotion of sexual potency, as celery, asparagus, and also the Spanish fly, is to be ascribed only to their diuretic and bladder-stimulating influence, as the indirect effect of which the genital reflex is to be regarded. Many aphrodisiacs are nothing but diuretics. The same effect, to a certain degree, is had by alcoholic drinks, which are often popularly supposed to stimulate the sexual desires. Also it must be considered here that alcohol at the same time sets aside the power of resistance, reason, while it blunts the finer psychic and sensory sensitiveness and capacity of reaction. With bladder illnesses such as stones, vesication, and after bladder operations, just as after operations upon the scrotum and penis, especially after a phimosis operation, a common phenomenon is a *priapism* wholly independent of the sexual urge.

I wish to tell briefly of a case from my practice which is pertinent here. A patient suffered of an intestinal carcinoma which had perforated through the bladder so that frequently he discharged feces through the urethra, mixed with his urine. One night the patient awoke with a strong erection together with a painful inner pressure in the penis and complete retention of urine. At catheterization I met with a hard resistance which finally proved to be a cherrystone which had worked its way from the intestine through the bladder to the urethra. With the removal of the foreign body, the erection disappeared at once.

Like the mucous membrane of the urinal passage, the

233

membrane of the rectum also, both having in their historical development a common origin in the cloacus, exercises a reflectory stimulus upon the nervi pudenda and erigentes. The rectal stimulus leading to erection usually appears with children, for example, from parasitic worms and not rarely affords the first motive for masturbation; also *digital manipulation* in the anal region, hemorrhoids, rectal massage of the prostate, and even slapping the buttocks can cause this, wholly or in part. Overfilling of the ductus ejaculatorius and above all of the seminal bladder causes an analogous reflex proceeding, which leads to erections and ejaculatory discharges in the form of pollutions.

As ovulation and menstruation with the woman, pollution with the man usually occurs without any *causal* participation of the brain and the sexual urge. The pollution dreams, which are of diagnostic significance for the determination of the inner direction of the sexual urge, are *secondary accompanying and consequent circumstances* and not the primary cause of the pollutions. Peripheral stimulation of the nervi erigentes can also result, which is particularly common and natural, from the overskin of the member and especially the pubes. The papillary bodies in this region are covered with so many, and such sensitive, nerve buds as is no other region of the skin.

The relative independence of the *cerebral* sexual center from the sexual apparatus makes it evident that the sexual urge can be completely maintained even when, through functional incapacity of the spinal nerve center through pathological changes, anatomical disturbances, and destruction, sexual-organic excitement, satisfaction, and possibility of propagation are excluded. Thus with tabetics and others suffering from spinal diseases in

234

which the reflex point is irreparably put out of action, we often find an almost *undiminished sexual lust*.

One case which I observed of *spinal priapism* with an increased libidinous excitability, is the following:

Dr. G., chemist, forty-five years old, infected with gonorrhea before he was eleven, childless, married seven years. In the last years exceedingly nervous, unstable temper, fatigued, but at the same time sexually sensitive with very easily aroused and *long-enduring* erections. Because of the progress of this complaint, he came to a doctor, "because in this condition he could not see any possibility of remaining faithful to his wife" and because the increased sexual excitability made him nervous.

In our diagnosis we established the following: staring, round, mitotic pupils; facial difference, stronger innervation on the right side; light, though distinct, spastic paresis of both limbs; hypertonic musculature of the upper thigh, spastic knee and Achilles reflexes; Babinsky both plus, more clear on the right. In the arm triceps reflexes right stronger, both spastic. Spasms of the arm musculature. Otherwise no findings, especially nothing in the way of bladder innervation; speech free. Psychically completely uninjured. Was quite weakly positive. We interpreted the not completely cleared case as luetic myelitis, which passed under the form of spastic paresis but did not indicate any purely motor illness of the system, although other disorders of the spinal system were indicated. We also interpreted the *increased erective excitability and the priapism* as symptoms of spinal stimulus. These would cause an increase of the libido and libidinous excitement as a secondary circumstance. Hypereroticism, as well as impotence, is often one of

235

the *first* symptoms of a spinal illness. We have repeatedly discovered such to be the case with persons who
had come to us for sexual-pathological reasons. It is a
serious mistake for a doctor, in any sort of case of
quantitative disorder of the urge, to neglect the spinal
condition.

In order to complete the picture of the independence
of the sexual urge and the sexual excitement, it must
finally be explained that a seminal discharge can result
from stimulation of the conducting channels between the
brain and the spinal center at any and every point of its
course. To prove this to people is difficult, but we know
several important points aside from animal experimen-
tation. (The oldest experiment to be mentioned here is
that of Segala who found that drilling the spines of
guinea pigs caused erection and ejaculation.) There are
the observations which were made on persons who were
hanged and decapitated, in whose clothing were traces
of fresh ejaculations. Similar observations were made in
cases of broken necks and fractures of the vertebral
column.

Still to be mentioned among the other causes of priapistic stiffening are insect bites, particularly scorpion
bites, polypus growth in the urethra, as well as throm-
bosis of the caverna corporosa. The relative, and but
rarely absolute enlargening of the member which is often
observed several hours after death, is caused partly by
stoppage of the blood, and partly by manifestations of
putrefaction. The erections found in hanged persons,
with whom there is usually only a thin ejaculation in the
fossa navicularis, arising in the prostate and going only
to the prepuce and scrotum, seldom a thicker ejaculation
containing spermatozoa, represent still an exceptional
236

phenomenon. Thus, from a number of persons hanged, whom I have observed in the course of a twenty-five years' practice, in no case have I been able to establish erections or ejaculations.

Also with severe fatigue, coupled with sleeplessness or very disturbed sleep as on long train rides, *priapism* has been observed, more as a very characteristic symptom of leucorrhea when connected with bleeding of the corpora cavernosa. With radiation of the spleen and of the penis, this leucemic priapism is seen clearly to recede. Another general ailment with which priapism often appears is epilepsy, and also tuberculosis and inflammation of the kidneys. In all these cases *toxic* influences upon the erection center may well play a considerable rôle, as with the priapism appearing after hashish and several other such drugs.

Remarkable also are the long enduring stiffenings of the member with small children of from six months to one year of age. Parents have repeatedly consulted me who had noticed this abnormality in infants and were upset about it. The lasting stimulus of the erection center, which is what we must consider priapism, can be brought about not only through peripheral and spinal irritation to arouse, but also by the cerebrum to decrease the erections. The following example may be cited in this relation:

The sixty-two-year-old Dr. R. assigned to us by Privy Councillor K., had suffered for about fifteen years from painful, enduring erections which set in every night immediately after he went to sleep, *continued the whole night,* and almost completely prevented sleep. During the day they completely disappeared. They were not accompanied by any sort of sexual conceptions, nor by

237

psychic phenomena of any other sort. The libido which was formerly thoroughly normal, has for years been very small. The patient, to whom this disturbance of his sleep was just as injurious as the erections in themselves were painful, had tried everything possible to free himself of them. Every night his attention was directed with increased anxiety to these erections. He tried to fight them through frequent urination. They actually diminished for a short time after urination. The result was an increased desire to urinate which was cultivated at the same time, and which, like the erections, only came during the nighttime. Then he submitted to all possible local therapeutic proceedings: perineal faradization, cold compresses in the sexual region, drawing blood from the vena dorsalis penis, high-frequency treatments, Roentgen rays.

The result was that his attention became more and more strongly focused locally, and the sensitivity of the whole sexual region increased to the utmost. The priapistic symptoms, however, increased.

Thus I became acquainted with the patient. The findings were as follows:

Light, general arterial sclerosis (blood pressure 150 mm Hg), no enlargement of the prostate, no pathological findings in the urogenital tract, especially no lithiasis or concretion. General functional neurosis, especially in the vasomotor region, slightly sympathetic (to hypnosis?). Important is the fact that there were no chronic kidney or bladder changes. For the therapist it was clear at once that any further local measures would be unsuccessful. A general treatment of the neurosis was instituted, avoiding all polypragmasy. On account of the increased splanchnic tonic spasms, atropina was tried in small quantities, and small doses of bromine and iodine.

238

The improvement was very noticeable after the passage of about four weeks, and after the course of several months was still more considerable. Patient slept about six hours every night without being troubled by erections; the urinal pressure decreased.

Epicrisis: the priapism in this case is the main symptom of a *functional splanchnic neurosis* and general vasoneurotic constitution, *made stronger* by psychogenous influences, part of which had been directly cultivated by the local measures. The direct cause of the priapism can have lain in the local changes which in the prostate region consisted perhaps of arterial sclerotic changes in the circulation, but only to a small and not perceptible degree.

Priapism may last for hours; cases have been established which lasted for days and even years. This long tension and strain becomes the more painful and agonizing the longer it endures and drives the patients to absolute despair. The feeling of pleasure is usually missing, but still they occasionally discharge secretions from the germ and genital glands but then there is also blood and bloody urine with severe burning of the member. There is usually no pleasure in coitus, but if it is undertaken, then its execution is accompanied to the end with pain and no feeling of pleasure. Decrease in the swelling of the member is caused neither by coitus nor by any other measures on the part of the patient, for example the blood stoppage is never eliminated by piercing. In general the priapism is even made worse through coitus.

In the literature on the subject, cases are described in which attacks of priapism enter immediately after coitus. Such occurrences have also been reported to me at different times by homosexuals who had gone through with cohabitation, with the utilization of some mechanical device, with no feeling of pleasure while suffering of this trouble. Often with these erections only the corpora cavernosa of the member is involved, but usually also the erectile bodies of the urethra and glans. The pain, which is in and of itself very great, is often still more increased through *retention of the urine*. Usually in the end recourse must be had to narcotic measures, of which morphine is recognized as the most useful; in other cases aid can be effected only through a chirurgical intervention, especially when foreign bodies and new formations are present as the ultimate causing factors.

Of not less practical significance than the aggravation of erections, is the aggravation of ejaculations, *polyspermy*. The *voluntary* seminal discharges, which are always psychically conditioned, are discussed in the section on ipsation. The others to be mentioned are the *involuntary*, usually unwished for, seminal discharges, which fall into the realm of *pollutions and spermatorrhea*. The pollutions take place with the stiffened member usually at night, occasionally also in the daytime; spermatorrhea, on the other hand, usually takes place with a dormant member, almost always during the day, and but seldom at night. Between the two are discharges from a half dormant member as are for example occasioned through riding on horses or bicycles, or with very sensitive persons in crowds.

Several authors, almost all advocates of the theory that sexual intercourse is superfluous for humans, explain the pollutions as a normal physiological condition; it represents a natural *valve*, a periodic discharge of germ cells which is to be likened to the ovulation and menstruation of the woman. Others consider every in-

240

voluntary seminal discharge as a pathological proceeding. We hold that here, as is so often the case, the truth lies between the apparent contradictions and the determination of illness is dependent upon various assumptions. Thus for example an involuntary seminal discharge with sexually abstinent persons is to be judged quite differently from that with persons who have sexual intercourse regularly. Usually an erotic dream is coupled with the jerky discharge of semen, in which case it cannot be determined whether it is the cause, or, as I hold more probable, it is a reflex result of the *seminal stoppage* and discharge.

Old authors speak of seminal plethora. This condition expresses itself in frequent erections, even in the waking state, sexual conceptions, and no little restlessness. In sleep, when the restraints are removed, the seminal plethora leads to erotic dreams which have the same effect as sexual experiences and finally, like them, cause a contraction of the seminal bladder. Almost all healthy men, who do not engage in other sexual activity, have pollutions from time to time, although in very differing circumstances. Its first appearance follows soon after the formation of the sperm, and like the first menstruation, often frightens unprepared young people. It is recommended therefore, although often neglected, that the parents instruct their children as to the appearance of these natural processes and at the latest by the eleventh year.

The *frequency* of the pollutions, like the time of its first appearance, is dependent upon various individual factors, especially upon the habits of life. How often any one can have pollutions without its doing violence to his health, can hardly be expressed in numbers. Whereas one abstinent person may be visited by seminal dis-

241

charges only once in four weeks or less, with others they may come every week, or several times a week. Not rarely these pollutions fail to appear for several weeks or days, and then appear, two, three, or more times in short succession. In regard to the number of pollutions, the individual measure can, in general, be regarded as not excessive when the discharges do not leave behind them either subjective or objective disturbances, or when they are followed by a feeling of satisfaction or relief.

On the average one can say that with temperate persons the pollution intervals vary from between ten and thirty days. Many persons regard periodical pollutions as essential for the relief of their nervous tensions; but for the favorable as well as the unfavorable criticism of the pollutions *autosuggestive and hypochondriac factors* are almost always contributory. Bonner cites a case of a physician who reports concerning himself that he was plagued by complaints every four weeks, which ranged all through his body, until he was freed from them by pollution. He took note of this fact, and from then on he always anticipated the complaints by a treatment which he himself described as "cito, tuto, et jucunde."

However, it also not seldom occurs that pollutions cause a great feeling of exhaustion and prostration with a lessening of efficiency. If it is stated that this shows these complaints to appear when the pollutions are more frequent than corresponds to the peculiar nature of the patients, then this is conclusive only within limits; usually it has to do with persons who are, in and of themselves, neuropathic cases, and whose sensitive nervous systems react unfavorably to the nocturnal seminal discharges. Those pollutions which are occasioned by minor external influences such as a full bladder, full bowels,

242

too soft a bed, etc., are based on a morbid hyperesthesia.

There are cases in which the pollutions appear every night, even several times in one night. In time the accompanying erections diminish. These losses of semen occur almost without sensation and only in the morning or at an accidental awakening does one find the traces which the discharge left behind in the bedclothes. Such pollutions in sleep often seem to pass off without any erotic dreams, at least there is lacking the remembrance of the discharge as accompanying a dream. They weaken the patient to a considerable degree, and often lead to lumbago, great weariness, heart troubles, nervous asthma, severe psychic depressions, and excessive sensitivity. They belong really in the section on sexual neurasthenia, which is the cause of these losses of semen and which they, at the same time, tend to increase.

More rare, but to a higher degree an indication of sensitive weakness, are the pollutions which *often occur during the day from quite trifling provocations.* They occur from light external rubbings and emotions, for example from the pressure of a saddle or some other support, and not rarely even from psychic influences such as the sight of an *adequate fetish.* Thus I had one patient who had seminal discharges whenever he saw ladies with high boots who had crossed their legs. Usually the patients claim that these pollutions arise without any physical contact. There takes place, however, *usually a more or less voluntary pressing together of the thighs which causes a welling forth of the semen.*

Of late years I have repeatedly seen cases in which patients complained of pollutions which befell them in the crowds on the electric trains. Thus a clergyman consulted me who said that earlier he had very rarely had erections and pollutions. Since the trains had become

243

so overcrowded during the war and the revolution, however, it frequently occurred that his genitals came involuntarily into contact with female buttocks so that now he suffered from innumerable pollutions.

Whoever is acquainted with the large group of *frotteurs* will probably regard the claim of involuntariness with a question mark after it. Most peculiar are the pollutions which with many persons occur in a *state of fright*. Usually this occurred first in early youth in some nervous excitement, and then repeated afterwards in similar circumstances. Probably all fear pollutionists develop in the course of time into metastrophic masochists.

To be considered quite differently from pollutions are those seminal flows which are characterized by the fact that they appear without a stiffening of the member and without sexual thoughts and preliminary excitation. They are observed particularly in connection with the emptying of the urine and feces, apparently because of the fact that the abdominal pressure extends its influence to the exceptionally sensitive seminal bladder and ducts. *Spermatorrhea at urination and defecation* frequently appears with persons who previously have suffered of nocturnal and diurnal pollutions, but it occurs just as often without this, particularly with persons who have been weakened through a severe general sickness whether acute or chronic. The name spermatorrhea is often used incorrectly, because it is usually no more than a prostatorrhea. The leakage of a certain amount of prostate fluid is an uncommonly frequent occurrence with all sorts of proceedings, as in the sexual excitements of lovers or at the sight of pictures which stimulate the libido.

Actual spermatorrhea is somewhat doubtful and it has been assumed that, for example, after emptying of urine

244

or feces there is only a secretion of fluid from the prostate. But microscopic examinations have shown that, although it may be only in rare cases, there were traces of semen in the flow. To be sure, there are often incorrect diagnoses in regard to spermatorrhea. Thus a time ago a soldier was turned over to me by a colleague, who was supposed to have suffered from an interrupted seminal flow for ten years. Microscopic examination, the omission of which is a grave mistake in such cases, revealed that it was a chronic urethritis, not of a gonorrheal nature, the so-called gonorrhea simplex.

Particularly often is the flow of semen found with a hard stool. It was believed earlier that the hard mass of the feces during its passage pressed out some of the contents of the seminal bladder. This however is very improbable because the seminal bladder is very mobilely placed between the great gut and the urinal bladder and could easily avoid the pressure. Aside from that, one finds the seminal flow at least as frequently, if not more frequently, without any strong pressure of the abdomen. Not seldom there is a seminal discharge immediately after urination; here the seminal bladder contracts in accord with the urinal bladder and allows a larger or smaller amount of seminal fluidity to escape, which the too sluggish seminal ducts do not hold back, and which thus is discharged with the urine.

However it also occurs that the semen escapes not in connection with a discharge of urine or feces, but with coughing, lifting of heavy objects, and other activities which exert a pressure upon the abdominal coat. Whereas pollutions occur with convulsive contractions of the urogenital musculature and sudden discharge of the semen, whereby at the same time is discharged the contents of the prostate and the urethral glands, in the case of

245

spermatorrhea it has to do purely with an atonic flow. The continual flow of semen of which so many tales were told of old, has never been established with certainty. With the many other secretions of the urethra, this could only be established with the microscope, and in the literature on the subject there are no wholly certain demonstrations of this to be found.

Just as it is so with pollutions, so the significance of spermatorrhea has been overemphasized, although at the same time it is not to be denied that it may have a great weakening effect upon the whole nervous system. A particular form of seminal discharge occurs when there is a contraction of the urethra with which it happens that the semen which has escaped from the seminal bladder is *regurgitated* into the urinal bladder and gradually flows out with the urine. A similar proceeding is sometimes intentionally brought about by persons who, shortly before a seminal discharge, squeeze together the member at the root to prevent fertilization at coitus.

One can say that pollutions are based more upon general causes, and spermatorrhea more upon local disturbances. Both demonstrate a circulus vitiosus insofar as the loss of semen has a weakening effect upon the general condition of the health, and the weakened nervous system has its effect upon the loss of semen. Some writers are inclined to the idea that the loss of semen should rather be regarded as the cause of the nervous disturbances, whereas others regard it rather as a result of nervous illnesses.

It is certain that the rise and the effect of all genital disturbances is to a great degree dependent upon whether there is in the start a stabile nervous system or a neuropathic organization. Moreover also there are often small local variations, inflammations, and rubbings

246

which cause seminal losses of all sorts, especially the ejaculatio precox which is still to be discussed. This *colliculitis seminalis* can be evoked as well through sexual excesses as excessive masturbation, coitus interruptus, sexual abuses generally, as well as through gonorrhea, and so one may probably say that, although in a circuitous manner, these ailments often lead to seminal flows.

In part it has to do with an immoderate stimulation of the peripheral terminations of the sexual nerves, and in part with an excessive stimulation of the brain and spinal reflex centers. The old conception of sexual over-stimulation has much in its favor in this connection if it also is not scientifically so circumscribed as the more recent conception of sexual neurasthenia, *sensitive nervous debility because of inadequate sexuality.* We will comprehend this whole subject in a special chapter and treat there also of the *local sexual neuroses,* among which the *ejaculatio precox, the too early appearance of the seminal discharge against the will, is of first rank in frequency and importance.*

The treatment of hypereroticism must be symptomatic and causal. It is rooted first of all in sexual hygiene and prophylaxis, but also medicinal and psychic sedatives must not be left out of the consideration. Etiological therapy lays the blame to the incretins; in the most severe cases it does not shrink back from their removal from the organism through surgical means (ectomy of the testicles), without concealing the fact, as is explained in the chapter on loss of the sexual glands, that through the removal of the testicles a complete extinguishing of the libido is as little guaranteed as through their congenital absence.

Not only for this reason, but also because I believe

that no second person, be he physician or judge, may go so far on purely humane grounds, I for my part have never yet advised castration, but to be quite truthful I must report that hypererotics who have *voluntarily* taken this course, and their number is greater than one would ordinarily believe, have agreed in reporting that they *have not regretted* this step, and that if there was not a complete disappearance, there was at least a considerable diminution of their passion to be noticed, and that the control of their sexual passion, insofar as it still entered the question at all, was far easier than it had been before the operation.

[III]

IMPOTENCE

THE mechanism of sexual potency with its different intersection points in the brain, spinal cord, and sympathetic plexus, and at the peripheries, with its trains of conception and restraint on the one hand, and the neuropsychic conducting trains and the internal chemism on the other, represents so complicated an apparatus that it is a miracle that an *instrument which depends upon so many previous stipulations and upon its own intactness,* does not break down more often than is in reality the case. At all events the physician who wishes to command the wide field of impotence must be as much a gynecologist as an andrologist, as much a psychiatrist and neurologist as venereologist and urinologist, but especially he must master sexual biology and sexual pathology in all their branches.

It seems essential to us to prologue this chapter with a synopsis of the sexual *nerve tracts* according to the most recent position of science, which is indispensable for an understanding of the disturbances to potency in man and woman. We will give a condensed summary which was prepared by Dr. Kurt Friedlaender in the Institute of Sexual Science.

249

If the inner secretions of the glands in general and those of the germ glands in particular are accepted as the ruling basic principle of the sexual pathological disturbances in the present work, then if we concern ourselves with *erection and ejaculation of the man and with the corresponding phenomena of the woman,* we may not neglect the anatomy and physiology of the innervation of these proceedings. It is sufficiently known that a great number of disturbances to potency in the man are caused by illnesses of the nerves or their tracts in the spinal cord or brain, or through direct injury to the sexual center, an absolutely unequivocal case in which there is no necessity of going back to the inner secretions or supposing any complicated psychic changes.

If we have studied innervation of the sexual processes in the woman, especially if we always draw comparisons to analogous disturbances to potency in the man, then we will certainly be able to explain many cases of impotency of the woman by injuries to the nerve tracts. These disturbances, as a simple consideration shows, will make themselves manifest in the feminine ejaculation, in the feminine orgasm, whether the nerves which bring about the orgasm are injured, or whether the erection of the clitoris ceases and with it the possibility of bringing about relief as the summation of adequate stimulus. The libido, a product of the inner secretions, can still be fully maintained. The genitals have a fourfold innervation: 1. sensory, 2. motor, 3. sympathetic, 4. parasympathetic.

Before we set out upon a division of the different forms of impotence, we might be allowed a few remarks of a more general character. What nature allows many in surplus, she completely withholds from other mortals, without asking the wish or consent of the individuals.

250

Thus on the one side we see many persons squander away their lives with the strongest love hunger, with an excess of procreative desire and power, while others pass away their lives passionlessly, or filled with a longing for productive powers which were denied them. How many married couples whose situation is otherwise ideal, try in vain to have children, while many poorer persons have for their own a whole brood of boys and girls whom they are scarcely in a position to feed!

Recently a married couple consulted me who had come to Berlin from Vladivostok in order to have an artificial fertilization performed. The man was forty-two, and the woman thirty-six; they had been married twelve years. The marriage had been thoroughly happy aside from the lack of a child. In order to make the marriage fruitful, a great number of cures had been attempted; thus the woman had visited many watering places, whose springs have a thoroughly unfounded reputation for removing feminine sterility. She had even undergone a climatic cure in Egypt for this reason. Careful internal examination of the woman revealed sexual organs which were somewhat hypotrophic, but otherwise quite sound and capable of fertilization; in the man however, complete azoospermy in a very rich ejaculation which arose exclusively from the prostate and the auxiliary sexual glands. The cause of this lack of any trace of semen lay in an inflammation of both testicles which had been caused by gonorrhea, which, as was only reluctantly admitted, had been contracted at the age of sixteen.

Relatives and doctors had repeatedly urged that they adopt a child, but the wife could not agree; as I have often found in my experience, the full mother instinct only in exceptional cases extends to a child which the woman has not received, carried, and borne herself. On the other hand, however, it cannot be denied that there are also cases in which childless couples can put an end to conditions of nervous depression and irritability, which had formerly bothered them a great deal, through the adoption of a child. I have been repeatedly convinced of this when I tried to lower, by a medical certificate, the age of adoption, which has been set unnecessarily late at fifty years.

I will introduce here a report which is pertinent as an example:

"I have been asked to give an expert's report on whether or not bodily issue is still to be expected of the childless couple Robert B. and Mrs. Hedwig B., from K.

"Mr. B. is forty-five, and his wife Hedwig is thirty-nine and a half. They have been married for eight years. They both work *together as dentists*. Their marriage from the start was based more upon comradeship than upon sexual attraction and affection. Mr. B. has naturally *very little sexual need;* up to the time of his marriage at thirty-eight, he had only attempted sexual intercourse twice, and one of these times it was at the advice of a physician. The attempts, however, failed completely; he had no erection whatsoever.

"In the marriage, even at the start, intercourse took place but rarely. Mr. B. found absolutely no pleasure in the act, but only *pains;* a cold sweat arose, with a deep psychic depression, so that for the past two years sexual intercourse has not been attempted again. Further questioning and investigation revealed that there is undoubtedly a case of sexual impotence with Mr. B. This ailment, however, has not disturbed the conjugal life of the couple, who are tied together by a *strong psychic bond,* and are thoroughly happy. They are bound together, and have a strong feeling of unity, not only through their common profession, but also by a similar outlook on life, a common joy in nature, music, and other common likes and dislikes.

"Mrs. B. does *not* suffer because of her husband's impotence, because with her, also, the need of sex is completely lacking. The lack of libido with her seems to be organically conditioned, for examination revealed atrophy of the womb and ovaries which do not seem to have developed beyond an *infantile stage.* Mrs. B. is the daughter of a dentist, whose profession she, as well as two brothers and two sisters, also follows. *The sisters are also childless.* The single sister of Mr. B., who has been married for eleven years, is also without child. This sister has been scrofulous from youth, while the father, as well as five of his brothers, died of tuberculosis.

"Thus from the point of view of heredity it was rather to be expected that Mr. B. be the last of his line. Mr. and Mrs. B. have now an ardent desire to adopt a child, whose rearing and education they will care for, and who shall bear their name. The desire has become especially strong since Mr. B. went to war. He fought on the Eastern Front, from which he has been temporarily withdrawn, but with the warning that he may be returned again later. The assumption upon which this wish is based is that the couple can no longer expect to have issue of their own. On the basis of a medical examination, the prospect of issue is excluded. There is a greater likelihood that a married couple of fifty, who are allowed by law to adopt a child without any further complications, may still have a child than there is in the case of

Mr. B. *I consider this, as much on psychic as physical grounds, to be absolutely out of the question.* Therefore this couple should be permitted the rearing of an adopted child."

The court accepted my report, and did so, as my later observation showed me, to the happiness of three persons, not only the foster father and mother, but also the adopted child whose real father had fallen in the war.

In former times inability of cohabitation, as well as sterility, were generally considered a disgrace, a point of view which in many regions, and not in the Orient only, cannot yet be regarded as completely overcome. I remember a number of cases from the earlier years of my practice in which married men were exposed to the chaffing of their fellow workers and other persons because their marriage had remained unfruitful. It frequently happened that they, in turn, directed their anger against their wives, and more than one woman has fled to us, who had been abused by her husband on this account. People in lay circles were only too ready to lay the *blame* of an unfruitful marriage upon the wife, with no further consideration. In many countries of the Orient, even today, a childless marriage after a period of time is regarded as invalid, and in others it is regarded as at least grounds for divorce.

Actually, in the majority of cases, the *blame,* of which, to be sure, there can be only an objective discussion, lies on the side of the man. Of one hundred and fifty childless marriages which I collected from my practice, thirty-six times the unfruitfulness was caused by azoospermy of the man based on gonorrheal ailments, fourteen times based on other organic changes, among which

254

were three cases of varicocele, and five of cryptorchism with which azoospermy is remarkably often coupled; thirty-two cases of impotence were psychically conditioned, in the majority of cases by homosexuality, three times the man was a heavy alcoholic, and twice a morphine addict. These eighty-two cases in which the cause of the childlessness was on the side of the man, stand opposed to forty-eight cases in which the woman was the responsible party. Twenty-seven times there were organic abdominal disorders, as severe catarrh of the womb or inflammation of the oviducts, usually caused by a gonorrheal infection; there were four cases of vaginismus, and seventeen times the women were psychosexually anomalous. The material which has come to my attention can produce yet other figures, among which is a statistical chart of sterile marriages at a women's clinic. In nineteen of one hundred and fifty cases it was not possible to determine a cause for the unfruitfulness because neither the male ejaculation nor the female function showed any variation from the norm.

From history, and from practical experience, there are enough cases known in which two persons were married whose fruitfulness and productive ability were proven through births which took place either shortly before or after the marriage, by the test of resemblance, and yet together they were unfruitful. Such cases not only show that beside the innate unfruitfulness there is also an acquired and temporary one, but also raises the thought that it may depend upon a certain harmony between the parties who are of themselves fertile. Here there are yet many things unclear, whereas the realm of impotency generally can be regarded as already rather thoroughly understood by science.

Of the earlier divisions of impotence, the old division

into *inability of cohabitation and of breeding,* the impotentia *coeundi* and *generandi,* still deserves to be mentioned first of all. This differentiation, however, is not a very fine one. It is true that many persons are incapable of cohabitation who are capable of production, and that many who are capable of cohabitation are not capable of production. Usually, however, the one is conditioned by the other. More often we find atrophied sexual glands which are lacking in both internal and external secretions. The result, for the person with such gonads, is not only an impossibility of propagation, but also often the absence of cerebral erotization, and thus psychic impotence. Of the many cases which I have observed in which aspermatism and andrinism, failing of the inner and outer secretions, were coupled together, I will choose as typical a report on a divorce case:

I have been asked in my capacity as an expert on sexual pathology to give a report on the ability of cohabitation of Dr. R. L., in Berlin. The cause of this report was the desire of the wife, Dr. L., née N. B., to contest the marriage because of her husband's incapacity for cohabitation, which was not known to her at the time the marriage was entered into.

Dr. L. is the only child of healthy parents, but in the families of both parents psychic ailments appear. His own psychic development was normal, he always attended the best schools (proficient in mathematics) and passed his final examinations in 1908 at the age of eighteen and a half. His student days revealed no peculiarities, only that L. refrained from sexual intercourse with women, because, as he said, "he was afraid of infection from prostitutes, and of pregnancy with other girls." The idea that he would *not be able* to go through with

256

sexual intercourse, had never occurred to him. As a boy he showed a preference for quiet games. For a short time as a student he practiced masturbation, not through any active urge but, rather, passively seduced to it by his fellow students.

At the age of twenty-two in a sanatorium in the Harz, L. became acquainted with the nineteen-and-a-half-year-old girl, who later became his wife, with whom he had a short secret acquaintance in the beginning and to whom he was later openly engaged. The basis of the engagement was first of all the psychic harmony. The marriage took place on the thirtieth of May, 1914. The first attempt at cohabitation took place several days thereafter, which turned out negatively. The same with further attempts which followed at long intervals (once every month). After an eleven-month marriage, during which the man was very busy at his professional work, he was called to the war. After a half year in the field, he was transferred to military office work. In between there was a *three-day furlough* at home, when he was busy at different things, *without any attempt at cohabitation*. July sixteenth and seventeenth he had his fortnightly leave in Berlin with *two negative attempts*. There always resulted just a *semi*-stiffening of the member, which would not permit of introduction into the vagina, and no discharge.

At the end of May he went on service in Berlin. During the three-day leave Mrs. L. explained to her husband that unless cohabitation could take place regularly, and bring about a pregnancy (both had been reported fertile from a medical point of view) she would have to press for a dissolution of the marriage. The husband then explained that with his physical condition a lasting inability for cohabitation and a lasting childlessness would have to be expected. Then the wife instituted divorce proceedings.

Detailed physical and psychic examination revealed the following:

The man is 1.8 meters high, and weighs one hundred and fifty pounds, musculature quite developed, hips of the relatively slim man are rather broad, buttocks small, only relatively stronger development in the breast region, voice not noticeably high in itself, but when trained for singing reaches a remarkably high falsetto. Beard slight on the upper lip and chin, otherwise normal bodily hairiness. Physical efficiency is limited, but the *mental keenness* on the other hand is *very great,* and the intellect without a blemish. Sexual urge is normal in its direction, but *weak.* Inner organs, with the exception of mitral disease, sound. For this reason he was assigned to garrison duty in the army. The sexual organs showed the following: scrotum *without* content on both sides, inguinal canal *closed,* testicles also not traceable through the rectum, but on the other hand a rather large prostate. Seminal bladder not tangible. Penis in dormant condition measured about three centimeters, and erect about eight. Now and then a few drops of fluid emptied out from the fossa navicularis, examination of which revealed that there were *no spermatozoa contained therein.* It was only a *secretion of the prostate* and other glands in the sexual canal. After the discharge, which usually occurred involuntarily, there was a feeling of weariness and fatigue as well as a feeling of *disgust* at the uncleanliness in the otherwise meticulous man. Aside from a slight tickling sensation no real feeling of pleasure was noticed.

Report:

In the case of Dr. L. there is a disturbance of the

258

inner and outer secretions, conditioned by an *organic underdevelopment of the sexual glands*. The testicles are absolutely not to be found in their normal place; if they should lie hidden anywheres in the abdominal cavity, then it must follow, from their apparent lack, that they are *completely atrophied*. Because of the lack of sexual incretions and excretions there arises:

(a) an impotentia generandi, because in the *external* secretions there are no semen cells to be found.

(b) an impotentia coeundi, because in the *inner* secretions is lacking that which causes a development of the secondary sexual characteristics and also of the sexual urge.

The peculiarity of the ailment is that the knowledge of its effects becomes apparent only gradually, both to the man and to his wife.

In ordinary speech, one understands by incapable of cohabitation, incapable of *erections;* this represents the condition which is usually spoken of briefly as impotence. The inability of erection can be organically caused and indeed peripherally, spinally, or centrally; after the genital organs, the spine or the brain is the place in which the processes of impotence will establish, themselves and through which those tracts are put out of commission which in their wide course from the brain through the spinal cord to the organs at the nerve ends, are necessary for erections. The erection-impotence, however, can be also of only a functional nature with apparent organic intactness. We will then have to regard it as a minor form of sexual neurasthenia if there is neither a physical nor psychic cause for it apparent.

Psychic impotence, which represents the most widespread form, as well with the male sex as the female

259

where it is not so clearly expressed, is conditioned by a *deflection* of the sexual urge, or by psychic constraints, which make themselves manifest in the most varied fashion, now severely, now lightly, from complete reversal or absence of the urge to mere autosuggestions. Whereas organic impotence is almost always *absolute*, the nervous, and especially the *psychic*, form is usually only *relative*, which is to say that it is present only in regard to certain persons, or more correctly that potency exists only in quite special circumstances.

Basically speaking, *every person is only relatively potent*, and thus at the same time also relatively impotent, for an absolute potency towards all persons, whether male or female, young or old, does not exist. It more often happens that the *potency is more limited, the more highly differentiated is the person and his love.*

Although a division of impotence as above into the absolute and the relative is only a very incomplete division, yet it has much in its favor. Thus a very disastrous and by no means rare form of impotence is the *matrimonial* impotence, which consists in the fact that a man is unable to go through with intercourse within the marriage, while outside he is able to have intercourse. I have often been asked advice by married persons in such cases, which have uncommonly peculiar psychic kinks as their cause. Many men give the explanation that their wife has too high a position in their regard for them to have sexual intercourse with her; the spiritual relationship which bound them together was of such a variety that the man considered it a degradation to the woman if he "used" her sexually. Here obviously there is a suggestive aftereffect of religious asceticism. The woman usually finds it hard to comprehend that the love and the sexual urge of the man in no way always

260

form a unity. If it is the woman who is affected this way, in the majority of cases it is because of her monogamous nature, but this is never the case with the man.

Of the many cases of matrimonial impotence with which I am acquainted, I will choose one which I have at present under observation. The wife consulted me first of all to find out whether there was any chance of her husband again being able to turn his affections toward her. She wished to make it dependent upon this whether she should leave her home and get a divorce, or remain with her husband despite his complete neglect of her. The husband was a physician, and the wife had also studied medicine. Since the beginning of their marriage she had assisted her husband, and they had discussed all his cases together. They were extraordinarily close in a comradely way, and besides that they were cousins.

For a year rather regular marital intercourse took place, which ceased when the woman was expectant. A child was born which, probably because of the marriage between relatives, was deaf and dumb. From the third month of pregnancy on, the man withheld from intercourse, and since that time, in a marriage of fifteen years, has no longer been able to perform the act. While in the field during the war he became acquainted with a nurse with whom he had sexual intercourse. Intercourse was not difficult and usually completed. When the man came home from the war he brought the nurse with him and demanded that his wife take her into the house. The wife consented; in the end the intimate relationship between her husband and the nurse could not remain concealed from her. With a heavy heart she agreed to it, and finally gave up her marital bed to the nurse. She did not complain about her husband, but was afflicted by the deepest psychic depressions.

Because in *all* cases of marital impotence I consider it necessary to have a conference with *both parties,* I called in the husband who told me that his wife was very dear to him, but just this great respect, against which he fought with all his intelligence and power, was the main obstacle to the execution of coition, according to his opinion. With other women who were of a lower moral calibre than his wife and not so lovely—his wife was a great beauty—he was thoroughly potent, whereas with his wife he was absolutely incapable. I suggested a trial separation of a half year, but could not conceal from myself the fact that with so deep-rooted a psychic complex, a return of the ability of marital cohabitation was scarcely to be expected. The result proved this.

Particularly in cases in which the *husband* consults the doctor because of marital impotence, it is advisable, with the consent of the man, to be sure, to ask the *help of the wife.* With the necessary tact, which is an absolutely indispensable characteristic for the practicing sexual physician, many things can be accomplished there. There are cases of impotence which can be cured through nothing so easily and quickly as through the woman responding to the advances of the man in the proper way, for example through digitovaginal guidance.

The division which has proven most practical to me in the course of years in my wide experience, which has extended to all forms of impotence, I will use as the basis of the remarks which are to follow. Even with these divisions there are no sharply defined division points possible, which can in any case be drawn only with difficulty in the field of impotence; at the same time

262

they have proven the most fitted to point out the cause of the weakness and thus the method for its cure. For *only etiological therapy achieves results with impotence.* The forms of impotence which I would first of all differentiate are:

1. *Lack of the sexual urge* (LIBIDO DĒFICIENS) a condition widespread with both sexes equally.

2. *Lack of the sexual pleasure* (ORGASMUS DEFICIENS) an ailment which seems to afflict the female sex more than the male.

3. *Lack of erections,* the actual impotence with the man which corresponds to lack of erection of the clitoris in the woman. When this is not present, the movements of the penis do not come into contact with the female organ of pleasure so that the peak of desire cannot be attained. (ERECTIO DEFICIENS.)

4. *Lack of ejaculation,* under which is to be listed with both sexes the EJACULATIO DEFICIENS AND SEJUNCTA.

5. *Lack of the sexual glands,* an anomaly which apparently occurs more often with the male than the female sex. (INCRETIO DEFICIENS.)

6. & 7. With the woman, allied to these forms of impotence, is still the inability to carry and give birth to a child, the IMPOTENTIA GESTANDI ET PARTURIENDI.

These phenomena may now easily be apportioned to the four main points of the sexual train: *brain, spinal cord, sexual organs,* and *sexual glands,* from which results the following serviceable division of impotence:

I. CEREBRAL IMPOTENCE

(a) Lack of the urge (*Aneroticism, Asexuality*).
(b) Lack of the pleasure (*Anorgasmy*).

263

II. Spinal Impotence

(a) Disturbances to erection.

(b) Disturbances to ejaculation.

III. Genital Impotence

(a) Defects of the *male* sexual organs which *mechanically* prevent cohabitation.

(b) Defects of the female organs which prevent

1. Cohabitation.
2. Fertility.
3. Birth.

IV. Germinal Impotence

(a) Male sterility.

(b) Female sterility.

Cerebral Impotence

If we turn first to a discussion of the *lack of urge,* then we must first of all answer the question, "Are there really anerotic persons, men and women of postpubic age *without* any desire for sexual activity?" It is often claimed by some persons, particularly women, but men also, that they have no sexual needs, they are asexual, *anerotic,* or as one can also say "atropic"; such representations are not seldom made by relatives.

It is also often claimed concerning persons whose professional work demands celibacy—an institution which is against nature from the standpoint of sexual hygiene, both biologically and psychologically—that they have no sexual impulses, and a tradition has grown up, through long endeavors of anti-erotic literature, that the great philosophers Kant, Schopenhauer, Nietzsche, Leibniz,

264

Spinoza, and others retained their virginity through life because they completely sublimated their sexual urges.

If one has the opportunity to examine these cases thoroughly, however, they represent themselves in a quite different light. Often these persons led an autistic sexual life, or they had sexual fixations on objects which they prudently concealed, or they may have actually been able to suppress their desire by exertion of all their powers. The problem also frequently has involved persons whose sexual urge is, in and of itself, very small, and usually for some organic reason, as those with germ glands which release only relatively small quantities of eroticizing stuff into the blood and nervous system.

The close connection between lack of the urge and lack of the sexual glands, in other words the dependence of the sexual urge upon the inner secretions, is most clearly shown in the case of the eunuchs and anorchized. Cases have been reported in which even with a *complete* lack of the germ glands there was a more or less strong sexual desire present, from which we must infer the participation of other endocrine glands in the supplying of libido-causing substances for the blood. It doubtless also frequently occurs that the eroticizing secretions of the germ glands are strongly curtailed by psychic and somatic influences.

Thus for example, strong psychic emotions and shocks, great physical exertions, have an anti-erotic effect through the *fatiguing substances* which form in the muscles and in the blood, quite similar to certain toxins, be they introduced from without like alcohol or morphine, or be they admixtures arising through some sickly disturbance, as for example in the course of a fever, uremia, cholemia, cachexia, diabetes, etc.

The experiences in the World War were very instructive here, which showed that the excitement and the danger to one's life usually silenced the sexual thoughts for a long time. On the other hand, during my experience in the war I also saw cases of exactly the opposite nature, in which suddenly, under the very heaviest fire, a condition of sexual excitement would arise which led to homosexual proceedings. Even the lack of adequate impressions will lower the sexual urge since it used formerly to be a means of controlling the sexual desires when hermits, monks, and nuns went into cloisters or solitary cells to avoid sexual temptations.

Here, again at times, the lack of activity merely proved effective in storing up an accumulation of erotic desires.

Krafft-Ebing once wrote:

"Psychically intensive activity (intensive study, physical exertion, moodiness, and sexual abstinence) has an injurious effect upon the stimulation of the sexual urge."

Bloch explained the impotence of scholars and artists during the periods of strongest mental activity, through the law of sexual equivalents; the active sexuality ceased functioning because it was converted into the latent form of mental production. Such correlation between the upper brain and the lower testicular hemispheres was also assumed by the ancients. However this abatement of potency in those who do heavy mental work, which at all events is not a general rule, may in the last analysis be explained less through a mental sublimation than through a simple psychasthenia, tiring of the brain, because of a process of chemical decomposition, often, to be sure, because of anomalies of the urge from which the person concerned takes refuge in his work.

266

Claims that certain mental activities, for example mathematics and philosophy, are especially likely to suppress the libido, and that for this reason prominent mathematicians and philosophers have usually been impotent, are in this meaning and generality scarcely in accord with the facts.

It seems as though almost all variations in the composition of the blood, influence the formation of the eroticizing elements. A great number of poisons, drugs, foods, and gases thus prove to be depotentizing. The influence of ardent spirits upon the potency is undoubted. With small quantities, to be sure, there often appears an apparent heightening of the sexual urge, because of the fact that the alcohol removes the restraints and the capacity of judgment even more than does the urge itself. Thus it is explained, as especially Forel constantly repeated, that very many sexual diseases have been contracted under the influence of small amounts of alcohol, just as the matchmaker, alcohol, very often plays so decisive a rôle in the first extramarital intercourse of females. This poison to the plasm may also be regarded as disastrous insofar as the alcoholized germ cells, in the sense of the injury to the germ known as blastophthoria, have a highly degenerative effect upon the posterity. With a stronger degree of alcoholism—and indeed as well with acute as chronic alcoholism, frenzy as delirium—there appears an abatement of the sexual urge and ability, extending to impotence.

On this account George Hirth spoke of *impotentia alcoholica*.

He writes:

"Above all no alcohol, particularly not as a means for the attainment of erections. In youth man does not

267

need any sort of stimulus, and in old age it affects him as it did the porter in 'Macbeth,' who called drink an equivocator: it causes the desire, and prevents its satisfaction.''

Morphinism has exactly the same effect upon the potency as has alcoholism. Here also after small doses there can appear a temporary heightening of the sexual excitability, but a wide experience has shown me that those who are strongly addicted to morphine are almost always impotent, and when this concerns the generative faculty, it is usually with the male sex. I saw several women addicts who became pregnant in quick succession. The depotentizing effect of morphine is not to be explained purely from a psychic point of view, but also through a paralysis of the nervi erigentes and thus a suspension of the glandular secretion of the testicles and the prostate.

According to Erlenmeyer, impotence will begin with a daily dose of one gram, and in case of longer addiction with less; according to my experience this varies greatly in every individual case. In general with the healing of the morphinism, the potency returns. Contrary to general supposition, morphine, just as opium, very strongly decreases the orgastic feeling. This last is also true of bromine. Similar to the effect of morphine is that of cocaine, which unfortunately has been spreading greatly for some years as a narcotic.

I have had the opportunity to observe many cocaine addicts who complained about the complete loss of their sexual urge and ability of cohabitation. Dupoy claims to have observed frequent cases of impotence with men who drink a great deal of strong *coffee,* five or six cups, every day. Potency returned when the coffee was removed from the diet, whereas impotence reappeared when a great deal of coffee was again used. To a certain degree *arsenic* also seems to prevent potency, whereby it is established that after elimination of the medicine the potency soon reappeared. Impotency has often been observed after carbonic oxide poisoning, carbonic disulphide poisoning, as well as smoke poisoning. However, there are two poisons to be mentioned here especially: *lead,* and *nicotine.* After chronic lead poisoning there is to be observed often a preliminary state of impotence, which is no wonder considering the general injurious effect of this poison. But nicotine also is not harmless as regards the sexual function.

Goncourt writes: "There is an antagonism prevailing between tobacco and woman. The taste for the one kills the taste for the other."

I consider it quite certain that cigarette-smokers, cigar-smokers less, not rarely suffer injuries to their potency. There are cases in which a return of potency could be made possible merely through renouncing the use of cigarettes. All of these disturbances have in common the fact that toxic changes in the composition of the blood stand more or less in the way of the formation of the sexual hormones, as almost all chemical substances which do not develop out of the body itself have a disturbing effect upon the chemism which causes the normal potency.

Quite similarly we have to explain the anti-erotic effect which arises from the toxins formed in the blood by almost all acute and chronic illnesses. Especially is this true of all *febrile* ailments. Different cases have indeed been observed in which coition has been carried out by men in a severe fever, but these are exceptional. During convalescence, after febrile ailments, one can often establish an increase of the libido with frequent pollutions. Among the other ailments which have an especially injurious effect upon the potency are malaria, diabetes, gall and kidney complaints. It is necessary that the urine be examined in every case of impotence, because it often happens that *sugar or albumen* in the blood will decrease sexual needs.

It often happens that these ailments are discovered through this, because the lack of sexual excitation appears as the first symptom to the sick person. It has been known for a long time that *corpulence* also diminishes potency, and this is so not only through the mechanical difficulties brought about by the corpulence, but through cessation of the sexual desires. It seems as though in the more severe cases the fatty degeneracy of the heart, liver, and kidneys finally also seizes the testicles; it is probable that in the last analysis here also disturbances of the inner secretions are decisive.

On this account the rules given corpulent persons for cohabitation are only of relative worth. Very indicative of the peculiar ideas of earlier writers on this question are the arguments with which Roubaud advises corpulent persons to coitus a posteriori; he writes:

"Morals and custom seem in this case to be in opposition to medical advice and so I will justify myself by the authority of Lisfranc. In order to help married persons attain the goal, he says, we may allow positions which are most comfortable. Religion does not discountenance them as long as they have to do only with generation of the kind. It is more against the spirit of the religious dogmas to give way to sensual joys merely on account of the vain pleasure, than it is to make use of the means

270

which nature and instinct dictate, for the purpose of propagation of the species.

"I do not wish to be misunderstood as though I had advised for married people such positions as will afford them the most unbridled sensual pleasure, means which will not only not eliminate sterility, but actually bring it about. These refined practices, which seem to afford pleasure to the sexually overexcitable, we will leave to those places where love tarries only with aversion, and where sensual pleasures are given way to only under outbursts of madness. Hymen, who increases the joy, but does not wish to increase the sacrifice, has banned from his service everything which outrages decency and good morals.

"For such exist, despite what the cynic may say against them. Every position which robs the pleasure of the fruits belonging to it, is contrary to the laws of nature, and every one which limits prevention of conception should be most recommended when the case requires. This seems to me to be the only admissible viewpoint because it runs counter neither to the natural laws nor to decency and morality."

It also is a result of the inner sexual chemism that the different ailments of the inner secretory glands have as a result a diminution of the sexual urge to its complete extinction. It is also understandable that *cachetic* conditions, such as are so frequent with *cancer* and other ailments, have at the same time a diminishing effect upon the potency, whereas many other ailments, among which *tuberculosis* is to be named first of all, have on the contrary a heightening effect upon the sexual desires. Besides the immediate influence and change to the inner secretory tissues, and increase of the Leydigan cells,

271

the slightly manic excitability plays a rôle, whereas a depressed state of mind and health generally lessens the potency considerably, so that with melancholics it can almost always be assumed as slight.

After all, every mental illness has a different significance as regards the sexuality. The sexual conduct of idiots, weaklings, and schizophrenics is naturally quite different from that of hysterics, epileptics, and paralytics, which is due just as much to variations in the sphere of the *urge* as in the sphere of the *restraints*. Often both are lessened, more often the urge is increased and the resistance weakened, but not rarely also, increased restraints appear with a diminished, increased, or unchanged libido. *Epilepsy* does not have impotence as its result, but occasionally sexual acts will evoke epileptic attacks. Cases have been observed in which the great sexual excitement of the bridal night caused epileptic strokes. A patient of mine, who suffered an epileptic attack on the occasion of every sexual activity, and who at the same time felt a powerful urge to engage in masturbation, had the semen cords cut through by a Berlin surgeon. This operation actually caused a complete disappearance of the ipsation as well as of the epileptic attack. It cannot be determined with certainty, though, whether this result was conditioned more through suggestion, or, as seems more probable to me, through the changes to the inner chemism.

On the whole, potency is to a considerable degree dependent upon the general frame of mind, whereby the paradoxical phenomenon must be mentioned that often sorrowful experiences, sad events, and accidents do more to increase than to decrease the sexual desires. A woman of about thirty stated to me that immediately after the death of her only child, who was very dear to her, she

272

had been subject to a desire for sexual intercourse which had been most painful to her. Even before the burial of the child she had had to ask her husband to sleep with her, so aroused had she been.

The defects of the urge are all just as common with the woman as with the man, only with the woman they are not of such great consequence because the physical hypotheses necessary to activity are suppressed. Complete *aneroticism,* dependent upon lack of the inner secretions, is a very rare occurrence with the woman, even though no more rare than with the man. This aneroticism, in the sense of a lack of desire, is not to be confused with the lack of sexual feeling, which is still to be dealt with, and which is, relatively, a more common condition with the woman. Defects in the urge due to ailments which alter the composition of the blood, are just as widespread with the woman as with the man. These are usually temporary and can be cured, whereas an aneroticism due to a deficiency in the *gynase* is uncommonly more difficult to cure. Attempts at organic therapy can have temporary results, implantations of sexual gland tissue can have permanent results.

The psychically conditioned defects of the urge, to which we will turn our attention in the following, are actually not so serious with the woman, who fulfills her marital duties more or less passively, as with the man, although to be sure the consequences to the nervous system of inadequate intercourse are no less disastrous to her than to the man. Impotence on the basis of *anomalies of the urge* assumes a special position among the forms of cerebral impotence, according to its peculiar nature, insofar as it is always only a relative, never an absolute, impotence. Thus if the conditions are proper for the anormal excitation of the urge, which, however,

273

is in accord with the peculiar demands of the situation, then usually potency will appear. Among the anomalies of the urge which lead to impotence, are first of all to be mentioned those cases in which the object of the libido is exclusively one's own person. More common than this *automonosexualism,* are the cases of homosexuality, in which persons of the opposite sex can cause no sort of desire or erection at all.

Here also, as we said before, it is not always a case of an absolute, but of a relative impotence, and not only in the sense that it is exclusively persons of one's own sex that are erotically effective, but also in the sense that intercourse with the other sex is often made possible only through homosexual conceptions. If, as explained above, we must advise against marriages of homosexual men and women to heterosexual mates, on eugenic grounds, yet it cannot be denied that cases occur again and again which seem to be in contradiction to all theoretical hypotheses.

Thus a short time ago I had the following case:

A patient of thirty-two who had been known to me for eleven years as exclusively homosexual, at the urgent request of his parents was to marry a girl who had been chosen by them. He, who had a firm fixation upon a friend, was very unhappy over the incessant urging of his parents who threatened to disown him if he should not comply with their wishes. The patient had returned to his parents' home, after four years service in the war, with his nervous system in exceedingly bad condition. In despair, after his mother, of whom he was very fond, had disowned him because of his homosexual relations, he decided to shut this friend out of his life. His intended

274

bride, who was a little younger than he, conducted herself very tactfully throughout the whole affair. She loved him very much and promised him that he could continue his relationship with his friend unaltered if he were willing to marry her.

The friend would be allowed to come and go in their home, and she would not regard him with jealousy; but the affection which she felt for her husband, and her husband for the friend, would from her side, also, although not erotically, be carried over to the friend. He agreed to this proposal, and to the greatest joy of the families of both, the wedding was celebrated. Two months later I saw him again. He was completely incapable of coition, and was still very much discouraged, although reassured by the attitude of his wife who was keeping faithfully to her promise. Then after a half year the couple visited me together. The wife was in the third month of pregnancy and very happy. Four months after the marriage took place, the husband, with constant thinking of his friend, had been able to go through with the first intercourse, and now he completed it quite regularly, twice a week, with increasing pleasure. A short time ago I received notice that a son had been born to them, whom they named after the husband's friend.

According to my extensive experience, such cases are quite rare in marriages of this sort. They always show that occurrences of life in the realm of sex are very much more manifold than can be imagined even on the basis of wide knowledge.

The anomalies of a *heterosexual* nature have a similarly exclusive effect as regards potency, in accord with the specific direction of the taste. First to be considered here are *fetishism* and *antifetishism*. Thus it rather frequently occurs that a man who feels himself very much attracted by the appearance of a woman, completely breaks down when he becomes more intimately acquainted with her in his bedroom. Small defects can have such an antifetishistic effect that they completely set potency aside. I was the expert in a case of contestation of a marriage, in which the husband explained that the fact had been concealed from him that his wife had false teeth. He had not noticed this during their engagement because the teeth had been very skilfully made. But when, on the first night of their marriage, the young woman placed them into a glass of water, he, who had loved her especially because of her beautiful teeth, was so repulsed that he could not kiss her again on the mouth and was no longer able to attain an erection.

Even more characteristic is another case in which I acted as expert at about the same time. A dentist had married a girl both beautiful and cultured. When she undressed for the first time, he noticed that she had innumerable pimples on her breasts and on her back. This aroused so strong a revulsion in him that he was completely cold, returned none of his wife's caresses, and just let her lie untouched. He wrote a letter to his wife's father in which he stated his intention to have the marriage annulled. The court granted his request. The most remarkable part of the case occurred when the dentist married again about a year later. Here again everything seemed to be in the best of order. On the bridal night, however, it developed that the bride had a psoriasis, of quite a small extent, on her thigh. The same proceeding was repeated as in the former marriage. In this case the dentist, whom I did not know up to this time, consulted me. Despite the fact that he was advised that the ailment could be treated and cured, this sensitive man could not

276

decide to keep his wife, and again he started annulment proceedings. The case was never decided because in the meanwhile the war broke out and the man fell in October 1914. In a third case the man's impotence was caused by the fact that his wife snored in her sleep and gave forth all sorts of remarkable sounds. In another case the man traced his impotence back to the fact that such a repulsive odor arose from his wife's genital organs, in another case because she had hanging breasts.

There are a great number of men who imagine that they are unable to have intercourse, that they would make fools of themselves at the defloration, or else conduct themselves so clumsily that the woman would be more injured psychically than physically. Very often excessive timidity causes the marriage night to pass without any sexual activity at all. In other cases impotence is caused by fear of infection or undesired pregnancy. Autosuggestions to the effect that the stiffening will not arise can actually bring it about. These impotences of *restraint* belong among the most important and widespread forms of impotence, but are also the most easily cured through suitable treatment, that is, through hypnotic and other psychotherapeutic cures.

The following report tells of a case which is pertinent here, treating of a phase of impotence that is of great importance in practice. This report led to complete restoration of a marriage which was on the point of dissolution. W. Z., teacher in the builders' technical school in M., has requested us, because of our specialized scientific experience, to prepare a report on his sexual condition from both the physical and psychic points of view. His wife, to whom he has been married since July of this year, has contested the marriage on statute grounds, because, according to her statement, he suffers from an impotence caused by abnormal inclinations, in connection with which he possesses certain personal characteristics, a knowledge of which, together with a true estimation of the nature of the man at the time of entrance into the marriage, would have prevented this step.

The suit was based upon the oral declaration of the lecturer, Dr. E. of Goettingen, to the woman, and confirmed by her, that "Mr. Z. stood on the borderline between man and woman, and it would always be an indecisive matter even if improvement should set in."

In a written report of October thirty-first, 1912, Dr. E. expressed himself somewhat less strongly, but even in this he termed Mr. Z. as a person who was nervously heavily burdened with somewhat feminine bodily construction, with whom it was very doubtful whether an improvement of the psychic impotence, which was possible, would be lasting. We have observed Mr. Z. thoroughly, examined him physically, and on this ground give our report as follows: *Previous history and findings.* Mr. Z.'s father died of an embolus in the lungs; the mother is still living, suffers of light nervous troubles, but despite her sixty years is still able to perform the household duties herself. Of twelve brothers and sisters, two brothers and one sister are still living; of the others some died in youth of diphtheria and other children's diseases, and some were stillborn. No psychic or nervous disorders were to be observed among close relations. But *the father of Mr. Z. is also supposed to have suffered at the beginning of his marriage (for about a half year) of lack of potency, which then disappeared so completely that the marriage produced thirteen children.*

278

Z. himself developed normally as a child and aside from an attack of diphtheria and occasional colds and bodily troubles, was healthy. He went through school and his studies easily, and apparently succeeded quite notably in his profession since he had brought it in its early years to a responsible and respected position. Shortly before puberty he had been led by his fellow schoolmates into masturbation but according to his statement had practiced it just a short time and in isolated instances. As to the rest, because of an especially moralistic attitude, he had remained completely abstinent in sexual regard until the time of his marriage, although his always active imagination continually busied him with sexual conceptions and pictures, which, *however, had an exclusively normal content, i. e., were concerned with the feminine sex.* According to his solemn asseveration he was able from the age of fifteen to completely refrain from self-satisfaction. Since then he had regular pollutions at intervals of three to four weeks, which were always accompanied by dreams *which depicted normal sexual conceptions, for example sexual acts with persons of the feminine sex.*

In December of the past year he became acquainted with his present wife, to whom he was attracted by a strong affection which was reciprocated, and led to the betrothal in March of this year. During the engagement, whenever the couple were not together, they were always in very close and intimate communication through correspondence. *Shortly before the marriage Mrs. Z. had a surgical operation performed for the cure of some abdominal disorder, which caused bleedings as its result, which were still present at the time of the wedding and during the first days made sexual intercourse impossible.* The mother-in-law had informed Mr. Z. that in the interest of his wife's health it was most urgently necessary that she did not have a child in the first years of the marriage. Then, when several days after the wedding he wished to attempt coition for the first time, he was filled with anxiety about conception. Aside from that, *the fear lest his wife's bleeding be not thoroughly cured, caused him an instinctive horror,* since he had heard that one should not have intercourse with a woman during the time of her bleeding.

The result was that in a way inexplicable to him his member would not stiffen and he was unable to complete intercourse. In the period following, despite medical treatment, potency did not set in. *According to his statement even the strong sensual appetite of his wife was repulsive to him and heightened his impotence.* This condition led finally to the wife's suit for annulment.

Mr. Z. is a powerfully built man who, aside from slight asymmetry of the skull and the facial construction, thinned hair on his head, and a slight phimosis, shows no signs of degeneration. Rather large buttocks lead one to expect a slightly feminine formation of the breasts, but due to the lack of the glandular tissues this is without any physiological basis or significance. The sexual parts are normally developed, the testicles large with rather tightly-stretched skin covering, the member in dormant state somewhat smaller than the average, but *in no way backward or stunted in a pathological sense.* (In aroused state, according to the statement of Mr. Z., it assumes a thoroughly normal size.) Aside from a slight aggravation of the optic reflexes and vascular irritability, there are no sickly disturbances of the nervous system.

In a psychic regard Mr. Z. gives the impression of being in every respect deliberative and conscious of his aims. He is free from morbid emotional weaknesses, logi-

280

cal and clear in his statements, shows a mature judgment in keeping with his education, keen interests, and mental liveliness. His manner and bearing seem somewhat restrained, but thoroughly manly. He states that of late, because of the constant irritation, he has suffered from nervous disorders, restlessness, fatigue, becomes easily tired, and does not sleep well, but said most definitely that *before his marriage he had been free from any complaint of this sort.*

Report: The *psychic impotence* present in Mr. Z. is to be understood as a *nervous restraining phenomenon,* which is due to *circumstances* and not to a congenitally pathological, abnormal, or weakened psychosexual constitution. Particularly *there are absolutely no deviations of the sexual feelings or direction of the urge in the sense of homosexual inclinations or any other morbid fixations.*

The total sexual abstinence up to the time of marriage caused in him, naturally, a condition of sexual overexcitability and oversensitivity, which unfavorable events transformed into a state of sexual weakness. These unfavorable circumstances were to a large degree responsible for the first unhappy marital intercourse. Restraints which had a reflex influence upon the sexual functions were represented by the *repulsion conditioned by the genital bleeding of the woman, as well as the idea of conception* and the caution aroused by this. In consequence of this first ill-fated attempt and influenced by the lustful attitude of the woman, which, experience shows, often has a disturbing and repelling effect upon the man, the constraints increased with every fresh attempt. However, it can be assumed without doubt that *under proper treatment Mr. Z.'s potency would set in completely and lastingly,* since, with him, there is absolutely no question of any organic or functional dis-

281

order which would be antagonistic to it. To be sure, for this is necessary, a completely understanding compliance of the wife, which, as in thousands of marriages and for similar reasons, must be exercised either on the part of the man or the woman, until a thorough adjustment and harmonious coöperation of marital functions is attained. This is already shown us through the example mentioned above of the father of Mr. Z. At all events the time after which the wife separated from Mr. Z. was *much too short* for a change in the conditions to have possibly been expected.

Therefore our opinion is:

I. Neither in physical nor psychic regard is there a lasting anomaly of the sexual constitution present in Mr. Z.

II. The psychic impotence with him at present, and particularly toward his wife, is conditioned through external circumstances, and through the present existing unfavorable relationship with his wife, and can be cured through appropriate treatment with suitable compliance of the wife.

III. There can be no talk of any kind of concealment of a sexual disorder or weakness on the part of Mr. Z. toward his wife, since he himself at the time of entrance into the marriage could not in any way consider himself impotent.

It has happened more than once that some one has hurried to us *immediately out of the marriage bed* in the utmost state of perturbation over the disappointment which his physical impotence had given him and his young bride. Thus, some time ago, a government office holder from southern Germany consulted me, who had celebrated his wedding the day before in a Berlin hotel,

282

and then retired with his young wife into the bridal chamber and had attempted copulation. He was all the more upset over the quite negative result of this attempt as he had prided himself on the chastity which he had up until then preserved; as reason for his abstinence he gave, besides his fear of infection, the fact that he was an opponent to the double standard of morals; in reality, he had a very small, and thus easily suppressed amount of sexual libido, and thus the failure of each attempt and *incorrect ideas concerning the difficulties of defloration.* A treatment combining psycho- and electrotherapy brought about, inside of four days' time, the possibility of the first deflowering cohabitation, and from then on a potency which was joyfully satisfactory to both parties. A frequent cause of psychic impotence is the feeling of *anxiety* with pangs of conscience which occurs particularly after masturbation or frequent sexual intercourse with prostitutes. Such men believe that because of their earlier lives they are defiling their wives through coitus, or they fear lest, through masturbation, they have rendered themselves incapable of cohabitation. Some people claim that *excess* leads to impotency, others *abstinence.* A strong sexual need and an all too strong sexual activity proceeding therefrom, will usually decrease in the course of years. But that it in itself will lead to a complete loss of the ability of cohabitation, is scarcely to be assumed; in such a case it is probable that organic illnesses, some sort of metaluetic processes, had entered in. Also, in a roundabout way, a neurasthenia which is acquired through sexual excesses can at times decrease the potency as a partial symptom of the general exhaustion of the nervous system. But that a frequent use of the genital organs causes inability of cohabitation, as is claimed, has as little basis on detailed investigation as the

283

claim that masturbation leads to impotency. Undoubtedly among the impotent persons the greater number of them have masturbated at some earlier time. But since count-lessly many more persons have masturbated than have become impotent, although there may be some causal connection aside from an autosuggestive one, yet it would be very difficult to demonstrate and even to dis-cuss.

Even as many other authors, I have observed a great number of cases in which men were able to perform coition *only with prostitutes*. Here also sexual anomalies are involved, partly of a fetishistic nature, and partly of a masochistic nature. In part this potency towards prostitutes is explained by the fact that these persons afford the men various aids, as for example manual aid during the act, which the wives usually will not do. In the case of one of my patients the potency, which up until the time of the marriage was present, and which formerly had led to strong erections at the caresses of the bride, was completely extinguished when on the bridal night at the attempt at defloration she was seized with an epileptic attack. A temporary form of restraint impotence is that which is bound up to certain times of the day and night. Thus many men can complete the act only in the evenings, others in the mornings; many only at dark, and others only in the daylight.

A particularly curious case of temporary impotence came to my attention a short time ago; a thirty-five-year-old restaurant keeper could only have intercourse with his wife when he was wearing a new suit. After he had owned a piece of clothing for about a week, he was completely impotent. Patient stated that he could remem-

284

ber clearly how as a child he had struggled and felt ashamed whenever he had had to try on a new garment. At the time of puberty, and at the time he got his confirmation suit, he perceived that he had erections thereby, and that at the same time the feeling of displeasure was transformed into one of pleasure, with the result that it gradually became for him an indispensable preliminary stipulation to every sexual union.

To the *lack of sexual urge* is added the *lack of sexual pleasure,* the want of sexual feelings with the man and the woman. We may regard the feeling of pleasure as a narcotic state, evoked by the chemical flooding and impregnation of the brain cells, comparable to the effect of an intoxicant introduced into the blood from without. With orgasm the substances supplied the blood through inner secretions flow at the same time as the external secretions. The lack of the feeling of pleasure is far more common with the woman than with the man.

The reason is obvious. The man as the active and aggressive party in sexual intercourse generally approaches the woman when he finds an adequate sexual goal, and when he can busy himself in a suitable fashion. Thus with him there is promised a greater probability that he will attain the orgastic feeling for which he is instinctively striving. The more *passive* woman, even in those cases where she does not regard intercourse as being nothing more than her *marital duty,* is in a far less favorable situation. Just as the germ cells with her, as opposed to those of the man, are released without any real activity, just as the fertilization usually takes place in her tubes without the wish or will of the woman, so also with the reception of the male germ cells she is, to some extent, nothing more than a receptacle for the deposit of the male secretions. The secretions which take place with the woman at the height of the sexual excitement are not germinal-corpuscular, but of a purely neutral mucous nature; they flow from the glandular tubes of the inner genitals whenever it happens through stimulation of these sensual bodies that such a summation of reflectory excitation is attained that a rhythmic, motor, propelling convulsion of the genital musculature arises from the spinal ejaculation center which is affected. This causes mechanically the mucous secretion with a simultaneous, cerebral, reflex-conditioned narcotic feeling of pleasure. *It is thus the task of the man to arouse the orgastic sensation in the woman,* although an analogous proceeding can at times be evoked through onanistic manipulations or other sexual stimuli, and even through dreams.

Intercourse without pleasure will, as well on the side of the man as of the woman, correspond really to onanism. Thus one reads often, that homosexual persons call intercourse between persons of different sex, vaginal onanism. The comparison is really not appropriate, because the feeling of pleasure which is evoked through ipsation, be it with or without mental conceptions, is actually stronger than that which is aroused by *non-cerebral* sensual participation. Often both sexes describe it as a feeling of numbness. Others say that they have a feeling of pins and needles as though their hands or feet had gone to sleep.

A Norwegian patient who consulted me some years ago, told me that the sexual act affected him like *gymnastic exercises*. This man was thoroughly normal in the direction of his sexual urge. Organically also there were no disorders to be discovered. On the other hand he had

286

overexerted himself a great deal; he had erections, to be sure, but never ejaculations with intercourse, although these occasionally occurred postcoitus in sleep, in connection with sensual dreams. This man, who was exceptionally powerful in all other respects, could continue coition at any time for as long as an hour without cessation of erection, and without having any sort of feeling of pleasure whatsoever. And in the same way there were no secretions whatsoever of the genital glands (ejaculatio sejuncta).

Far more common than the lacking ejaculation, and just as disastrous for both parties, is the reverse situation, the premature ejaculation of the man. In this case, the woman almost never attains her goal because there is lacking the necessary heightening and summing up of the nerve tracts which cause the final climax. The pleasure curve of the man is different from that of the woman insofar as both the rise and the fall run more steeply, whereas the pleasure curve of the woman in sexual intercourse both rises and ebbs slowly. For this reason the coveted accord in the time of the ecstatic climax is by no means to be termed the general rule. Often, with certain manipulations of the man, the feminine orgasm appears before the acme of his pleasure. It happens more often, however, that with the woman, almost immediately after the ejaculation of the man, there results a rhythmic contraction of relief. Not every intercourse, not every sex act, not every man is able to arouse the pleasurable sensation in the woman which should accompany the mechanical frictions of the pleasure bodies. *For that is the thing which most differentiates this reflex proceeding from most other reflexes,* that the mechanical stimulation of the glans clitoridis or penis does not in itself suffice to centripetally release the sensual titillation and

287

conduct it over to the centrifugal trains. *This stimulation will frequently depend upon a personality who is psychically effective.*

This basic rule, which is still somewhat unclear in its ultimate causes, but is indispensable for the understanding of sexual reflexes, is often not realized even by physicians. I remember, as very indicative, a declaration which a legal expert made to me concerning the proceedings in one of the great political homosexual trials of the first decade of the twentieth century. The argument was submitted that a man, accused of perjury, had submitted to onanistic manipulations from another man. The accused was married. My colleague expressed his great surprise over the fact that the accused had turned to another man for such a trifling affair; since it was nothing more than onanism, he could not comprehend why the accused had not turned to his wife who was accommodating in every respect, or why he had not done it himself. When I told him that it was exactly this which constituted the perversion of his sexuality that the desired partner must be of the same sex, he started, in support of his argument, a long, as well as very incorrect, lecture on the feminine vagina: "I cannot understand that. A hand is a hand, and a member is a member."

W. Nagel came closer to the kernel of this matter when, in his handbook on the physiology of mankind, he said that a state of excitement which for the present could not be more exactly defined, which he termed as a *tuning of the nervous system,* must accompany the mechanical stimulation. When a woman feels no love for a man, this tuning of the nervous system will usually not be attained, and when a woman has no inclination towards men in general, or has, for example, only homosexual feelings,

288

then, likewise, the feeling of pleasure can never be attained.

When Otto Adler, one of the foremost investigators in that field put the number of frigid women at forty per cent, this figure indicates, surely, only a relative, and not an absolute frigidity. The individualistic character of the sexual reflexes is responsible for this, which accounts for the fact that prostitutes only rarely feel any pleasure during the cohabitation. Many men are subject to the illusion that they can awaken pleasure even in these women, and many prostitutes simulate such feelings of pleasure, "to make better business."

In reality there is little doubt for the expert on prostitution that it is only in the exceptional case that there is any real sexual satisfaction. If, aside from her profession, a prostitute has a strong sexual relationship, as often occurs, with a man or a woman, and it be that this person acts as her protector or has a lover's agreement with her, without any monetary considerations being involved, then the greatest significant value could be laid on this companionship, though in all of the mercenary cases of sexual intercourse she maintained a complete indifference. Without doubt there are many women who, despite strong sexual urges, have never in their entire lives become acquainted with a real feeling of pleasure. Hammond has correctly stated that the physician who wishes to be of assistance in such cases must first of all *turn to the man.*

In cases of ejaculatio precox the man has already passed the climax while the woman is still in a state of strained expectation. The sexual act is at an end for him, and he lies there physically and psychically relaxed while the woman is still far removed from the height of her sexual paroxysm. Especially does the so-called

289

decent woman, who becomes accustomed to sexual intercourse only gradually, suffer from the suddenly precipi-
tated course of the affair. It sometimes occurs that the
woman's loss of sexual feelings takes form, for the first
time after one or more pregnancies, or after a long marriage, because she now feels indifference or coldness
towards the man. Are there absolutely *cold women* as
such, who remain constantly without feeling towards all
persons and every act? The proof for this has not yet
been brought forward, and even in isolated cases is very
difficult to establish. Of course there are physical ailments which strongly diminish the feeling of pleasure.
Of this more will be said in the section on genital and
germinal impotence.

In order to show what influence the completion of the
act by the man, especially ejaculatio precox, has upon
the woman's feeling of pleasure, I will cite a technical
opinion from my divorce practice; it was really drawn
up by my colleague Otto Adler, with whom I was working
on this case. The case has a certain similarity to the one
described on pages 277ff; here as there the wife filed suit
for divorce because of her husband's impotence, here as
there she falsely accused the man of homosexuality. But
whereas in the above case we strongly advocated main-
tenance of the marriage, here we came to another
conclusion. Whereas in the first case there was a temporary and curable disorder, here it was a chronic case
and one which, under any circumstances, could hardly be
cured.

The husband X. had suffered, in all probability, from
the beginning of the marriage from impotence, in a
relative-chronic form with lack of ability of erections
and premature seminal discharges (ejaculatio precox).

290

All statements of Mrs. X. bear this out. Her statements were supported to a great extent by the documentary evidence which was available insofar as it originated from the husband himself. (Treatment by Dr. N. N. and refusal by this same doctor to reveal confidential communications to a third person, contradicts the claim that the wife was very sensually organized and yet shunned marital intercourse.)

The form of impotence of the husband (ejaculatio precox) is without doubt in itself sufficient ground for the contestation of the marriage in the sense of the statutes. Impotence is above all "such a personal characteristic as would have prevented the marriage taking place had a knowledge of the situation and a correct estimate of the nature of the marriage, been possible before the time of entrance into the marriage." It is sufficient ground in itself, and is still more so since the woman is a widow who, in her first marriage, had normal sexual intercourse and bore children.

As regards statute 1339. The "period of six months' time" is to be reckoned from the time when the deception is first discovered, and not from the day of the marriage. The fault of the husband is established only when the failure of the attempt is recognized as "relative-chronic impotence" i. e. as incurable. This realization is easily arrived at with *absolute* impotence, but it is slower, on the contrary, with the *relative* form which can have sudden erections and even regular (premature) seminal discharges. The *lasting* failure of the attempt, which at the start was considered by the wife as a temporary weakness, finally, *after waiting for months and years, opened her eyes. She was first convinced through professional medical declaration.* On that account there is no doubt that, if the claims of the wife, which already are made very probable through the existing documentary evidence, can be further crystallized by more proof, then the marriage is with justice being contested on the basis of statutes 1333 and 1339.

Either: there is an erection, complete to be sure, but lasting only a few moments, which disappears completely with the *attempt* to perform coition, while the seminal discharge takes place simultaneously (ejaculatio precox). In such cases, *usually no regular sexual union takes place.* The discharge takes place outside the vagina, (*ane portas*) or the introduction may have succeeded for a moment so that the discharge may reach its goal. In the latter instance a fertilization (pregnancy) is possible, but for the woman, because of the speed with which it all occurred, the whole proceeding occurs without arousing any feeling in her whatsoever. She is nothing more than the victim of the momentary pleasure of her husband. *She herself feels nothing* and of the whole purely animal proceeding she retains a memory only of the brutality and the uncleanliness.

Or: the erection is only partial, half, allowing no definite introduction, and thus is unable to cause the sexual satisfaction of the wife. The discharge can take place either immediately or not at all. *For the wife the proceeding is painful, having as its result an unnecessary excitation, but never any satisfaction. After frequent repetition there arises dislike, opposition, and disgust both for the sexual act and for the person responsible.*

Both forms, absolute and relative impotence, can appear *temporarily* (acutely). In such a case they are partial symptoms of a temporary *general* nervous condition, or the aftereffects of some illness, particularly of severe infectious diseases such as malaria. Moreover it is to be noted that the potency of the man is more or less

292

dependent upon the frame of mind, mood, opportunity, etc. The proceeding is under the influence of the psyche, in which the world of conceptions and thoughts plays a leading rôle. Even the man who is normally potent will at times, especially if he is no longer in the flush of youth, be temporarily impotent. Then so-called psychic restraints which are usually rooted in some unpleasant conception interfere. An unpleasant odor, a repulsive sight, some uncleanliness, or perhaps some quite unimportant skin blemish such as a small pimple, will be enough to awaken in the mind of the other person a suspicion of some ailment, and through this render potency impossible. Temporary exhaustion or overexertion, sorrow and trouble, can in the same way cause impotence at times. A very common example of *temporary (acute) impotence* is the *"psychic impotence of young husbands,"* which is very familiar to physicians. It appears only too frequently on the bridal night and can last for several days, even for weeks. When the embarrassment and the awkwardness have subsided, and the two persons have become accustomed to each other, the self-confidence and potency will usually return.

In no case do these transient disorders to potency constitute a basis for annulment in the sense of statute 1333. Only a lasting (chronic) condition justifies the application of the annulment paragraph. Justification therefore is afforded at the very earliest after *several months* have gone by with no result. It would be very hard to establish firmly the length of this period of deprivation. *A wide scope must be allowed the feelings of the woman in this regard.* A woman who wished to have a marriage annulled, after about one or two months of *relative impotence,* might be considered lascivious and impatient.

On the other hand one must consider how much time is

necessary for the *woman's train of thought to arrive at the realization that the husband's impotence is sufficient ground for an annulment.* For several months she fights out this question alone. She does not discuss it because she fears lest she compromise herself or her husband. She had never discussed such a subject with other people. And to that is added the hope that everything may still change, and the attempts, although up to that time abortive, still arouse in her the trust that in the course of time the awkwardness will pass and make way for a normal marital life.

This chain of thought is important in judging the paragraph according to which the annulment can take place only within a six months' period. This six months' period can naturally be reckoned only from the time when the wife first realizes her error or the deception. The error, or deception, only becomes apparent when the *impotence* proves to be *chronic.* To arrive at this conclusion, the woman must first have abandoned all last traces of hope. It speaks for the woman's decency and delicacy of feeling if she does not give up hope immediately in the first weeks or months but allows a trial period of a year or two. It was when even medical treatment could bring no aid to the man, and the woman's eyes were definitely open by Dr. N. N.'s declaration, "Where there is nothing, even the gods must fight in vain!" then for the first time she began to lose all hope. She first gained information about *relative impotence* as a ground for annulment when she came in contact with expert medical advisors.

One must really enter psychologically into the thought-world of the woman. The *matured* thought of *chronic, incurable* impotence, which had first run through the woman's head in all stages from thoughts of "awkward-

294

ness," a temporary "weakness," a temporary "nervousness," "overexertion," "the result of years of celibate
youth," etc., really needs a long time to ripen, for which
one or two years was certainly not too much.

The question can be raised whether the wife should
not consider the impotence of the husband as an ailment
to which she should be indifferent and submissive, and
which merely prevents the bearing of children. This
notion must be thoroughly contradicted. The sexual act
does not serve merely for the mechanics of propagation,
it serves a still greater function in a harmonious marriage in affording a mutual sensual satisfaction. Every
wife as well as husband has a right to the feeling of
orgasm (the acme of sexual enjoyment). Moreover
people are generally inclined to the opinion that a woman
is from birth less sensually organized, that her more or
less passive sensuality must first be awakened by a
man. There are actually a great number of *feelingless
"cold" women,* such as Adler described in scientific
detail in his monograph. There may be women with
this innate or acquired coldness who lead a bearable
married life. They are in the situation where they do not
miss the pleasure because they had never become acquainted with it. It is with them as it is with persons
born blind, they are usually not so very unhappy because
they have never seen the light. These women perhaps
even shun marital intercourse which brings them only
uncleanliness and the pangs of childbirth. They would
perhaps be very happy if married to an impotent
husband.

It is another matter with *sensually organized women.*
In this case one should not understand *oversensually*
organized women, a misconception, that unfortunately so
frequently occurs, and which seems to be the idea of the

husband in the case under consideration. *The normal woman also has a normal, natural, sensual desire, although it is not so tempestuous, and is limited through the nature of feminine restraint and through millenniums of custom and morals. The normal woman has a right to satisfaction of this sensuality,* which in a marriage presses to a natural fulfillment in companionship with the attracting power of the male body.

The wife of normal feelings who steps into the marriage bed as a *virgin* has this right. How much more is it then due a *widow* who has already been happily married and given birth to children. When she decided on the second marriage, she had a double right to expect of her second husband a normal sexual ability. *A man who, conscious of a small sexual ability, enters into marriage with a widow is guilty of a doubly serious deception.*

Six years ago in the monograph already cited, the expert Adler said:

"The fact of a thoroughly *developed* sensuality may probably be regarded generally as sufficient reason for the same to be occasionally satisfied. A constant battle against this can lead to serious disorders of the psyche. Nervous disturbances from slight exhaustion and a feeling of displeasure to severe attacks of spasms and cramps—stomach and bowel disorders and muscular weaknesses—in short all the different forms of neurasthenia and hysteria, all too frequently have their main basis in sexual disorders, in missing sexual sensations. Gattel, in his work on the sexual bases of neurasthenia and neuroses, describes this connection in one hundred cases. Some sort of sexual anomaly is almost always

296

present, especially *the lack of satisfaction because of ejaculatio precox or coitus interruptus.*"

Under this hypothesis those lacks, assuming that they really exist, which were the reason for the wife's finally taking the matter to court, appear in a quite different light. It was not an excessive lust and sensuality which led to this step, but the instinctive craving for relief. She must have felt as imminent the phantom of inner disquiet and displeasure, and of threatening nervousness which was aggravated by the abortive attempts of the husband. *It is much easier to refrain entirely than to constantly have the sensuality, which was awakened in the first marriage, aroused and tormented through the ineffectual assaults of the second husband.* Here, finally, even the strongest person gives way and casts convention aside. The *unsuccessful attempts* caused by this *relative-chronic impotence* (ejaculatio precox) must have a more repelling effect upon the wife than would the complete inability of an absolutely impotent man. This point is of importance for the psychological investigation although it does not come into the annulment suit as a point in itself. But the brand of lasciviousness and loose morals must be lifted from the woman.

The husband termed the wife as "especially sensually organized" and at the same time he claimed that "according to her whim she completely forbade the complainant the exercise of his marital right, or allowed it only in the *most reluctant manner,* and finally, during the last months of their living together, she shut herself up in her bedroom with her son." How is this contradiction of sensuality and reluctance to be explained? Obviously only through the dislike of the wife for *this*

297

form of intercourse which she has with her husband! If she is really so sensual as the husband represents her, then she would welcome with joy every opportunity which the husband offered for her satisfaction. Only, this satisfaction never appeared! It was always just a repellent and abortive attempt. Her nerves were in a frazzled state and she decided finally that it was better to refrain completely than constantly to suffer from fresh unnecessary excitation, tension, disgust, and uncleanliness.

Finally must be considered the remark made by the husband according to which, at the time of reconciliation, the wife is supposed to have said that "she considered a permanent life together as out of the question." This remark is psychologically important. One must consider that at this time the wife was not bringing suit for *divorce,* but *for reëstablishment of the married life.* And despite this, quite contradictory to the spirit of her suit, she said that life together was impossible. This contradiction arises from the unhappy wording of the statute (1567) concerned. The wife actually desired a separation, and wilful desertion seemed to her the most fitting and least harsh basis for the suit. The paragraph, however, presupposed a suit for reëstablishment of the marriage. Thus the law brought this woman, who wished a divorce, into the muddle where she was asking for a reëstablishment of the marriage. When at the time of reconciliation, despite the fact that by law she had demanded a reëstablishment, she admitted that the marriage was hopeless, she was merely following her simple, healthy, natural feelings. She was shy of telling the true reason, and she was shy of basing her divorce suit upon sexual grounds, attempting to avoid scandal and cruelty.

298

SPINAL IMPOTENCE

In order to understand the nature of spinal impotence it is necessary to form a completely clear picture of the mechanical realization of erection and ejaculation. The stiffening of the member which affords the male organ the rigidity, form, and size necessary for intercourse, is caused by a repletion of blood; this is the result of varied vascular tension, dependent upon vasomotor innervation through an intermediary center which is set into action by sensitive nerves. Thus it is a typical reflex proceeding, which is different from most bodily reflexes in that here the relationship is far more finely differentiated both in the *quantitative summation* and in the *qualitative ability of reaction* than is the case with any other reflex action in the human body.

The anatomy of the male sexual organ teaches that on the foreskin and the glans there are a great number of free intrapithelial nerve end bodies as well as particular nerve end organs; among these are to be mentioned: the thick end bodies, tactile buds, vatersche bodies, Krause's genital nerve bodies. The latter, in particular, are thickly developed on the under side of the glans. Because of their great sensitivity they bear the name of pleasure bodies. Mechanical friction of these leads a strong nerve current centralwards, which, however, *is felt as pleasurable only in quite special conditions,* as cannot be strongly enough emphasized. As has already been mentioned in the chapter on hypereroticism, this excitation of the genital nerve endings can also arise mechanically through stimuli which have little or nothing to do with the sex life, for example through acute inflammation of the mucous membrane of the urethra. Contact with this mucous membrane through probes, catheters, or objects introduced for masturbational purposes often causes erections.

Particularly will rubbing and stimulation of the pars posterior urethrae cause the reflex proceeding, whereby is also explained the fact that a stiffening will arise with pressure on the prostate for examinational or therapeutical reasons, as for treatment of strictures, a similar mechanical stimulus is evoked through the taut filling of the urinal bladder and the seminal bladder. In accordance with this, as Ricke correctly pointed out, is the fact that innervation of the member appears after an ejaculation has resulted even as the common impotence appears with spermatorrhea, in which case there is no accumulation of seminal fluidity in the seminal passages. Exceedingly important is the fact that the sexual conducting tracts cannot be set into motion through the sheer exercise of the will, but that for this there is always necessary *involuntary stimuli evoked through particular impressions and conceptions.* It was already demonstrated in the seventeenth century, through experimental injections in a corpse, that the erection depended upon the arteries being filled with blood. In dormant condition the arteries of the member, particularly the small arteriae helicinae which form the *trabecula* of the corpora cavernosa penis and the bulbus of the corpora cavernosa urethrae, as well as the cavernous space itself, are under the influence of a tonic contraction of the smooth muscular apparatus. The long muscle fibers are so situated that the vascular lumina are narrowed so that only an inconsiderable influx of blood is possible. *Warmth and cold, and other influences, even psychic influences such as fear, anxiety, and fatigue, cause variations of the bloodflow in the dormant member.*

300

Thus, through cold such a strong contraction of the smooth long and cricoid vascular musculature results that the arterial lumina are almost completely closed up and because of this the *penis appears completely shriveled up*. However, when the vascular partitions become innervated through vaso-dilatory effect, the blood flows spontaneously from the arteriae dorsales and the arteriae profundae penis into the dilated supply basin of the similarly dilated tissues of the corpora cavernosa. The speedy filling of the cavern at the arising of the erection, as well as the speedy emptying at its disappearance, depends in part upon the peculiar arrangement of the smooth musculature. This is arranged in the form of the so-called Ebner Intimapolster, longitudinal muscular pads which are usually in tonic contractions. With dilation of the tissue an equal pressure is exerted on the one side upon the arteries of the penis and on the other upon the urethra, whereby both channels are dilated. The opening of the urethra which is thus produced cannot be without some significance for the ejaculation.

Formerly, it was generally supposed that through the sudden dilation of the cavernous space the aperient venous channels are compressed and through the influx of the blood, so to speak, the efflux of blood is decreased. The anatomical proof for this attractive theory, however, has not yet been brought forward. François Frank demonstrated an increase in pressure in the peripheral ends of the vena dorsalis penis during erection. Haehnle assumes that there is a compression of the veins through muscular contraction, and indeed in such a way that the musculus perenei exerts a pressure upon the venae profundae penis, the musculus trigonalis and the musculi bulbo- and ischio-cavernosi upon the vena bulbo-caver-

301

nosa and vena dorsalis penis. Opposing these conjectures, however, it has been proven that even with long enduring erections the penis shows neither the cooling which always results with a swell of blood, nor cyanosis. On the contrary, accompanying the erection there is always a considerable *increase in temperature* of the member, an indication that an increased circulation of blood is taking place in the whole member during the erection.

Therefore, when it is present at all, the damming and stopping within the veins can be only of quite secondary importance. The raising of the stiffened member, which usually occurs with the increased filling with blood, may be caused through the tension of the fasciae at the root of the penis and along the back of the penis, since the back is shorter and more tense than is the ventral side. Beside the erection itself, the slightly concave curvature of the erect member may also be explained through this. Here also, to be sure, the muscular fasciae of the musculus bulbo-cavernosus and ischio-cavernosus may be effective, since through their contraction they cause the stiffening, but at the same time, in relation to the other factors already named, this is of merely incidental significance.

This analysis seems necessary in order to be able to correctly estimate the disorders to potency. This is not always so simple, which is the unpleasant hypothesis in all therapy. Spinal impotence is *partly organic* and *partly functional*. First to be mentioned among the organic forms are injuries to the spinal cord, such as, unfortunately, could be observed in such great numbers in World War I.

Of those cases which I saw during the World War I will describe one in some detail. R. was wounded by a

302

shot on the twenty-eighth of April in Poland in the battles on the Rawka River, which went through the lumbar region of his body from the left to the right, and pierced the spinal cord at the top of the lowest lumbar. There was a crippling of both limbs, which disappeared again after about ten days. There was almost no feeling as high as the thigh. In sexual regard the libido, as well as the facultas erigendi and ejaculandi, had completely vanished. Every feeling of pleasure was also lacking.

About three months after his severe wound of which no external trace was apparent aside from a slightly visible scar where the bullet passed in and out, his libido made itself noticeable again to a high degree. However, when the patient was in the company of a person who was psychically very attractive to him, he had *no sign of an erection,* and was extraordinarily depressed thereover. It was at this time that I saw him for the first time.

First, all sorts of electrophysical, chemical, and psychic treatments proved to be of absolutely no avail. After about six months of general massage treatments, thus almost one year after the time of wounding, in bed one morning, for the first time, there was a spontaneous erection. A few days later when in company of the lady whom he desired, the patient also had an erection. But despite extensive manipulation, there was no ejaculation. Twice already, in the fifth and eighth months after the wounding, there had been pollutions in sleep without erection or any feeling of pleasure. Six weeks after the first erection he had his first ejaculation at coition with his beloved, but the orgastic sensation was completely lacking thereby. He had only a dull feeling, and later a slight tingling. This numbness was removed somewhat

303

through diathermic treatments, but a restitution of the former powerful feelings of pleasure has as yet not been achieved.

His last report, four years after the wounding, reads:
"Since May, the sexual feelings have again increased to some extent. The member stiffens more often of its own accord, but still, when I have sexual intercourse with any one, there has as yet been only one seminal discharge. But there is often a discharge at night. I have the same sensation at that as I did formerly. There is no feeling in the right side of the abdominal region, in the member, the testicles, and the right hip. On the left side, the feeling is normal as formerly. After the wounding the abdomen was entirely without feeling. That however has improved to this extent. I cannot cause an erection of the member myself, but as soon as I am with some one who attracts me psychically, the member becomes stiff. But after a short time it is again relaxed. Then I have pains in the abdomen. But of late these have diminished, and they no longer appear so violently as they did before."

This case is exceedingly instructive, as it shows the relative *independence* of the different sexual tracts from each other. Of the organic changes to the spinal cord, *spinal consumption,* which almost always has present symptoms of impotence, demands consideration first of all, because of its prevalence. At the beginning of this metaluetic affection there can usually be noticed an increased sexual excitability, just as other reflexes show an increase with tabes, at first. But after a very few months the ability of cohabitation becomes less and less until it is soon completely extinguished. I have seen very many cases in which tabetics, and their mates as well,

304

have suffered far more psychically from this symptom than from any other at all. The women find the impotence of their tabetic husbands so much the more unpleasant because it is usually preluded by a period of *priapism* and satyriasis. Also other spinal disorders lead, according to their situation, sooner or later to complete inability of erection and usually ejaculation, most frequently after a temporary condition of high excitability. Almost all forms of myelitis, even infantile paralysis as well as innate defects of the spinal cord like spina bifida, are to be named here.

A further illustration will serve as an example which is similar to many other cases of spinal impotence in our practice: W., chorister, thirty-four years old, comes with the complaint of failing of the stiffening of his member and decreased pollutions. These still occur, however, without erection preceding them, and still amount to "something" although much less than before. The libido has not decreased much. The trouble arose a year and a half ago. Previous to this he was quite healthy. No previous sexual diseases and nothing particular could be remembered of importance. The rather drawling and choppy manner of speech of the patient was surprising even in conversation. Examination revealed: *Nystagmus* horizontally at the extreme side positions of the bulbi, fast looking to the left and slow looking to the right. *Speech scans metrically.* Brain nerves and ocular background otherwise free. Reflexes of the arms and legs spastically *heightened;* clonic spasms in both feet; spasms of the thigh musculature; no marked paresis, but pronounced *pyramid symptoms* (Oppenheim, Gordon, etc.). *Missing abdominal skin reflexes.* Sensibility, bladder and great intestine without manifest symptoms.

Quite *slight ataxy* in reaching finger to nose, or finger to finger.

The case concerns a *multiple sclerosis* with all typical symptoms most clearly developed. How long the ailment dates back, cannot be definitely established because the peculiar patient *claims to have noticed nothing at all of this ailment—with the exception of the impotence which brought him to the doctor! This impotence is undoubtedly of spinal origin and a symptom of the multiple sclerosis, and in this case the one which was subjectively most felt and first noticed.* In another case which I saw, which concerned a thirty-eight-year-old merchant, a case of multiple sclerosis which had been treated twelve years before in the Charité Hospital had completely died away for the last six years. The patient was free from paralysis, intention-tremors, nystagmus, and so on; he had been in active service throughout the war; the only thing still to be found was a temporal pallor. At the same time, however, there was an impotence of erection and a reduction of the ejaculation frequence, which had remained since the time of the illness as a lasting *residual symptom.*

Among the ailments of the spinal cord, with which I have had the opportunity to observe considerable disturbances to potency, particularly during the war, is that form of concussion of the spinal cord which is described under the name of railway spine, the traumatic myelasthenia with which, in general, anatomical-pathological variations are not manifest. This brings us to saying something about the other forms of functional impotence which are comprehended under the group name of *nervous impotence.* Under this name is included a miscellany which would be difficult to explain and to arrange in any other way, as by no means all afford an absolutely clear

306

and unequivocal explanation, as wide experience in the field of impotence teaches.

As regards the "nervous impotences" I have come to the conclusion that the *greater part of them are purely psychically conditioned,* and so in these cases are involved countersuggestions and autosuggestions of a *more subtle* and unknown nature which counteract the automatic activity of the spinal cord center. Eulenberg has already shown that nervous impotence is usually caused by the effects of abnormal reflectory and associative stimuli. His division of spinal impotence into peripheral-sensory impotence, which has its basis in functional disorders of the affluents to the symptomatic centripetal central tracts; and spinal-sensory impotence, which is conditioned by functional disorders in the spinal part of the rising genital conducting train, will in all events be as satisfactory as Krafft-Ebing's threefold division: that of a sexual neurasthenia connected with impotence in a local genital neurosis, a neurosis of the lumbar cord, and a general neurasthenia. This will be treated in more detail in another section.

The greater the experience in the field of impotence, the more it is shown that a nervous impotence in the sense of a functional disorder of the peripheral genital nerves is extraordinarily rare, provided in exceptional cases. Of one hundred cases of impotence which were first of all assumed to be nervous and were reported as such by the experts, *eighty proved to be psychically conditioned,* although by no means all based on anomalies of the urge, but frequently evoked through simple psychasthenia, *phobias,* and autosuggestive oppositions. In five per cent there were spinal cord disorders, in six per cent there were organic disorders in the region of the genital organs, whereas in nine per cent a definite cause

307

could not be ascertained, with the preponderance of probability pointing to psychogenous origin.

Coinciding with spinal and nervous impotence is also that form which goes under the name of *"paralytic* impotence" in the literature on the subject. It can be cursorily described by saying that every sexual expression is lacking, neither erections nor pollutions are present, and often even the libido is missing. As objective indications can be mentioned: striking pallor, a livid coloring, flabbiness of the external genitals, reduction of the skin sensitivity, oversensitivity of the urethra and the mucous membrane, smallness and weakness of the testicles, extinction of the cremaster reflexes, and the patients complain of a feeling of coldness which proceeds from their genitals. Apparently there are concerned here forms of impotence which are partly psychic and partly spinal in connection with sexual neurasthenia, and therefore I consider the special designation of paralytic impotence as superfluous.

Moreover, according to their nature, the disorders to erection show very different characters. There are some with which the member does not become stiff at all, others with which there appears a temporary stiffening which, however, soon yields place to a debility. As a minor group are to be mentioned the forms in which the man first of all approaches the woman with a complete erection because of a strong libido, which however disappears completely as soon as the member comes near the vagina. But here also there is usually a relative psychic impotence involved.

There is usually, secondarily connected with impotentia erigendi spinalis as well as with psychic impotentia coeundi, an *ejaculation impotence,* without there being a direct disorder of the ejaculation center. The normal seminal discharge has a previous stipulation of at least a relative stiffness of the member, so that with the failing of this there is also a failing of the ejaculation as a consequent phenomenon. There are also disorders of the ejaculation with which the sexual urge and the erections are completely normal and even the semen production leaves nothing to be desired. They are based upon reflex anomalies in the ejaculation center of the spinal cord, and have either the character of a reflex paralysis or of a reflex spasm. Objectively and subjectively the one is just as serious as the other, the one is the premature seminal discharge, the ejaculatio precox, the other is the *omission of the ejaculation,* be it at cohabitation, or be it generally, the *ejaculatio sejuncta* and *deficiens.*

The premature discharge, which is just as unpleasant for the man as it is for the woman with whom he is having intercourse, is based upon an irritable weakness of the sensible genital nerves, and thus it is a partial symptom, and indeed one of the most important symptoms of sexual neurasthenia, in the detailed discussion of which we must still engage. As with ejaculatio precox the impression of the sensory disorder predominates, so with ejaculatio sejuncta that of the motor disorder predominates. Without doubt the sexual anomaly here is one of the most curious and difficult to explain. The anatomical basis may be a cicatrization or sticking together, or at least an excessive *spasm* of the ductus ejaculatorius, especially cases in which, although they are relatively rare, the semen flows for a long time after the member has become dormant.

I have seen a considerable number of males with whom there has never been a seminal discharge at intercourse. Many have involuntary pollutions in their sleep; there are, however, some who have absolutely never had either

309

pollutions nor ejaculations, despite the fact that their testicles seem in no way to vary from the norm. Thus many years ago I was treating a married engineer who had tried different means to attain an ejaculation, but without ever having been able to achieve his result. Since the couple wished a child very much, they were doubly unhappy. At the same time the man had erections which lasted for an *indefinitely long period,* and he had already continued the act in different positions for over an hour. Two more examples, selected from many similar ones, may give us a complete picture of this sexual disorder of which practicing physicians have only too little knowledge.

Dr. M., chemist, thirty-three years old. Married for two years, he complains, in an otherwise happy married life, of the following. At intercourse he has a strong libido and powerful erections, but *there never is an ejaculation thereby.* He has ejaculations only periodically in sleep without erections beforehand, partly with, and partly without sensual dreams. Because he wished to have children, this condition towards his wife had gradually become unbearable to him. Patient expressed these complaints with strong psychic abhorrence. He proved to be *physically quite healthy,* no hereditary burdens, sensitive psychically, and intellectually a very gifted man.

The more exact analysis of the disorder which troubled him is given in the following: Patient was reared strictly and with a strong feeling of modesty. Until the time of his marriage, at the age of thirty, he lived an *entirely chaste life.* He had, as he stated in the most positive and entirely credible manner, forcibly suppressed every desire for masturbation. He was enlightened as to sexual

310

things, about which, as he himself said, he had no instinct, at about the age of fifteen. His only love affair before his marriage was with a cousin of the same age, which lasted about five years. They both used to cycle about an hour's distance into a small wood where they would kiss each other and manipulate each other's genitals. Patient had strong erections on the ride out at the thought of what was to happen, but a feeling of shame prevented an ejaculation at this mutual masturbation. After the marriage of his cousin, he still had very strong erections at the thought of her kisses, etc. His present wife *resembles the cousin.*

The treatment consisted of a series of hypnoses which heightened the desire for immission through imperative suggestions, and foretold the ejaculation as immediately coupled to it. After a long time the treatment had results. A proof of the psychically conditioned nature of spinal reflex disorders.

A similar case:

Dr. L., editor, twenty-eight years old, married for four years and had lived a happy married life. He complained that he could not satisfy his wife. His erections at sexual intercourse were very slight in strength, and the ejaculation was missing. Despite his great love for his wife, his desire for sexual intercourse was very small. On the other hand, he had ejaculations as pollutions, usually with specified dreams. Also (and this is a contrast to the case of Dr. M.) he could attain powerful erections and ejaculations through masturbation.

It was the couple's desire for a child which brought the patient to a physician. Physical examination revealed indications of a functional neurosis, previous history had many neuropathic points. Patient is mentally a very alert and sensitive person, with a great feeling of modesty. After long hesitation he stated: he had ejaculations with his sensual pollution dreams and his attempts at masturbation as soon as he imagined that he was wrestling with a woman and was beaten by her. It was a particular movement of the battle, the conception of which would arouse him to an ejaculation. The female partner in this remained quite uncertain. L. had first experienced the effect of this conception at the time of puberty. Also, as in the case before, through a feeling of shame he had excluded this whole complex from his waking life as far as possible, had tried to suppress his desires for masturbation, and had *lived chastely* up until the time of marriage.

The marriage was based on an enthusiastic platonic love. Treatment through hypnosis. Indicative is a dream, which he will dream now upon suitable suggestion, and which he dreamed in a hypnotic state. He finds himself in a long narrow corridor which is dark. He wishes to penetrate deeper into the corridor, but a block of ice prevents his passage. The block is small, and any other person could easily get by; but no matter how he tries, he is unable to get over it. A figure is imbedded in the ice block, like a fly in amber, a human figure, but much smaller. This dream signifies himself, so to speak, as a symbol of the excitation of feelings, apprehensions, and wishes which agitate the patient at sexual intercourse.

Here also a few hypnotic treatments achieved a relative initial result, because the ability of cohabitation underwent an improvement; but since the cohabitation still proceeded entirely without ejaculation, there can be no talk of a cure, which is generally very difficult with these disorders and requires great patience on the part of the patient and physician.

Epicrisis of both cases: in both cases the ejaculation mechanism is separated from the erection mechanism. In both cases this took place *after a total sexual abstinence extending over a period of years, during which masturbation was also suppressed.* In both cases the total sexual abstinence is the result of sexual timidity. This sexual timidity and modesty has also modified the nature of the libido in both cases. It has placed the greatest amount of pleasure of a libidinous sort in the imaginative life, especially in the involuntary dreamworld. The content of the dream is far removed from the conception of the sexual act; it is related in part to the preliminaries of the act, and in part to quite other things. Toward the wife there is an idealistic sort of love feeling; at sexual intercourse with their beloved wives both lose their frankness and sureness of ejaculation and on this already set stage the symptom of separation makes its entrance. It is noteworthy that many of these patients are not quite clear in their minds whether or not they have ejaculations at intercourse; the doubt is caused by mucous secretions of the woman during the act, and so even the woman is often not able to make this clear. To make the diagnosis certain, coitus condomatus is necessary.

GENITAL IMPOTENCE

We come now to the *genital* impotence which is conditioned by organic changes of the male and female organs of copulation and the surrounding region. There are a great number of anomalies to be considered here,

313

each of which is in itself a rare thing. Collectively, however, they considerably impair the ability of cohabitation and fertility. In the following, we give a cursory synopsis of the disorders belonging in this group:

1. *Complete inborn lack of the penis.* In this case, with a normal libido sexualis and, usually, potentia generandi, there is an impotentia coeundi, or, at least, complete impotence of immissio penis. The lack of the penis is more common than is generally believed if one includes those cases in which it is connected with hypospadia of the scrotum. Thus they encompass all the variations of pseudohermaphroditism with which, under the external feminine front, there are male germ cells. That such persons can be capable of generation is not to be doubted according to my own experience, and also that of earlier writers. In this connection it must be stated that a relative ability of copulation is possible. Not, to be sure, in the sense that an organ of copulation is introduced into the vagina as far as the mouth of the womb, but that the *efflux opening of the man is laid upon the influx opening of the woman.* Through the motions of cohabitation the secretion is forced into the open vaginal channel, which in no way excludes sensations of pleasure for both parties. This observation has a practical significance since the query is almost always raised by hermaphrodites as to their ability to marry, have intercourse, and progeny. This question, assuming certain previous stipulations, is in no way to be answered negatively. The lack is less common with a bifurcated scrotum than with a completely normal scrotum. But even in this case there are examples and exhibits in the pathological-anatomical museums. Whereas with scrotal hypospadia the testicle usually lies behind the inguinal channel,

314

where the scrotum is not bifurcated the testicles are usually in their normal position.

2. More common than an inborn lack of the penis is a partial or total lack of the penis *acquired* through injury or evoked through a severe illness. Such cases could be observed constantly during the war, as also some which were caused by necessary amputation. Such losses of the organ render potency more difficult, but do not completely remove it. The claim, assumed by one writer after another, that a stump of fifteen centimeters is necessary for cohabitation, is arbitrary. The libido, ability of cohabitation, and even the orgastic feeling are not eliminated through total or partial lack of the penis.

3. Not essentially different from complete lack of the male organ, is the condition of an *abnormal smallness of the penis*. Here it must first of all be remarked that many people are of the opinion that their organs of copulation are unusually small, and are therefore hesitant about approaching a woman. In reality, however, these doubts are almost always unfounded; and, as most conceptions regarding a too large or too small member, or a too narrow or too wide vagina, are untenable and based on a sexual reluctance. *Small members* usually appear in connection with small genital apparatus generally, especially with small testicles. It is occasionally to be observed, however, that the scrotum is thoroughly normal in its construction as regards its content, whereas only a diminutive, bump-like rudiment represents the penis. The most common case is the type of the eunuchoid, which I have described in the section on the lack of sexual glands. Here the libido sexualis, although weakened, is often present and not rarely is ipsatorically satisfied. There are no spermatozoa, but there is usually a rather sticky glandular secretion. Orgasm is present to a small

315

degree, but on the other hand the potentia generandi is lacking. I have also seen isolated cases in which with eunuchoid persons there was a certain postdevelopment after the twentieth year, together with a certain increase in growth of the penis. Moreover, with abnormal smallness of the penis, usually other organs, and the mental life also, show variations from the norm, and usually in the direction of psychic and psychosexual infantilism.

4. Just as with abnormal smallness, so also the *abnormal largeness of the member* is often considered a hindrance to cohabitation. To set a normal size, or even an average size, for the penis, is not feasible. There are occurrences of persons who, accused of having gotten a young girl with child, claim that even the size of their organ made this improbable; but expert investigation has usually revealed a more or less conscious deception. The remarkable ability of dilation of the female genital channel shows that even a very large penis would hardly afford a permanent obstacle to copulation. In this case it would show that there was either *vaginismus* or some other pathological condition in the woman. At all events, the disproportion between a member which, in erection, is too large and the female vagina, too narrow, is often presented as a reason for divorce, can always be accepted with a degree of suspicion.

5. A very rare anomaly, of which mention should be made, is the innate *doubling* of the penis. Usually in this case both penes lie side by side, rarely one above the other. There is also differentiated a total or partial duplication, when the organ is fully duplicated, or just the glans is duplicated in the upper part. By *diphallus spurius* is understood a deformity with a shape like the penis which, however, has no anatomical relationship to the member. Connected with the diphallic formation are

316

also duplications of the urethra, among which is the especially remarkable case cited by Ricke, in which a young man urinated and ejaculated through both members. The very rare doubling of the urethra is very closely connected with abnormal paraurethral channels, which, however, scarcely ever have any significance for potency. More serious as obstacles to ejaculation are other urethral deformities such as total and partial strictures of the urethra, innate strictures, different formations in the urethra, as well as the complete lack of the urethra with lack of the penis; abnormalities which are usually coupled with other restraints of development.

6. Much more common than the last-named congenital anomalies are those variations of the urethra which are known under the names of *hypospadia* and *epispadia.* Hypospadia, which according to my observation is almost always present with variations in the secondary sexual characteristics, and not rarely with variations in the sexual psyche, must be differently estimated according to whether it involves an opening of small degree from the upper point down, or whether it goes still further down towards the scrotum, and furthermore according to whether it involves a hole, or a slit of greater or lesser length, which also frequently extends to the scrotum. That hypospadia prevents neither the ability of cohabitation nor of generation is shown by the many cases in which this variation from the norm is hereditarily transmitted from *father to son.* However, with the more developed forms of *hypospadia peniscrotalis* and *perinealis,* cohabitation is rendered very difficult, if not impossible. Often with hypospadia there are other genital anomalies such as atrophy of the testicles and of the prostate. Moreover with the more severe forms of the hypospadiac penis there usually appears in erection an

317

abnormal splitting, the so-called "verge condée" of the French, which represents a considerable obstacle to cohabitation. So far as I have seen, the frequently attempted surgical cure of this deformity has thus far been able to show no real results.

7. Still more uncomfortable for cohabitation than hypospadia is the condition of *epispadia*. With this also there are usually other deformities of the penis, for example abnormal smallness or misplacement of the member. Also the corpora cavernosa is usually weakly and imperfectly developed. All these abnormalities, which are often allied with disorders to the development of the urethra and the bladder also, naturally cause a considerable obstacle to cohabitation.

8. We come now to one of the most widespread of the disorders in the region of the genital organs, *phimosis*. Usually this peculiar formation of the foreskin induces conceptions of a hypochondriac autosuggestive effect. I have repeatedly had the opportunity of observing persons who traced their impotence back to an excessively narrow foreskin. Despite the fact that *objectively* this idea was in no way justified, I considered it best, finally, to cure the strongly anti-erotic condition, and often saw, after a little treatment, a disappearance of the impotence. Particularly in several cases in which the clumsy attempts at cohabitation of young married people were constantly negative, this treatment had results. Usually phimosis is caused by an epithelial *cohesion* of the glans to the prepuce, which physiologically is present in early childhood, and gradually withdraws at the time of maturity. Erections, and even masturbation, accelerate this separation. When because of cohesion the foreskin will not allow itself to be drawn back, the preputium can become so strained at an erection, that the violent pain

318

will counteract the stiffening. This strong tension of a narrow preputium frequently causes an attenuation, the atrophic form of phimosis. While this form through its pressure on the glans draws this also into common suffering, with the hypertrophic form of phimosis it usually results in bleedings because of stoppage of the urine, or in the formation of preputial stones because of the deposit of calcium from the urine, which mixes with bacteria. Hence there arise conditions of irritation in the foreskin sack which lead to edematous swellings, phenomena which make themselves felt particularly with erections and lead to the quick disappearance of them. In other cases the balanitic conditions which arise through the stoppage of secretions exercise a tickling effect which brings on erections and sexual excitations. Such conditions of irritation are, in the long run, not without significance for the nervous system, so that in this respect also phimosis is not to be disregarded. But before all else a severe phimosis demands cure for this reason—and not, as one occasionally still sees done, through incision, but through circumcision—because at coitus the strained narrow foreskin can easily be slightly torn, which affords an entrance point for infectious germs, gonococci, staphylococci, and spirochetes.

9. A shortening of the foreskin ligament can lead to pains and variations of the glans at erection. Here also, with strong erections, there can be tears, which again increase the possibility of infection. This condition can be relieved by cutting through the foreskin ligament, but the fact must be emphasized that *here also many baseless worries arise* as a result of a completely normal ligament being regarded as too short.

10. Paraphimosis, which is usually only a temporary condition, forms a still greater obstacle to the ability of

cohabitation than does phimosis. Paraphimosis usually arises from a more or less phimotic condition through forcing the foreskin behind the glans through some masturbational, rarely a coitional, way. It leads to severe subjective and objective complaints which manifest themselves through severe pains, ulcerations, swellings, and inflammations. The small ulcers and erosions of the tight ring of skin will often lead to gangrene formations. But the whole affair usually seems more dangerous than it really is. Also the violent symptoms can soon be ameliorated through rest and suitable treatment. However, cases have also been observed in which the ravages spread finally from the corona glandis to the urethra and the erectile bodies.

11. *External injuries* of the penis are not so common as one would be led to expect from the accessible situation of the organ, but still they are frequent enough to be mentioned as a further basic obstacle to the ability of cohabitation. Besides contusion, which occurs for example at gymnastic work, there are different sorts of wounds that come from stabs, as from an open knife carried in the pocket, tears, bites, cuts, and particularly in the war, through shots. In my special practice I was able to observe several cases in which the organ was half or more destroyed through shot wounds. If these wounds should heal well, then they present a better presage than the unfortunate wounded man would in the beginning have believed possible, if, to his horror, he had seen the secondary swellings and discolorations from the blood discharges. Here are to be mentioned even self-mutilations of the member from sexual-hypochondriac or hypererotic motives as well as injuries from trimming the hair.

12. Beside the external injuries there are also *sub-*

cutaneous injuries, as well of the lighter sort with which the blood flow is soon reabsorbed, as the more serious ruptures of the erectile bodies which not seldom lead to cicatrization, destruction of the tissues, and lasting variations which are a great hindrance to erection. Sometimes, because of the bleedings there result partial erections with a bending of the member, such as is observed with other bleedings. If the rupture involves the main parts of the erectile bodies, particularly the albuginea, then one speaks of a *fracture of the penis*. Such fractures occur with the stiffened member through forcible use on the part of the sexual partner, occasionally, although very rarely, through *too violent coitus* as well as through accidental contact with hard objects. Cases have also been described in which persons have themselves broken their erected penis. It also happens that the urethra is torn, which is then termed a compound fracture. If one considers that man, different from the dog, has no bones in the penis, it is obvious why the expression fracture of the penis is seldom used.

13. Also there has been talk of a *luxatio penis*. Nelaton understands by this, a condition in which the penis is drawn back under the skin of the abdomen or has crept into the scrotum. These cases influence the ability of cohabitation to the extent of making it impossible when it comes to shriveling of the skin of the penis and to its degeneration.

14. By *chapping* of the penis is understood *accidents* through which the skin of the member is wholly or partly torn or ripped. Such happenings are occasionally caused through industrial disasters as getting jammed in machine wheels, machine belts, etc., also through being run over, etc. These wounds, indeed, heal relatively well, but

321

they often leave considerable scars which cause pains at erections. Cases have also been observed in which no functional disorders at all were left behind. Thus I have repeatedly observed cases in which jealous lovers would make deep cuts into the member of a sleeping partner, which healed completely. But because of the constant use of the organ for the discharge of urine there is an especial danger of infection with injuries to the erectile bodies and the urethra. The member is not only open to attack by accidental injuries, and deeds of violence because of anger or jealousy, but it is often the object of manifold attacks with sharp instruments, be it from religious fanaticism, or emasculation through other reasons, as from ipsatorical or automasochistic grounds. Also bites from horses, dogs, rats, etc., have been observed as well as pinching in drawers and doors. Experiments have shown that to tear the penis in a dormant state 125-145 kilograms are necessary, with young people 160, and with the erect member 40-60 kilograms are enough.

15. Especially to be mentioned are the *tying* of the penis and the result. This is done partly with some *playful* idea, and partly to prevent pollutions, erections, ipsations, and nightly wettings. For this reason parents and nurses have not seldom tied up the penis of young people with ribbons, elastic bands, twine, and thread; even iron rings have been used. Through this tying can appear a severing of individual tissues, or even a stricture which may extend to gangrene formations. Such bindings of the member also occur through masochistic intent. Thus during the war a woman consulted me whose husband, an officer, had asked her to tie up his member tightly for him, through which he had repeatedly suffered considerable injuries.

16. Priapism is not rarely caused by foreign bodies in the urethra, for example small stones which have worked their way from the bladder or from without. But there are also cases in which the intense pain will a priori prevent erections.

17. *Freezing* of the penis will also cause intense pains which will stop erections, particularly when infiltrates arise through them in the cavernous tissues. Such cases occur with drunken persons who after urination leave their member hanging out in great cold for a long time and go to sleep. I once saw a freezing of the member with a metastrophic man who was sexually aroused by running about in extreme cold in the snow with exposed penis. In opposition to freezing, burnings of the member occur relatively seldom.

18. Herpes progenitalis (praeputialis); just as inflammation of the glans, has no influence upon potency worthy of mention, these irritations, rather, evoke erections and premature ejaculations. Disorders of the potentia coeundi occur only when there are involved chronic ulcerous formations with consequent deformities. This is particularly true of diphtherial and diabetic forms of glans inflammation.

19. We come now to an ailment which is very rare, but which is very important for the ability of cohabitation and stiffening of the member, the more or less extended, acute or chronic, inflammation of the erectile bodies, the *cavernitis*. The most common cause of this ailment is a gonorrheal inflammation which transfers from the urethra to the follicles and the parafollicular connective tissue. But peri-urethral abscesses occur also as the result of injuries and not gonorrheal inflammations. The cavernitis more commonly affects the corpora cavernosa than the trabecula of the urethra. Usually this results in

323

serious destruction of the tissue with cicatrized shriveling of the member, which has as its result a complete inability of cohabitation. This scar formation usually appears in the form of cavernous tubercles. It often leads to the shriveling of the penis with the concavity toward the lower side, the so-called *chorda,* which is usually accompanied by pains and allows only a partially stiffened member which is unsuitable for copulation. Since the *chronic plastic induration of the penis,* which has been studied mainly by Finger, appears especially with old people, many have chosen to believe that it is a hardening of the sexual parts due to old age in connection with hardening of the arteries. But in contradiction to this is the fact that this transformation of the connective tissue has been observed with young and otherwise healthy individuals, and indeed with persons who could not be proven to have suffered from either gonorrhea or syphilis. Although we are in no way completely certain as to the origin of the plastic hardening of the penis, yet this much is certain, that this ailment has a serious effect upon the general condition and the potency. Usually the section of the penis from the focal point of the illness to the tip of the member remains limp. This ailment is generally regarded as incurable, but several cases have been reported in which successful surgical cures have been attained.

A short time ago I had the opportunity of observing a case of excessive plastic induration. A lady, at the end of her forties, consulted me because she had noticed violent nervous disorders with deep psychic depressions, which she traced back to the fact that her husband had remained away from her for a year and a half, because his sexual organ had "stayed three-quarters dormant."

324

The woman had already been married twenty-eight years and had children who were already married. Her husband had had very frequent intercourse with her up until the time of his illness, and, as she said, only "rarely had a day been skipped." The woman, who had a fresh youthful appearance, would never have been considered over forty years of age, menstruated regularly, suffered far more from her husband's condition than he did himself, and explained that she was still too young to cease sexual intercourse for good and all, and that if he should no longer be able to exercise his marital duties, she would have to decide upon a divorce and remarriage. When the woman came to me for the first time, the husband was at a spa to cure his ailment; previous to this, at the instigation of his wife, he had taken several cures at different spas and under different doctors, without having been able to cure the hardening. There was involved a plastic induration of about four centimeters in length and one and a half in breadth. The member very seldom became stiff, and then only in a ventral section of about two centimeters. I only had the opportunity of seeing the man, who was otherwise quite healthy, three times because at the third meeting he explained that he had decided to institute a divorce action himself since for twenty-eight years he had fulfilled his duty and obligations to the fullest degree and he was of the opinion that that was enough; after he had been forced to bear the unceasing reproaches of his wife for a whole year, his patience was at an end. He did not wish to be treated any longer, and he would not allow an operation, because he himself did not miss the cohabitation and was so enraged over the continual demands of his wife, "who is already a grandmother," that he no longer desired a continuance of the marriage.

20. Still rarer than induration of the connective tissues are *bonelike cartilaginous* formations in the member. They usually arise from the septum of the penis. Here also almost always it is old men who are afflicted. They cause deviations of the member along the length of the erectile bodies, and also violent pains. The chorda which is present here causes impotence. The ailment can be cured surgically. Apparently there is a senile ossification, such as often occurs in old age, but there may well be other causes also, such as cavernitis, which bring on this condition.

21. Beside the secondary formation of gangrene on the member, there is also a spontaneous gangrene. Its causes are not yet fully explained. The ailment is rare, extends, regularly, from the penis to the scrotum; there is then usually a suspension of the gangrene and a cure, but there are also cases of death through septicemia. Permanent impotence appears as a result of this only when the process extends more deeply into the erectile bodies.

22. The same is true of the corroding chancre ulcerations which often cause great ravages to the member, but usually do not permanently affect the potency because, as already mentioned, short stumps will usually suffice for cohabitation.

23. *Elephantiastic* thickening of the member and the scrotum hinder cohabitation, just as do *edematous* swellings of the organ, during their presence; this is less true of the rather rare spasmodic indentation of the *varices* of the vena dorsalis penis.

24. Among the results of sexual diseases, the pointed *condyle* is prominent, which, if it is not treated at the right time, often leads to an overgrowth of flesh which so envelopes the member and the glans that it prevents the introduction of the organ. Also strictures after gonor-

326

rhea, partly because of their painfulness and partly mechanically because of the considerable narrowing of the urethral lumen, affect the stiffening and the passage of the semen.

25. Of the swellings of the penis which make cohabitation impossible, *carcinomata* are to be mentioned first of all, whereby it must not be forgotten that small particles of ulcerated tissue can be transmitted to the female organ in intercourse. Similarly important as regards potency are sarcomata and endotheliumy. Special mention should be made of the cornea cutanea of the glans, with which long pointed horny excrescences hinder the penetration of the member into the vagina. This horny formation, which is often first apparent after the cure of phimosis, demands surgical cure, so much the sooner, as it can develop malignantly; in general, *horny protuberances* seem to have existed in the beginnings of time on the human organ in the same way as on that of many beasts, to be considered as rudimentary vestiges.

26. Beside these many sickly depotentizing variations of the male genital organ, which have been mentioned here, there are still other changes in the vicinity of the member to be mentioned which can afford obstacles to cohabitation. To these belong inguinal ruptures, which cause the penis to disappear because of the abdominal skin being drawn over. A similar disappearance of the member occurs with hyrocele, and with a paunch, as well as with elephantiasis. Usually, if the extent of the ailment is not too great, the erect penis will project forth from the folds of skin, but rather often this is not the case. A similar mechanical obstacle to copulation can be caused by a very marked pot-belly, whereby it is to be noticed that the obesity which causes this is in itself sufficient to decrease the potency through internal de-

327

generation and indirect influence upon the inner secretions.

GENITAL IMPOTENCE WITH THE WOMAN

Just as common as the local deformities and new formations in the male organ of copulation, are those in the copulative organ of the woman. There are known to be disorders to development in almost all parts of the female genital apparatus; for the act of copulation, to be sure, only those are of significance which concern the pudenda and the vagina. If these are in order, then as far as the woman is concerned the ability of cohabitation is assured, even though the uterus, tubes, and ovaries are not normally constructed. The anomalies which arise in the last-named parts, naturally, also influence the sexual functions of the woman, but in the sense that they influence the conception, carrying, and giving birth to the child, so that it is sufficient just to mention these abnormalities.

Inability of cohabitation with the woman is *even as little connected with inability of propagation* as with the man. The establishing of this fact is important because it is frequently assumed that a fertilization can only take place with complete introduction of the member into the vagina, and thus after defloration. The usual proceeding, to be sure, is that the semen is discharged into the inner vaginal chamber, and from there makes its way immediately into the womb which is right next to the fossa navicularis. But even spermatozoa which only come to the lower part of the vagina, even those which touch only the external sexual parts or their vicinity, can, through their own mobility, make their way to where they come into contact with the female germ cells. Thus Gerard

328

reports one of many cases in which a young girl came to him with a complete and in no way injured hymen, who had been attacked at the house door by her escort, and who stated that she had noticed dampness only on her linen and external sexual parts. Completely conclusive in this respect are the observations which were mentioned earlier, according to which many pseudohermaphrodites without external organs of copulation effect a fertilization through simply lying with their urethral outlet upon the female vaginal opening. Thus are also to be explained many cases of inborn or cicatrized contraction of the vulva and vagina, which did not prevent pregnancy, although scarcely affording passage to a fine surgical probe. However, in the literature on the subject, there are authentic cases described in which, with a closed vaginal entrance, pregnancy took place through cohabitation in the urethral and rectal openings, indirectly, through fistulae in the urinal or intestinal channel. Admittedly, these are cases of great rarity. Here again we will give a synopsis of the main genital basic obstacles to normal copulation:

1. First to be mentioned is the *hermaphroditic formation,* the feminine pseudohermaphroditism, with which there is externally a preponderantly masculine configuration, particularly as regards the clitoris, but behind the masculine front there are feminine conditions. Most typical of these is the case in which the vagina, together with its annexes, empties into the rear part of the urethra with apparent external male habitus and twofold cryptorchism. Usually a person so constructed passes as a man through life, but even if the sex is correctly determined as feminine, regular copulation cannot be had with her. Although it is suggested from several sides that the inability of cohabitation be cured through curing

the hypertrophy of the clitoris in these cases and separating the large pudenda which have grown together, yet it very seldom occurs in actual practice. It is unnecessary to go into further detail on this question because it is treated thoroughly in the section on hermaphroditism.

2. Aside from the field of hermaphroditism, there are membranous closings of the vulva, which are not the same as the physiological closing of the hymen. Several years ago a case was submitted to me in London in which the vaginal opening was completely covered with a silver white sinewy skin which extended wing-like from the rectum over the labia vulvae. The woman was married but was unable to have intercourse.

3. Besides the inborn membranous cicatrizations and closings of the vulva, there are, and far more frequently, acquired ones which can be traced back to injuries and illnesses of various sorts, such as burnings, acid burns, gonorrheal vulvitis, and other ailments.

4. The shriveling of the vulva which Breisky describes as *craurosis* usually causes a strong contraction of the vaginal channel which, in connection with the great roughness of the skin and painfulness, arrests the ability of cohabitation. This shriveling appears as the final symptom of an inflammatory swelling which has been existent for years, particularly with younger women; the ailment is usually curable through excision of the affected parts.

5. *New formations* which present an obstacle to cohabitation are either of the nature of elephantiasis, which affects the clitoris as well as the large labia, or they are based on carcinomata, sarcomata, or lues; also irreducible labial hernias, lipomata, fibromata, and lupus are to be mentioned. Although these do not usually ex-

330

tend so far as to completely exclude copulation, yet they often form a mechanical hindrance to cohabitation and they are particularly liable to arouse disgust so that in the majority of cases an erection is rendered impossible.

6. In this latter sense there are a great number of other disorders which would not hinder copulation organically, but are *psychically depotentizing*. Thus several times I have seen cases in which men were repelled from intercourse because of breasts which hung too low, another in which a similar repelling effect was exercised by an overlarge clitoris. *Even small growths like warts and pimples can be disastrous in this regard.*

7. A very common illness of the external female genitals, which also has considerable influence upon the ability of cohabitation, is the *pruritus vulvae*. The itching which is present with this ailment is uncommonly intense and torments the patient to the utmost. Especially often have I seen this ailment appear with women who had recently lost their husbands. I was once consulted by a widow, about thirty years of age, whose husband had suddenly died of a stroke. Shortly afterward an irritating itching of the vulva had set in so that she constantly scratched the greater and smaller lips of the vulva, as well as the clitoris, until the blood flowed, causing severe inflammations to set in. In these circumstances cohabitation was impossible. At the beginning of the pruritus, one usually finds an increased craving for sexual intercourse. Despite all treatment, the ailment of the patient did not disappear until she entered into a second marriage. Sometimes the small painful *excoriations* at the vaginal entrance cause, upon contact with the male member, or even at its approach, a spasmodic contraction of the vaginal musculature, a condition infrequently passing under the designation of *vaginismus*. This condition,

331

which is caused to the greater extent psychogenously, is one of the most important sexual neuroses of the woman, and is treated in the section on that subject.

8. Still more common than in the vulva, are all sorts of *atresias* and *stenoses* in the vagina itself. However, too narrow a vagina makes sexual intercourse difficult. It is extraordinarily rare that the organ, in and of itself, has too narrow a lumen. A pathological condition in the vicinity of the vagina, or in the vagina itself, would narrow the vaginal opening. Neugebauer mentions cases in which the disproportion between abnormally large male members and innate, or acquired, narrow vaginas have led to fatal bleedings as well as fistulae of the entrails.

9. The normal closing flap of the maidenly vagina,. the *hymen,* can be so thick and resistant that it forms an obstacle to copulation. But here, also, the *excessive fear* of the man plays a rôle that is not to be ignored. Men who have read that it is the custom with many primitive tribes to break the hymen before the bridal night with ivory goads, or by some other method, are apt to set the difficulties of defloration very high. Men frequently come to physicians with the request that they open a hymen which is allegedly too thick or resistant, which is really in no way stronger than usual. At all events psychic causes, on the side of the man as well as on the side of the woman, will at the defloration form greater restraints than will the purely physical action. It should seldom form an obstacle to cohabitation with regard to the normal nervous system and potency of the man. For a cure for this resistance, outside of an operation, is more forceful stretching.

10. A greater consequence is when there exists a second *closing membrane,* as an addition to hymen, in the vagina. This condition, called atresia vaginalis, is rare,

332

and may be caused by disorders in development; however, it is not always inborn but often acquired through some outside influence. Very often there are inflammations in childhood which are scarcely noticed, but as a result of which closing of the vagina secretly takes place. Behind the vaginal atresia there often forms a hematocolpos. Neugebauer, to whom we are indebted for so many important disclosures in this field, has also made valuable contributions to the study of inborn and acquired closings of the vagina. They appear in connection with a colpitis adhesiva ulcerosa and perivaginitis phlegmonosa dissecare, especially after such infectious diseases as scarlet fever, diphtheria, measles, typhus, smallpox, articular rheumatism, lues, etc.; also after injuries, burns, scaldings, or the introduction of pieces of wood or iron into the vagina. Finally, through puerperal infection, this also develops into ulcerous formations which cause a cicatrization of the vagina. Similar cicatricose closings of the vagina have been observed as a result of injuries from instruments at childbirth. Permanent contractions of the vagina have not rarely been caused by injuries of the vagina from suicidal, therapeutic, and usually abortive reasons, through different chemicals such as sulphuric acid, nitrate of silver, and infusions of cayenne pepper.

11. To mention some of the rarer causes of contraction of the vagina, there may be mentioned a sewing together of the vaginal opening, after a ripping of the same, at the request of an unsatisfied husband, which must be cured again. A brutal cohabitation, particularly with very youthful individuals, can easily cause destruction of tissue and as a result cause inflammation of the vagina, cicatrization, and contractions. A disorder which should be mentioned, which makes cohabitation com-

333

pletely impossible, is absolute lack of the vagina, which is usually accompanied by defective development of the ovaries and the uterus. But since in these cases there is usually, in the place of the vagina, a thin connection tissue between the rectum and the bladder, the skin can be forced in, through repeated attempts at cohabitation, so that a proceeding similar to cohabitation is possible, and even at examination it will seem as though there were a vagina. In such cases sexual intercourse has taken place in the gradually dilated urethral channel.

12. Double formation of the vagina, when the septa reach down very deeply and are very firm, can be an obstacle to cohabitation. In such cases usually only one half of the vagina is used. Surgical removal of the septum, in case it should divide the vagina into two halves which are too small, will remove the obstacles to cohabitation.

13. Swelling of the vagina occurs very rarely, but the vagina can be afflicted with tumors, which extend from the womb, and especially by myoma. These, just as vaginal cysts, which can become rather large, can make cohabitation impossible. Dropping of the womb and vaginal prolapsus prevent copulation only when they cannot be reduced, which is seldom. Franqué even mentions cases in which cohabitation took place with a prolapsus of the uterus, where the male member was introduced directly into the inner channel of the womb so that pregnancy occurred.

Germinal Impotence

(Sterility of the man and the woman)

Although we are not to be numbered among the theologians who, identifying result and aim, consider fertili-

334

zation to be the exclusive significance of sexual union, we would rather believe that love is, for the lover and the beloved, so powerful a thing in and of itself that, in comparison, propagation is a secondary matter. Yet this effect of cohabitation must be regarded as so important that when intercourse is damned from the beginning to unfruitfulness, at all events a very important attendant phenomenon is lacking. In this matter impotentia generandi has up to now been commonly considered together with impotentia coeundi, whereas in practice inability of cohabitation is considered as very different from inability of generation. Inability of cohabitation is usually considered as far more unpleasant, but often on the other hand inability of generation has far more practical consequences.

The ability of generation of the man is dependent upon the discharge of a normally effective seminal fluidity. Without ejaculation there can be no generation; without erection it occasionally occurs. The mechanical peripheral skin irritation which causes the erection, at its summation releases the ejaculation also. Central excitations from the brain, which so commonly cause erections, will rarely suffice to cause ejaculations.

We have already emphasized the fact that erection and ejaculation involve two separate centers in the spinal cord, from which proceed, also, separate centrifugal tracts. At ejaculation the sperma is rhythmically emptied from the spermaducts, through whose fine openings at the top of the seminal tubercles it flows into the urethra, and from there is discharged by muscular contraction to the outside. Accompanying this is the orgasm, whose culmination is simultaneous with the exit of the semen through the very narrow ductus ejaculatorius. The excitability of the ejaculation center admits of many variations. With many the ejaculation results after a few pulsations, while with others the discharge appears after several minutes. Also the length of the period of preceding abstinence, as well as the fullness of the seminal bladder which is partly dependent therefrom, has its influence upon the duration of the act of cohabitation. The ejaculation center lies at the height of the fourth lumbar.

According to Mueller, there is another in the sympathetic ganglia of the pelvic basin. It is assumed that the first takes care of the bulbus musculature, which serves to force out the semen, whereas the other brings about different glandular secretions into the urethra. As far as the locomotion of the testicular secretions from the testicles into the spermaducts and the seminal bladder is concerned, peristaltic movements are assumed by some, whereas others believe that the semen is pushed forwards by pressure from the point of secretion, and by the motions of the legs generally. The entrance of the seminal fluidity into the urethra seems to be taken care of, in the main, by the muscle fibers of the prostate, whereas the musculi ischiocavernosi and bulbo-cavernosi and the musculi perinei superiores et profundi cause the seminal discharge through spasmodic contractions.

The ejaculation is of two parts. First, the forcing of the semen from the spermaducts, the seminal bladder and ductus ejaculatorius into the urethra. Secondly, the discharge of the seminal fluidity which has been made complete by the different glands, through the urethra to the outside. The seminal bladder has for a long time been regarded as the reservoir for the semen, but recently another opinion has been formed on this question. Steinach demonstrated that the sexual urge is present even with an empty seminal bladder, and that with the extir-

336

pation of the seminal bladder there was revealed no lack of the sexual desires and functions. The opinion of Exner that the seminal bladder is used only for storing semen is shared by few investigators.

It is the claim of most all writers that the seminal bladder is an independent glandular body whose secretion is of great significance for the vitality of the seminal bodies. It is probable that the seminal bladder mainly fulfills the function of mixing together the seminal bodies and the fluidity. It is possible through massage of the seminal bladder through the rectum to force the semen fluidity outwards, which also happens rather often with massage of the prostate. Before the secretion of the testicles, spermaducts, and seminal bladder are discharged into the urethra through the ductus ejaculatorius, they are mixed with the secretion of the prostate. Since the secretions of the Littré and Cowper glands are also mixed in, semen fluidity is represented to us as a combination of six different glandular secretions. Of the mixture, after the testicular secretion, the secretion of the prostate is of particular importance. It is a milky, almost always acid-reacting, fluidity containing protein, from which arises the specific odor of sperma.

In the prostate secretion there are, of corpuscular elements, large roundish and cubic epithelia and cylindrical colloids, also there are small lezithin bodies, filmy amyloid, and yellowish irregularly formed prostate grains. From the prostate secretion comes also the so-called Boettscher crystals. The odorous substance of the semen, the spermin, is identified with this. The spermin is also found in the testicles, the ovaries, the thyroid gland, in the pancreas, the spleen, and in benignant festering. Fuerbringer has also named the spermin, and correctly it seems to me, *prostatin*.

337

The same investigator verified the vivifying influence of the prostate secretion upon the spermatozoa. It can actually easily be demonstrated that if one adds a drop of prostate fluid to immobile seminal bodies, they become very agile. The secretion of the seminal bladder is rather thick, sticky, yellowish, and appears in the semen in the form of swollen tapioca grains which liquefy within a short time. The testicular secretion itself is thick, viscous, completely without odor, and consists, for the greatest part, of countless thickly crowded seminal bodies. For certain identification of the seminal bodies, a microscope is necessary. Only through this can it be established in isolated cases whether human sperma is involved. According to Eberth ("The Male Sexual Organ," Jena, 1904) the human seminal body is about fifty-five micra in length, of which about fifty micra form the tail. Head, body, and tail display a number of individual differences, so that a highly trained eye can distinguish the sperma of different men almost as well as he can the men themselves.

With *germinal* impotence we must distinguish between those forms with which there is no formation of germ cells, and those in which no discharge of semen takes place. In the literature on the subject we find different terms which do not express so clearly what they mean. Thus a lack of sperma fluidity is usually understood by the expressions *aspermatism* and aspermy, whereas a lack of seminal bodies in the ejaculation is called azoospermy, which is usually in conjunction with oligospermy and necrospermy as transitions and variation. It would be more correct to designate the lack of sperma as such as aspermatism, and to choose other expressions for disorders of the ejaculation, as we did earlier when we spoke of ejaculatio deficiens and sejuncta.

338

I saw many cases in which there were rich and *profuse discharges,* which under the microscope revealed *not a single germ cell.* Obviously in such cases some intermediary fluidity took the place of the normal ejaculate. Orgasm, as the libido, was seldom noticed. According to my observation azoospermy and sexual desire are in no way exclusive of each other, but there is frequently a certain diminution of the potentia erigendi. In comparison to the lack of ejaculation, the lack of semen cells in the seminal fluidity is relatively common. Azoospermy can be caused by a lack of production of semen cells, but also it can be caused by the fact that the testicular secretion cannot be secreted. A complete lack of testicles, anorchism, is relatively rare, more frequent is microrchism, inborn shriveling of the testicles. These important anomalies are discussed in detail in the section on the lack of sexual glands.

We have seen that in such a case feelings of pleasure, and indeed in the double sense of libidinous and orgastic pleasure, are not necessarily lacking, but that the lack in inner secretions has, as its result, a great number of variations from the norm. To be sure, besides the *extrasecretory* there is an *innersecretory impotence,* which however cannot be exclusively attributed to the sexual glands, since despite a complete lack or complete atrophy of the sexual glands, there is still a considerable libido, so that without question other endocrine glandular secretions are also effective here; on the other hand the coincidence of animal heat with the stronger growth of the interstitial puberty cells shows that there is a parallelism between the proceedings in the gonads and the sexual psychic strain.

With lack of the testicles the external secretions arise from the seminal bladder of the prostate and the urethral glands. Also with inborn lack of the testicles and the vasa deferentia the formation of the spermatozoa is usually lacking. With defective development of the testicles there are involved disorders of development which are both more deeply rooted and more effective than would appear from superficial observation. With local disorders of development there are probably in all cases general somatic and psychic disorders connected; the primary one seems to be a restraint in the development of the genitals, but it is still not fully explained in how far the psychic and the *generative* constitution are coupled together, and in what causal relationship they stand to one another. What is true for anorchism and microrchism, which is usually only a disguised *unilateral* cryptorchism, is true especially for cryptorchism. This is also commonly accompanied by infantilism and very commonly by sterility. With bilateral cryptorchism, as much as it concerns inguinal or abdominal testicles, there is frequently azoospermy. But there may also be positive findings of sperma, so that in isolated cases an examination of the ejaculate is indispensable, which has heretofore been only too commonly neglected.

In *most* of the cases of azoospermy the testicles give a *normal* impression when regarded outwardly. One would scarcely consider it possible that even in cases of disputed paternity an examination of the semen is almost never suggested and undertaken. We consider this a serious omission. The following cases, laid for report before the Institute of Sexual Science, may show of what decisive significance the examination of the ejaculate is.

Mr. L. W. was accused by Miss R. of having gotten her with child. W. stated;

340

1. That he absolutely did not know this person and suggested that some one had misused his name to her.

2. That he had no affection for women.

3. That at two examinations in the years 1916 and 1918 his semen had been declared *unfertile*.

His wife, to whom he had been married since 1914, despite his homosexual inclinations of which his wife was informed, also testified to this. Since she was very anxious to have a child by him, he had sexual intercourse with her under the conception of a male person. There was no pregnancy. Then his wife persuaded him to have his semen examined with the negative result mentioned.

We then examined, microscopically, semen acquired through ipsation and established the fact that no seminal bodies were present. Even macroscopic observation showed that the secretion, which was very small in quantity, consisted *only of secretions of the prostate and the seminal bladder*. Therefore we considered it as *out of the question* that W. should have impregnated the person who accused him.

The following report shows that the seminal examination is not less decisive in cases of *doubtful paternity:*

F. M., metal worker, thirty-two years old, married two and a half years, turned to us for establishment of his ability of generation. M.'s wife, née E., twenty-four years old, was in the third month of pregnancy. M. doubted the paternity claimed by his wife, and for three reasons: first, in frequent sexual relations before marriage without any preventative measures being used, no girl had ever become a mother through him; second, he had only one testicle and the discharge of semen had always been

341

very sparse, besides which there were other bodily defects such as catarrh of the lungs, palpitation of the
heart, anemia, etc.; third, his decision was based upon
the fact that from the start his marriage had been very
unhappy, it had frequently come to quarrels and even
blows between them, and his wife had always behaved
with absolutely no feeling whatsoever at intercourse,
which had, despite this, taken place on the average of
three times a week. At the advice of the physician Dr.
E., who was treating him for his lung ailment, M. turned
to our institute with a specimen of his semen in order
to have it established microscopically whether or not it
contained semen cells.

We instituted a threefold examination: first of all we
examined the ejaculate which M. brought us which he
had acquired twelve hours before at home by use of his
hand. In the fluidity, which consisted of about two
grams, in which the individual secretions could not
clearly be distinguished one from the other, no spermatozoa were apparent. Because of the importance of the
case, we immediately obtained a second ejaculate from
M. in which the prostate and seminal bladder secretions
could be clearly distinguished one from the other macroscopically, but in which neither macroscopically nor
microscopically were testicular secretions (semen cells)
to be found.

In order to be quite certain, we suggested a punction
of the testicles to which M. agreed. In the scrotum only
the left testicle, of normal size, was found; the right
testicle was missing from the scrotum; there may have
been an inguinal or abdominal testicle (cryptorchism)
from which it was impossible, according to the above
findings, that a spermatogenesis should take place; the
fluidity obtained through punction and aspiration con-

342

tained no semen cells whatsoever. Since spermatozoa could not be established either in the ejaculate or in the well-developed left testicle, we considered M. in no way capable of generation.

In order to establish whether the claim of the wife that she was three months pregnant, in which claim she was joined by her physician, was true, M. came to us with his wife; and the examining physician, Dr. Wertheim, was able to corroborate the statement of the woman as well as her physician in regard to her pregnancy. That M. is the father of this child of his wife's is, according to the above establishments of fact, *absolutely excluded*.

Hidden testicles, which later wander down, may often be capable of function, but the chances of this are more unfavorable the later this wandering takes place. Receding testicles have generally a greater inclination to malignant degeneration than scrotal.

Very much more common than inborn lack of testicles is the *acquired* lack, as well if intentionally carried out through castration as unintentionally caused through injuries, particularly through shots. In both cases azoospermy is the rule, but there are most rare exceptions. With castration this is caused by semen cells which, it seems, can still lead a long life in the spermaducts after the removal of the testicles; various writers have reported of pollutions after castration. I have myself had patients who many days after severing of the spermatic cords have reported pollutions. The longer the period of time after the removal of the germ glands, the less is the chance of the semen containing spermatozoa.

Although the statements from ancient and recent times of the ability of cohabitation and generation by eunuchs

343

are to be accepted with suspicion, an historical legend is that the mother of Aristotle was the daughter of a eunuch.

It is not to be denied that live seminal bodies have been found in the spermaducts of both animals and men long after the removal of the testicles. With azoospermy acquired through injuries, it must be considered that even remnants of the normal testicular tissues suffice for the testicular functions. It is often claimed that swellings in the region of the testicles, hydrocele, variocele, or enterocele influence the formation of sperma through pressure upon the testicles. It seems, however, according to the observations made to now, that in the main these are merely theoretical conceptions.

Of by far the greatest significance in the question of azoospermy is the bilateral *inflammation of the testicles*. In the course of this gonorrheal illness there results a cicatricose growing together. Thus a thick connective tissue forms around the channel which leads the semen outwards. The inflammatory infiltrate causes cicatricose shriveling in all regions of the testicles. Particularly when it seizes the caudae of both testicles, it leads to sterility because thereby the passage for the seminal bodies formed in the testicles is blocked. It is not so serious when the head and middle section of the testicles show shrinkage; luckily, in the great majority of cases, the testicular inflammation is only *unilateral* (Finger, in 3136 cases of testicular inflammation, found only 211 which involved both sides) so that the danger of gonorrheal sterility is greatly lessened.

It is still great enough since, for example, Souplet could discover no spermatozoa in thirty-one out of thirty-four cases of bilateral epididymitis, and White in one hundred and four out of one hundred and seventeen

344

cases. Lack of semen cells in the ejaculate is in no way conclusive proof of lack of semen cells in the testicles themselves; punction of the testicles has established beyond doubt the presence of living spermatozoa in such cases, so that the idea of effecting an artificial fertilization through such a punction, in case of an intense desire for progeny, has much in its favor.

Kehrer reports that of ninety-six sterile marriages, childlessness in twenty-two of them was the result of male azoospermy; and that in two-thirds of these the cause was bilateral inflammation of the testicles. Finger and others are of the opinion that over eighty percent of the cases of epididymitis duplex have a permanent loss of seminal bodies as their result. The *unilateral* gonorrheal inflammation of the testicles is claimed by some writers as cause of sterility, but this can scarcely be the case when there is not, perhaps unnoticed, an inflammatory process on the other side also, at least of the *vas deferens*. Moreover, definitely established cases occur in which, several years after a mature bilateral inflammation of the testicles, there appears a profusity of semen cells; although Fuerbringer's opinion may be correct: that an azoospermy lasting three months, with epididymitis bilateralis, may be regarded as definitive.

Temporary lack of semen may often appear with acute febrile illnesses as well as with severe conditions of exhaustion; or constitutional anomalies, such as obesity as well as lues and alcoholism. Of greater importance, with the last of these ailments, is the qualitative influence, blastophthory, rather than the quantitative. Simons found, however, in eighty-seven cases of chronic alcoholism fifty-three cases, sixty-one percent, of azoospermy. Although the semen production is often checked with serious wasting diseases, such as cancer and advanced

345

tuberculosis (which is certainly *a favorable selective process* from a eugenic point of view), yet this is in no way a universally true rule.

The synopsis would not be complete if we did not mention an influence upon semen formation with which we have only recently become acquainted. That is the damage done to the germ cells, and their production, through the *Roentgen rays*. First of all the sensitive epithelium of the seminal ducts wastes away. In the beginning there appears necrozoospermy, which usually passes away again until a permanent azoospermy results. Simons found with guinea pigs that subjection to the rays for three seconds destroyed only isolated germ cells, six seconds destroyed one-third, twelve seconds one-half, and after eighteen seconds almost all. Scholtz found the same with subjection to radium rays. Not only the patient, but even persons near the Roentgen apparatus, are subjected to this danger.

It was earlier thought that the effects of the Roentgen rays affected principally, if not exclusively, the skin and its cellular elements. The idea arose that the Roentgen rays, which passed through the body, would be able by their passage through it to influence the inner organs. Treatment of pulmonary phthisis and carcinomata of the stomach through Roentgen rays was tried. The attempt was given up because, aside from a result in stilling the pains of cancer of the stomach, no result could be ascertained except injury to the skin. Thus we met with the idea of a penetrating effect of the rays less and less often. So it is not surprising that the Roentgen rays were used exclusively for dermatotherapy.

With the important observations which Albers Schoenberg made of conies and guinea pigs subjected to the rays, there set in a change of opinion. And after the

346

results of Heineke had extended the horizon still further as regards the penetrating effect of the Roentgen rays, the opinion as to their penetrative effectiveness was completely changed. Albers Schoenberg had already found in 1903 through experiments on conies and guinea pigs that the *Roentgen rays made animals sterile,* without, however, taking from them the *ability of cohabitation* or influencing their physical well-being.

After long penetration of the Roentgen rays, the seminal glands of the experimental animals contained no more *spermatozoa.* A. Schoenberg verified no macroscopic variations of the testicles. Frieben, who conducted histological investigations on the same sort of sterile animals, was able to establish no changes to the other organs of the animals concerned (lungs, liver, spleen, and kidneys). When we cite Frieben's report, we understand from his microscopic slides that in place of the testicular ducts which are normally padded with many epithelial layers, and conducting countless spermato-blast, there are wide empty spaces which, as remnants of former epithelial layers, possess a very small amount of small shriveled cells. Since there were no symptoms of inflammation, Frieben had to assume a process caused by the Roentgen rays. Seldin was able to substantiate the findings of Frieben and Albers Schoenberg.

Fundamentally important are the labors of Bergonié and Tribondeau who studied the effect of the Roentgen rays on the testicles of white rats. The histological changes were quickly perceptible after subjection to the rays, and were marked at first by the fact that the *mitoses* were lacking. Through cytolysis the cells are destroyed. The semen cells form the point of attack for the Roentgen rays, of which first the spermatogony are destroyed, then the spermatocytes, and finally the

347

spermatids. With stronger subjection to the rays there are, as a final result, only the Sertolic cells left in the destroyed testicular ducts. *Only the intermediate cells are left intact.* In contrast to the destruction of the spermatogony, the mature spermatozoa have a high capacity of resistance, as was proven also through further experiments with human sperm *in vitro.*

On the basis of their experiments, Bergonié and Tribondeau came to the following conclusions: The Roentgen rays have *a direct effect upon the epithelial cells of the tubules. Sterilization* results through destruction of the *spermatogony.* Subjection to strong rays destroys even the Sertolic cells and all *intermediate connective tissues.*

The process of degeneration takes place in about six weeks. Then all the degenerated cells have disappeared. Only in such cases as there are still several layers of epithelium present, do symptoms of restitution appear, and then through the entrance of mitosis. To draw from these findings the practical significance, through graduated Roentgen doses we can effect a temporary sterility, and through stronger doses a complete castration. (Bergonié and Tribondeau.)

Villemin, for his part, established the fact that the interstitial tissues were not attacked by the Roentgen rays. From the immutable continuity of the sexual urge, despite the extended degeneration of the seminal epithelium, Villemin concluded that the general functions of the testicles were connected with the interstitial glands which remained unharmed, an opinion which was corroborated by Ancel and Bouin.

Thus the effect of the Roentgen rays is not yet completely explained. More recent experiments have taught and demonstrated that the Roentgen rays are capable

348

of effecting a *stimulation of growth,* as it is believed, through stimulus on the inner secretory organs (Stettner), and thus, especially, would have a rejuvenating effect. (Steinach.)

As the experiments and observations conducted by Dr. August Bessunger in the radiation division of our Institute for Sexual Science have shown, all these findings have considerable practical significance, especially as regards the treatment of sexual pathological abnormalities, both qualitatively and quantitatively. To be able to give a conclusive judgment of the *permanent* effect, a long time is necessary for the collection of purely objective findings and experiences.

Connected with azoospermy as a condition of germinal impotence of equal importance, is necrospermy, with which there are, to be sure, seminal bodies in the ejaculate, but in an inanimate state; oligospermy, with which the number of seminal bodies is considerably smaller, has, on the other hand, a smaller significance from the standpoint of possibility of fertilization, since even with the millions of sperm which are normally in the ejaculate, only a single one can perform the function of fertilization. With oligospermy there are only isolated seminal bodies within the range of vision. This phenomenon is found particularly with a state of exhaustion, but then it is only temporary.

Fuerbringer has shown that often there are deceptions here which arise from the materials used in the experiments. Erroneous conceptions can arise from the disorder, which has been called *asthenospermy* by Fuerbringer, in which the normal or limited number of sperma show a strong decrease in their mobility; with this disorder the particles creep sluggishly and slowly through the field of vision, soon to lose their mobility

349

completely. Since it has been found through experiment that the vaginal secretion considerably increases the mobility of the seminal bodies, it is very difficult to determine whether or not an asthenic semen is capable of fertilization. At all events an ejaculate which is to be examined must be handled very carefully, since even small amounts of semen-destroying substances have an influence upon the mobility of the semen cells, as have also variations in temperature. Receptacles in which the semen is caught should neither be damp, powdered, nor impregnated, since this all has a harmful influence upon the semen.

In order to exclude every doubt that an ejaculate for examination comes from the person whose report it concerns, we consider the old method, of giving the physician a discharge which has been caught, in some receptacle, as *absolutely not to be relied upon.* Just a short time ago a judge, who was conscientious as he was unprejudiced, wished to be shown expressly, in the attestation concerning a man who was disputing his paternity because of infertility, the *undoubted origin of the semen.* This is, in general, possible only when manually obtained. At the Institute for Sexual Science we proceed in this matter in this way: we give the examined a clean glass basin with the request that he ejaculate into the same, through mechanical release of the reflex by means of manual friction, be it with or without imaginings which might be adequate to him. For this purpose the patient goes into an adjoining room and reports for presentation of the fresh ejaculate, still warm from the body, which is usually followed in about five or ten minutes by the examination.

Experience shows that almost without exception this simple, sure, and in no way dangerous proceeding is

350

more agreeable to the patients than obtaining the semen in a condom through intercourse with their wives or some other woman. Aside from coitus condomatus and ipsation, there is still a third way of acquiring the testicular secretion, *punctions of the testicles.* The technique is very simple; one testicle is pressed tightly against the skin of the scrotum, while it is pushed upwards with the thumb and forefinger from the bulge of the scrotum and a simple Pravaz syringe pushed quickly and deeply into the tissue. If a fine needle is used, the pain caused is astonishingly little. Then a very small bit of the testicular secretion is aspirated and sprayed on a stage for examination. Usually we allow the patients the choice of the method of obtaining the sperm, whereby we have noticed that almost always they decide in favor of ipsation, shunning the punction on account of sensitivity and the catching in a basin on account of the bother.

In addition I will briefly summarize the methods and experiences which in the course of time have been shown to us, as examiners of semen at the Institute of Sexual Science, as especially practical. First of all we make a microscopic examination of the ejaculate, which, for the expert, already allows certain important conclusions as to its composition. Particularly when there is no testicular secretion in the ejaculate, the secretion of the seminal bladder shows up very clearly against that of the prostate, whereas with a discharge containing spermatozoa, the testicular and prostate secretions can be recognized, while the secretion of the seminal bladder cannot be defined. The testicular secretion consists macroscopically of large glassy, thick-flowing lumps with fine white stripes drawn across; the secretion of the seminal bladder consists of coiled bodies, about two millimeters thick, of glassy, translucent, viscous character, appearing

351

in a fresh ejaculate like connected grains of *tapioca*. The prostate secretion is a watery, somewhat milkily opaque fluid. The secretions of the Cowper and urethral glands appear usually with strong sexual excitement as light thread-like drops from the opening of the urethra, especially when the penis is dormant after long excitation without relief (orgasmus interruptus).

In order to make a microscopic examination, one draws a drop of the liquid semen, places it on a stage, and puts a glass cover over it. The examination is made with medium strength magnification, and narrow shutters, best of all on a *dark ground*. I have made it a rule to demonstrate this to the persons of whom the seminal examination is made, because experience shows that the sight of their own, living spermatozoa in active movement is *uncommonly instrumental toward increasing their sexual reliance*. I have often seen patients, who suffered because of sexual scruples of a *fear* of impotence, which is only too often a basis of actual impotence, and of deep psychic depression, influenced through this method in so favorable a way that one could actually speak of a cure.

As regards necrospermy it is not to be left out of consideration that long standing, changes in temperature, traces of disinfecting mediums, mixtures of urine, blood, festering matter, and many other admixtures can cause the semen cells to seem dead, whereas in reality they are thoroughly capable of fertilization.

Fuerbringer first showed in this matter that often in fresh sperma there are a number of seminal bodies congealed in the jelly of the seminal bladder, in the gelatinous secretion, which prove to be thoroughly normal after the liquefaction of the gelatinous conglobulation. As with the inner secretions of the germ glands,

352

so with the outer secretions also, every disturbance of the physiological proceeding is shown to be injurious. Whether there is a necrospermy, which can be traced back purely to sexual excesses, seems quite questionable to me. Here, in the main, there may be a question of a sickly change in the prostate secretion which destroys the seminal bodies. But necrospermy is not observed with prostatitis chronica glandularis, so that the prostate secretion has a deadly effect only when altered in a particular manner. Especially do suppurative cells seem to kill semen cells. Also when swelling, stones, or dystrophy of the prostate prevent the egress of the prostate secretion, there is a probability that the seminal bodies will be unfavorably influenced in their function.

Deformed seminal bodies occur not as rarely under similar etiological conditions, as the completely destroyed semen cells. Thus one finds seminal bodies with crooked or rolled-up tails, with two heads, and other remarkable deformities. They are often only youthful, immature semen cells which show such changes in form, and this finding does not exclude the possibility of completely normal and vital spermatozoa also being present.

Quite commonly the sperma is colored red through an admixture of blood. The blood can arise from injuries, inflammations, and stoppages, and can have been mixed in along the whole way, from the testicles to the outermost orifice. Even arterial calcification, through the bursting of small blood ducts, can have a similar effect. Also, not rarely, the blood arises from the bladder. Hemospermy is not always unconditionally connected with pyospermy, with which suppurative admixtures is almost always necrospermy.

They are seldom coupled together in a pyohemospermy, with which the semen is colored greenish. In

353

several cases I have had the opportunity of examining a yellowish colored ejaculation which was secreted by exceedingly icteric persons. Here also seminal bodies, which were very sparse, proved to be mostly dead, so that with *cholospermy* the semen mixed with bilious coloring matter may in most cases be regarded as not capable of fertilization.

Besides azoospermy and the spastic lack of ejaculation already described in the section on spinal impotence, there is still another form of lack of semen which can be termed mechanical aspermatism. Its most normal form is that which can appear after repeated intercourse when the whole supply of germ cells present in the spermaducts and their annexes is exhausted, a condition which is always only temporary and of different duration according to the individual. On the average, the same degree of fullness of the seminal channels as before the discharge, will be reached after about ten or twelve hours, so that a *relative* fullness will appear rather soon again.

Therefore we may question with justified doubts the claims of some persons that they have been able to go through with intercourse ten times and more in the night without decrease in orgasm and amount of the ejaculation. Organic obstacles to the egress of the seminal fluidity occur with inborn closings, defects of the ductus ejaculatorius as well as with *shriveling processes of the excretory ducts of the prostate gland*. Also involved here are stone formations in the prostate or the ductus ejaculatorius; most common is the *stricture of the urethra,* be it inborn or gonorrheal, also occasionally spastic and traumatic.

Here, at intercourse there is a normal orgasm, to which are added, not rarely, painful feelings as will often occur
354

with orgasm when there are inflamed parts in the
urethral channel, especially in the upper part. Usually
with stricture of the urethra the sperma flows through
the seminal tubercules into the urethra, but it is checked
behind the stricture and goes upwards toward the bladder. After the relaxation of the member, the ejaculate
usually flows slowly outward. It has been advised with
strictures to leave the penis in the vagina for a longer
time after the act, but because of the relaxation, this
advice is easier to give than to follow. It is still more
common, especially when the stricture is highly developed, for the sperma to be regurgitated into the bladder and later for urine, containing sperma, to be discharged.

Germinal Impotence with the Woman

With the woman also there appears complete lack of
the germ cells, inborn as well as acquired on some pathological basis, and also evoked through extirpation of the
ovaries. The inborn lack is considerably more difficult
to demonstrate with the woman than with the man, because the secretion is not so easily available for examination as is that of the male germ cells. However, in the
menstruation we have a rather conclusive medium from
which we can draw conclusions as to the production and
repulsion of the ovules; these usually remain constant
even though only small pieces of the ovaries remain.
Fertilization, which had occurred after bilateral removal of the ovaries, shows that even very small particles of the ovarian substances can furnish eggs capable
of fertilization. On the other hand the fact of menstruation is not a conclusive proof of the presence or repulsion of eggs capable of fertilization. Particularly atro-

355

phic ovaries, such as we find so often with virile women, only very rarely produce fertile eggs.

Germinal impotence or sterility of the woman is, however, not dependent upon the repulsion of fertile germ cells alone, but also upon the capacity of conducting these to that place where they will be able to come into contact with the male germ cells. To the conception of female fertility belongs also the possibility of being able to bring the germs to mature development and to discharge them as being capable of life. Therefore, with the woman, besides the inability of cohabitation and receptivity, we must distinguish the inability of bearing and giving birth to the fruit.

The most common cause of female infertility, just as with the man, may be ailments of the conducting channels, inflammations, changes, and closings together particularly of the tubic connective ducts from the ovaries to the uterus. Here also should be considered only bilateral impassableness, especially pyosalpinx and hydrosalpinx, which *by no means always condition permanent impotence,* but are curable so that they may be observed at the same time as, or after, conception. In general, in such cases, there is only some slight sickly process of the tubes, whereas a *larger bilateral hydro- or pyosalpinx* almost always permanently checks the ability of generation. In most cases these inflammations of the tubes can be traced back to a *gonorrheal* infection, less often to a puerperal infection, so that here again *sexual diseases must be named as the most common cause of infertility.*

The inborn shriveling of the ovaries is almost always connected with shriveling of the uterus. If these atrophies of the uterus, of which we deal in the section on infantilism and in the section on the preliminary forms of hermaphroditism, are highly developed, then in them-

356

selves they cause an inability of reception, even though there are rudimentary forms of the uterus which will possess no cavity, because the genital tubes are incompletely developed. Double formations of the uterus do not generally prevent conception. We differentiate between the uterus *fetalis* with two to four centimeters extent of separation, uterus *infantilis* four to five, and the uterus *pubescens* or hypoplastic uterus with five to seven centimeters extent of separation.

The adult state of the fetal uterus is distinguished by the relative largeness of the cervix as opposed to the corpus, as well as through its limpness and the thinness of its walls. The ovaries are then usually very small and the menses are lacking. With this condition the ability of reception can be considered *out of the question*. The infantile uterus forms the transition to the hypoplastic. Here the relationship between the corpus and cervix is usually normal, but the ability of reception is naturally decreased. Just as with the hypoplastic uterus, the defective development of this organ is usually accompanied by a backward state of the whole body especially of the *vascular system*. However, it sometimes occurs that after the age of twenty the belated uterus shows an afterdevelopment, which happens, though, only rarely in those cases with which there is a genital hypoplasy because of virilism. Most noteworthy for the inner secretory relationships of these phenomena, as well as from a therapeutic standpoint, are the experiments of the gynecologist Professor Schroeder in Rostock.

Cases are cited in the literature on the subject in which, even with an originally closed up vagina, the belated uterus and ovaries developed after the twentieth year to such a complete extent that pregnancy entered. In such cases, however, it often results in an abortion. In

357

lay circles one often hears talk of too narrow a womb as an important cause of infertility. Although this phenomenon is less common than it is often supposed to be, yet frequently both inborn and acquired stenoses of the mouth of the womb are obstacles to fertilization.

Acquired contractions of the uterus are often formed because of misuse of medicaments, which are used for the purpose of getting rid of a child. These contractions occur more rarely after extirpation. They are often accompanied by a swelling-like accumulation of blood behind the cervical duct, the so-called hematometra. Most commonly these closings together, desolation, and shriveling of the uterine mucous membrane are accompanied by endometritis. To be differentiated from the hypoplasy of the uterus which was described before, is the atrophy which occasionally develops after severe confinement illnesses and general infections such as lues; an ailment which quite frequently resolves into inability of generation, and of reception, and has inability of bearing as its result. But here again we come to questions which are to be answered not by sexology, but by gynecology.

TREATMENT OF IMPOTENCE

Several summarizing remarks over the *treatment of the disorders to potency:* the indispensable preliminary stipulation for the successful treatment of the different forms of disordered potency is an exact diagnostic establishment of their pathogenesis, their origin. The treatment of organic and of functional disorders to potency is naturally basically different. With *organically* conditioned disorders to potency the general treatment combines with that of the ailment which is at the root of the matter. We have to regard these disorders to potency as a symptom of the illness and thus to treat the basic illness. One should, however, be on his guard against too many local measures which will unnecessarily focus the anxious attention and apprehension of the invalid upon the sexual region and thus work as increasing psychogenous factors of the illness.

The *spinal* disorders to potency, such as we see appear especially with tabes and multiple sclerosis, may occasionally be cured through treatment of this ailment of the spinal cord. A treatment of *tabes* with a combination of salvarsan and mercury, somewhat after the method of Leredde or Gennerich, can at times revive the erectional function. With multiple sclerosis, besides arsenic, we give strychnine especially. We noticed absolutely no results whatsoever from a fibrolysis treatment. Impotence, as so many other symptoms, with multiple sclerosis, is occasionally checked spontaneously after a longer or shorter duration. On the other hand I saw one case in which it remained as almost the only residual symptom for ten years. In such cases of spinal impotence we give strychnine on the theory that it heightens the reflex excitability. The qualification of this consideration is naturally a different one from case to case. On absolutely the same basis, purely as a symptomatically effective aid, we also resort to physical therapy with spinal impotence; galvanization of the vertebral column, faradization of the perineal region, high-frequency treatment of the latter with, if necessary, rectally introduced effluvium, and subjection to Roentgen rays with infrared doses of special filtering. According to our experience, with these organically conditioned cases of spinal impotence we have no reason to share the skeptical opinion of

359

Lewandowsky, as though it concerned suggestive workings.

The *functional* forms of disorders to potency we consider practically as *organic neuroses* of the genital apparatus, and in accordance with this viewpoint our therapy must always be accompanied by a *general treatment of the neurotic condition of the whole.* If this important basic rule is overlooked and a number of local measures applied willy-nilly to the sexual region, then as a rule the invalid becomes worse instead of better. A sensible moderation in the application of local therapy and the most exact individualizing of the general treatment are the indispensable prerequisites to results. There is here still a third prerequisite: patience for both parties, the invalid as well as the physician. A firmly established parafunction of so complicated a variety that with its concatenation of psychic factors, vasomotor and secretory reflex mechanisms, it represents a functional disorder to potency, cannot be cured over night. Many therapeutists, on the other hand, limit themselves only too much in their methods of treatment of functional disorders to potency. Proceeding from the correct assumption that psychic components of an effective sort have a decisive influence in the cure of disorders to potency, they seek to render these abortive through assuring the invalid in a suggestive manner that the matter will pass of itself, he has to do nothing, the *habit,* for example, of the marital bed, and the increasing experience will carry him over all the difficulties. I cannot advise this rather summary form of psychotherapy. To be sure, in some cases, it may suffice, where the normal potency is checked purely by the feeling of inadequacy, shyness, and timidity; that is, however, an exceedingly small number. Thus I have in mind several marriages of recent date where the husband, psychically impotent—who had received this advice before entering into the marriage—still possessed an undisturbed virginal wife after years had passed. In one case after such a marriage, the woman was still virgo intacta after three years, in another after five years. The painful married life for both husband and wife can be imagined.

Thus in every case of functional impotence or disorders to potency, I am in favor of *active* therapy. This means, first of all, psychotherapy. However, it must make use of physical as well as medical means for the attainment of its object. In other words, then, it is necessary in every case of functional disorder to potency to institute a cure, a régime, which is in accord with the psychic individuality of the invalid and the ailment, which will regulate his general manner of living and his sexual relations, and will subject the disordered function to specific means of treatment.

As far as the *psychic treatment* is concerned, there must be taken first of all an exact inventory of the previous sexual history with no reserve, and a summary of all the emotions which are displaced by a feeling of shame or shyness; thus suitable information can be obtained as to the nature of the illness. I have never seen final cures result from *psychoanalysis alone*. However, in the literature on the subject many psychoanalysts make use of hypnosis in their treatment of disorders to potency. (Gouleschew, Wyrubow.) An exhaustive psychoanalysis is an excellent means of bringing to light all the restraining psychic factors which are involved in the disturbances to potency and are often seated in the unconscious mind, and thus of depreciating them for the sick person. I myself, however, have never attained complete results without suggestive treatment. In the

361

majority of cases this suggestive treatment can be masked behind physical methods, but in a certain number of cases direct *hypnosis* leads to results. The suggestion in the hypnosis must be of a threefold variety: it must extend to the *general* condition of the invalid; it must eliminate the occurrences, memories, and timidities which restrained and disturbed the potency; it must express the positive assurance of success in an imperative form. Every single case of disorder to the potency requires a different individual formularization of the suggestions.

Furthermore there is added the regulation of sexual relations with treatment of functional disorders to the potency. In almost every case, *first of all,* all sexual intercourse is forbidden. Thus is checked the source of psychic restraints from which the functional disorders to potency derive their nourishment. Even with an increasing libido one does not abandon this prohibition. The libido, which is dammed up in this way, can, in certain circumstances, and with certain forms of impotence, achieve a curative result by itself.

At times *medicinal* and *local therapy* serve the purpose of a masked suggestive treatment. But it is worth little if its significance is exhausted in this. Far more must the treatments chosen possess some direct symptomatic value as a method of treatment. Therefore they must be chosen differently with the different forms of disorder to the potency. With the *erective* impotence one should combine general stimulating and tonic medicines with those which have a vasomotor and reflex-stimulating effect. Arsenic in connection with nux vomica, ergotine, and adrenalin belong here. The yohimbine, which is so famous, has proven of little worth to me. With functional impotence we will also make use of the different kinds of local electrizations, high-frequency

362

and Roentgen stimulus treatments. It is to be emphasized, however, that these local treatments should never predominate the general treatment.

As concerns the *organic extracts* which are much used in the treatment of functional impotence, they have not lived up to the expectations which people pinned to them at the time of their appearance. There is hope, however, of obtaining in them substances which correspond to the natural inner secretory *sexual chemism* which activates the functions of the sexual center. I prefer the injection to internal administration through capsules or tablets; it is possible that the *implantation method* will take the field here, and it is claimed, as is also possible, that we can still so far improve the organic preparations that administered *per os* or subcutaneously they will fulfill *in practice* what has been *theoretically* promised for them. Also other surgical interventions such as separation of the semen ducts from the sexual glands can, at the cost of the generative capacity, through the transformation of the connective substance into proud flesh, have an eroticizing effect and thus one which will increase the potency. The latest publications of Steinach on "Rejuvenation through Experimental Revivification of Aged Puberty Glands," are of an importance not to be underestimated in this respect.

INDEX OF SUBJECTS

INDEX OF SUBJECTS

367